A FEW CHOICE
MARK LEYNER

"You can bring me ten contemporary novels with HILARIOUS! stamped all over their covers and I will show you ten pages of Leyner that are funnier than all of them combined"

—Adam Sternbergh, *New York Times Magazine*

"I laughed out loud in the bathroom." —David Byrne

"Leyner is the original charged particle, formally inventive, hilariously funny, completely original. Think Beckett on acid. Read this book." —Darcey Steinke, author of *Sister Golden Hair*

"Will blow away your expectation of what late-model literature has to be." —David Foster Wallace

"Mark Leyner is a mad genius, one of the smartest and funniest humans since Aristophanes. A twisted wizard, a genre-busting virtuoso, working at the outer edge of narrative convention."

—Jay McInerney

"His books are compulsively readable, created by a literary mind that seems to have no precedent, proving that fiction can be robust, provocative, and staggeringly inventive without for a moment forfeiting entertainment."

—Ben Marcus, *New York Times Book Review*

"Like Franz Kafka on speed or Hunter Thompson on Valium."
—*Chicago Sun-Times*

"Big-ass brilliance on every sun-kissed page."   —Sam Lipsyte

"There is no one like Mark Leyner in fiction today."
—Charles Yu, author of *How to Live Safely
in a Science Fictional Universe*

"Kicks with the amphetamine-addled impact of a Hong Kong gangster flick."   —*Village Voice*

"The most intense and, in a certain sense, the most significant young prose writer in America."
—Larry McCaffery, coeditor, *Fiction International*

"A writer willing to decorate the room with the contents of his own dynamited head."   —*Entertainment Weekly*

"The literary love child of a bizarre menage à trois of William S. Burroughs, Hunter S. Thompson, and Mark Twain."
—*Los Angeles Reader*

"Mark Leyner may be the most insanely inventive writer working today."   —*Willamette Week*

"One of the most singular, wild-ass and brilliantly fearless voices in American literature...equal parts Roth, Joyce, *Scientific American*, and the Marx Brothers."
—Jerry Stahl, author of *Permanent Midnight*

A
SHIMMERING,
SERRATED
MONSTER!

A SHIMMERING, SERRATED MONSTER!

THE MARK LEYNER READER

Edited by Rick Kisonak

BACK BAY BOOKS
LITTLE, BROWN AND COMPANY
New York Boston London

Copyright © 2024 by Mark Leyner
Compilation and text copyright © 2024 by Rick Kisonack

Hachette Book Group supports the right to free expression and the value of copyright. The purpose of copyright is to encourage writers and artists to produce the creative works that enrich our culture.

The scanning, uploading, and distribution of this book without permission is a theft of the author's intellectual property. If you would like permission to use material from the book (other than for review purposes), please contact permissions@hbgusa.com. Thank you for your support of the author's rights.

Back Bay Books / Little, Brown and Company
Hachette Book Group
1290 Avenue of the Americas, New York, NY 10104
littlebrown.com

First Back Bay paperback edition, December 2024

Back Bay Books is an imprint of Little, Brown and Company, a division of Hachette Book Group, Inc. The Back Bay Books name and logo are trademarks of Hachette Book Group, Inc.

The publisher is not responsible for websites (or their content) that are not owned by the publisher.

The Hachette Speakers Bureau provides a wide range of authors for speaking events. To find out more, go to hachettespeakersbureau.com or email hachettespeakers @hbgusa.com.

Little, Brown and Company books may be purchased in bulk for business, educational, or promotional use. For information, please contact your local bookseller or the Hachette Book Group Special Markets Department at special.markets@hbgusa.com.

Copyright acknowledgments begin on p. 439

Book interior design by Marie Mundaca

ISBN 9780316591652
LCCN 2024942644

Printing 1, 2024

LSC-C

Printed in the United States of America

Editor's dedication:
To my people — Nancy, Lane, and Ash

CONTENTS

CONTENTS

Usually the word "monster" signifies some sort of unaccustomed harmonizing of dissonant elements. I call "monster" every original inexhaustible beauty.

— *Alfred Jarry*

You'll never be able to keep this up, Mark!

— *Alan (American Mischief) Lelchuk, 1975*

FOREWORD

HERE'S A FACT: I once started a Mark Leyner cult in Providence, Rhode Island. This was in the late '80s, which was maybe a silver age for cults. I was a junior at Brown, snouting around in the college library for something to read, when I stumbled upon some issues of *Fiction International,* found a few stories by some guy named Mark Leyner. I was tsunamied by these sentences. They were the answer to the question I'd been asking for a long time: "When will I find writing that can stand up to, and make art of...this?" And by this, imagine my arm sweeping over the whole of the late '80s. And everything that came before.

Leyner was my instant hero, and it seemed that he was just getting going with his corpus as I was preparing to be a superfan. Right away I found *I Smell Esther Williams,* in which those stories I discovered appeared, but by my senior year he was publishing his next books, including his early masterwork, *My Cousin, My Gastroenterologist.* I turned everybody I knew on to Leyner's prose. We read aloud from his work at parties, quoted him in lieu of quips of our own. He was our Wilde, our Burroughs, our Monty Python, our Woodstock, our Seka. We really were a cult, and one of us, after moving to Brooklyn, made contact with our god, told him about us. Leyner informed his publicist, as any savvy god would, and next thing there was a camera crew up from New York to do a story on this young phenom's oddball following. I knew this was my big moment and got ready for my head-apostle close-up. But it never came. Instead of interviewing me, they filmed my much more photogenic girlfriend reading *My Cousin* under a tree.

I got over my disappointment and never stopped reading Leyner with awe. *Tetherballs of Bougainville* was another astonishment, and after a Hollywood lull there has now been a full flowering of mature genius: *The Sugar Frosted Nutsack, Gone with the Mind, Last Orgy of the Divine Hermit.* I really believe that if there is a future literary culture of any worth, these books will have an ever-growing importance in it. He was branded early as some sort of amoral postmodernist, but his project has always been much more powerful than that.

Leyner—in temperament, in vision, in his belief in the aesthetic (and, yes, moral) worth of his endeavor—is an artist of the dawn of modernism, not its end. But his material is the detritus in the craters of our imploded world, all the junk that is us and our language and our disembodied existence and our fractured views of reality. Because if you just stop squinting, or pretending the last hundred years never happened, and go to the gym a little more, you will begin to understand precisely what needs to be picked up and bent and twisted and welded into new shapes. Mark Leyner is one of our great sculptors. Stack all his books together and you get literature's most magnificent Watts Towers of the mind. As for why they are so funny, and so full of genuine feeling, well, that's what happens when you truly understand tragedy and love.

—*Sam Lipsyte*

ENTER

Rick Kisonak

THE STORY OF the story of Mark Leyner begins at the beginning of the last century's last decade. In the early '90s, I did in succession three things by which my life is now defined. First, I came to possess a copy of *My Cousin, My Gastroenterologist*. Second, I read it. Third, I got married and raised a family in Vermont.

That third part consumed a quarter century. Then one day I looked around the house for the peculiar little paperback with the strange comic-book panels on its cover. Why it had remained on my mind all that time I wasn't quite sure. So I read it again. Oh, yeah.

I'd never encountered anything remotely like it. The writing was as breathtakingly unhinged, visionary, erudite, and utterly fearless as I'd remembered. It was the kind of writing I'd vaguely dreamed of doing but never quite gotten around to. I reread passages at random for days ("I was an infinitely hot and dense dot"), marveling at their mind-bending blend of the lyrical and the laugh-out-loud hilarious.

It went without saying, I thought, that the world had rebuffed him. Eaten him up and spit him out. No way could an artist so revolutionary have made it.

I montaged the fates allotted to literary genius in America: Delmore Schwartz–style ruin and madness; John Kennedy Toole's suicide; poor Richard Brautigan. Poor Anne Sexton. "The vector of my movement from a given point is isotropic," he'd written. "All possible directions are equally probable." Poor New Jersey naïf. How mercilessly the marketplace must have rejected his stab at a new, mutant literature. Mark himself seemed mystified as to what the future might hold when he wrote the "about the author'" piece that closed the book and ended:

> When I saw the Beatles on television in 1964, I decided that I'd like to be an artist…In high school, I was in a band that broke up over artistic differences—I wanted us to go "glitter," a la T.Rex, Bowie, the New York Dolls; the other guitarist, Tom Cacherelli, wanted us to be a more workman-like band like the Allman Brothers…While working on *My Cousin, My Gastroenterologist*, I supported myself by doing advertising copywriting. Recently I've written ads for biodegradable incontinence briefs and artificial saliva. No one knows what the future holds in store for me.

No one knew in 1990. But this was the future. I stopped rereading passages at random. Between the time when I'd bought the book and the point at which I'd raised a family, then reread it, that whole information superhighway deal had, of course, magically materialized. I could learn Mark Leyner's tragic fate with a tap or ten on a Mac. Fingers trembling, visions of homeless poets dancing in my head, I girded myself to google.

I couldn't believe my eyes! "American postmodernist author?" "Movies?" YouTube videos of appearances on Letterman and

Conan? And that was just the *Wikipedia* blurb that gives you the nutshell skinny. Unbelievably, there was more. Rows of book jackets, each bearing a title as fabulously improbable and lovely as the one I'd assumed was his one and only.

Profiles in the *Paris Review* and the *New York Times*. Decades of adoring reviews in the country's most prominent papers and magazines. Awards. A column in *Esquire*. Experimental work on MTV. A film starring John Cusack and Ben Kingsley. A novel recently released and racking up more adoring reviews. Mark Leyner wasn't homeless. He was infinitely hot!

Here, of course, is where a well-adjusted fan of fine writing would maybe order a few books, shake his head at fortune's capriciousness, and move on. Really, after all, what did this have to do with me? I wasn't the one who followed his bliss, beat the odds, and birthed a brilliant body of work. I was a mere movie critic from Vermont.

Upon learning what Mark had been doing with himself for the past quarter century, I didn't move on. Clearly. Something in the back of my maladjusted mind relayed ridiculous signals that all this did have something semimystical to do with me. "Fate," as Mark wrote in *The Sugar Frosted Nutsack*, "is the ultimate pre-existing condition."

Paul McCartney has a Twitter account. What do you guess happens when a fan direct-messages him? To my surprise, I saw that Mark was on Twitter as well. What do you guess happened when I messaged him on May 20, 2017? He messaged me back. He also shared his phone number and said he'd be happy to chat the next day. We did. And for me, at least, nothing's been the same since.

Okay, I still live in Vermont, now with my wife and daughter. And until the pandemic shuttered cinemas, I still worked as a film critic, as I'd done for more than three decades. And until COVID, I still directed the annual Burlington Book Festival, which I founded in 2005 (I've met everybody). So sure, some things are the same. What I mean is that getting to know Mark, getting to talk to him regularly and at length, having access to his interior life, his ridiculously unpredictable, exuberantly playful creative process—basically being given a backstage pass to his brain—has upgraded my existence in every conceivable sense and has led, as fate would have it, to the development of this book.

I entitled this opening section "ENTER" because Mark is a human amusement park and this, dear reader, is your all-access ticket of admission. He's a bottomless repository of mystical acumen and fun facts, a seer for whom the words *unfettered imagination* are laughably inadequate. Mark is and always has been avant la lettre, deep in the woods, as far as he can get from the citadel. He devotes himself to making fun to this day. At sixty-eight, he gets up in the morning, goes to the gym, shreds it to within an inch of his life, then declares a multimedia fatwa on everything standard-issue. And I don't mean knocking out the next exemplary bit of literary fiction. I'm talking about waging a life-and-death jihad to do the unthinkably new. The same one he was waging before *My Cousin, My Gastroenterologist* was a twinkle in his mind's eye.

I'd like to share an observation I made some years back concerning his literary superpower, one that I believe will add to your appreciation of the excerpts you're poised to sample. It's a kind of key: Mark's narratives aren't *set against the backdrop* of anything. Everything he's ever written is a complete, self-contained world unto itself. I don't know of another author who does what he does, starting with an infinitesimal element—a dot of an idea—and unspooling it page by page, creation by creation, until it fills a book. It really is a kind of magic.

And amazingly, he just keeps getting better. How often can one say that about a writer? There's an emotional weave and an embrace in the work of his maturity. There's a humanity and poignancy to it now. When you read one of these unforeseeable books, it's not only going to blow your mind, it's also going to break your heart.

Hop aboard with me, then, and take a tour through Mark's extraordinary novels, stories, and other writing. I bet you'll find getting to know him and his work as marvelous as I have. And since the twenty-first-century analogue of the traditional literary biography is the celebrity interview, that will be the form much of our investigation takes. (See page 441 for directions to our career-spanning chat.) If you've never read anything by him before, I envy you.

Let us do some Leyner. Take a hit of high-grade Mark. Visions of everything from drug-dealing gods to kung-fu-fighting squirrels will dance in our heads. Cerebral cortexes will twist and shout. Medulla oblongatas will do the ontological conga!

On the seventeenth of May, 1996, Mark appeared with David Foster Wallace and Jonathan Franzen on the PBS show *Charlie Rose* to discuss the Future of American Fiction. YouTube it. Seriously, the talk's titanic. The hair is hilarious!

Well, here we are in the future that the three of them were attempting to imagine, and Mark's oeuvre stands apart. It's entirely without precedent, a universe conjured from his subconscious.

Here's what Jonathan Franzen had to say about the uniqueness of Mark's voice (I interviewed him on July 15, 2020):

> I think Mark was running something that was different from anybody else's work that comes to mind. It's less apparent with Mark where he comes from than with Dave or me. If you're a student of DeLillo, you have a pretty good idea where Dave Wallace comes from. If you've read modern fiction—that is, modernism and nineteenth-century fiction—it's pretty clear where I come from.
>
> Mark came out of nowhere with something that didn't feel like anybody else's. And I think that's partly just the stamp of his own personality. But formally, it's like, What is this? What am I reading? *Antic* is a word for it, but it doesn't really do justice to the uniqueness of his voice, the

uniqueness of his method—or his lack of one. Literary context is tricky with Mark's work. I'm not sure who you would point to exactly…

When I think of his work, I see how it sits on the page, particularly *My Cousin, My Gastroenterologist*. Yes, there are some riffs in there that I remember specifically, Walid Jumblatt and his Druse Militiamen, et cetera, but mostly what I remember is the combination of what the words were doing and the way they sat on the page.

I can't really think of anyone else like him.

I can't really think of anyone else like him, either. Which is why I proposed the idea of a Mark Leyner reader to his publisher. And here it is.

The goal of the book in your hands is to provide a kind of greatest hits collection, pulling together some of the most dazzling, heartbreaking, superunique human communiqués you've—ever—encountered. Each of these excerpts stands on its own and is introduced by an appreciation from one of Mark's innumerable admirers along with a brief account he composed of his life at the time he was writing the work that follows.

And speaking of greatest hits collections, this one even comes with an all-new bonus track that Mark actually wrote (gulp) for me!

Working on this book, corresponding with and talking to people who love Mark Leyner's work as I do, has been an undreamed-of blast. It's my hope that you'll share that delight, that you'll enjoy what you discover in these pages and promptly run out to discover more.

1

I SMELL ESTHER WILLIAMS (1983)

THE STORY SO FAR

January 4, 1956   Born in Margaret Hague Maternity Hospital, in Jersey City, to Joel and Muriel Leyner

1960–1966   Entranced by nuns (and ants, of course, always)

1967   Immerses himself in the world of professional wrestling: Bruno Sammartino, Baron Scicluna, Haystacks Calhoun, Gorilla Monsoon
   Profoundly influenced (i.e., traumatized) by several movies, including: *Attack of the 50 Ft. Woman, A Song to Remember, Pride of the Marines, Jason and the Argonauts, Mutiny on the Bounty* (any movie in which mutineers are whipped on ships), etc.

1967   Moves to West Orange, New Jersey, where he makes a series of transformative pilgrimages to Thomas Edison's laboratory
   Entranced by squirrels (and the smaller chipper-munks)

1969   Moves to Maplewood, New Jersey

January 12, 1969   Bar mitzvah party on the day the New York Jets defeat the Baltimore Colts in Super Bowl III (as personally guaranteed by Jets quarterback "Broadway" Joe Namath)

1970   Ejaculates for the first time and begins stealing his grandmother's Marlboros

1970–1973   Attends Columbia High School; writes column for school newspaper (*The Columbian*) called "This Side of Paradise"

1973–1977 Attends Brandeis University, in Waltham, Massachusetts
    Upon graduation, receives the Dorothy Blumenfeld Moyer Memorial Award for creative writing

1976 Begins obsessively humming the ABBA song "Fernando"

1977–1979 Completes the graduate writing program at the University of Colorado at Boulder as a teaching assistant. Begins work on several of the texts that will eventually comprise *I Smell Esther Williams*

1980–1981 Lives in Washington, DC, and works as a document analyst in Beltsville, Maryland, and then as a cashier at a drugstore and a bookstore and a record store in Chevy Chase
    Develops a passion for chicken livers in cream gravy
    Works on *I Smell Esther Williams* in a room full of bees (one can't possibly overestimate the impact of the bees on his evolving style)

1981 Moves to Hoboken, New Jersey
    Works at Panasonic in Secaucus as a copywriter and then as a waiter at the Summit House restaurant in Jersey City
    Spends a considerable amount of time at the Mudd Club, Danceteria, the Roxy, etc. (nights frequently culminating with a knish and an egg cream at Dave's, on Canal and Broadway)

1983 Publication of *I Smell Esther Williams*

WRITING SO TRULY UNIQUE THAT CRITICS HAVEN'T KNOWN HOW TO TALK ABOUT IT

An Email Conversation with Larry McCaffery

November 6, 2020

Dear Larry,

It was great to connect on the phone today. Sincere thanks for your time. I look forward to working with you in whatever way works for you. Can't wait to see the interview you did with Mark.

Cheers,
Rick

November 19, 2020

Yo, Rick,

Sorry I've been so delayed in getting back to you—it's my sense, then and now, that Mark's work has always been so truly unique that critics haven't known how to talk about it; but certainly, he deserves more serious attention. At any rate, I'm interested in hearing more about your plans.

Cordially,
Larry

November 22, 2020

Hi Larry,

As I understand it, you're responsible for pulling the pin from the grenade of his career. You published that piece in the Mississippi Review, Harpers picked it up & the next thing Mark knew, he was offered a deal by Harmony Books. Who knows whether he ever would have happened without you.

Mark was extremely glad to get your greetings.

Hope you have a great Thanksgiving.

Cheers,
Rick

April 13, 2021

Hi, Rick,

I know I'm prejudiced, but I absolutely loved *LAST ORGY OF THE DIVINE HERMIT*! Not only did it keep me laughing throughout, but I actually wound up also being very moved by Mark's sweet treatment (it IS sweet) of the father-daughter motif. I just sent a copy to my son, Mark—his daughter Ella, who is my beloved granddaughter Ella, is a senior in high school, and so Mark is understandably concerned about how their relationship will change once Ella takes off for college, so

I thought *LAST ORGY* would be the perfect novel to offset his worries.

It's so great to see Mark continuing to write with such…poetic and utterly timely outrageousness and passion (as you know, it's hard to describe Mark's work).

aren't we lucky to have him around?

best,
Larry

April 14, 2021

Hi Larry,

Thanks so much for the wonderful message and beautiful photos. What a great story about sending your son Mark's book. Maybe it will become the standard text for father/daughter separation a la *What to Expect When You're Expecting* for childbirth!

Yes, I agree. We're lucky to have him still around and still innovating. It was such a privilege to watch that novel come together. You know, the way you did in the case of *Esther Williams, My Cousin* and *Et Tu, Babe.*

Speaking of which, you're mentioned a number of times in the book we're working on. I quote from your interview with Mark in *Frequency* and he alludes to several memorable moments involving you.

Any chance you might be willing to contribute a few memories or observations if I sent you text for comment? It would be an honor to have your voice in there.

All the best,
Rick

May 29, 2021

Hi Larry,

I hope you're well. And thought you might get a kick out of this astonishing review by Bruce Sterling. In a science magazine of all things.

Really beautiful.

Cheers,
Rick

May 31, 2021

Dear Rick,

I am resting up nicely after a "small stroke," my "rest" being made more cheerful by the bruce sterling review. i'm expecting my rest to start really getting going after my doctor gets around to operating (the actual operation is supposed to be routine, i'll be back in touch shortly when all this is taken care of), in the meantime, we have bruce sterling's review...

bruce has been a leyner fan ever since i chose mark's piece ("i was an infinitely hot and dense dot...") for the mississippi review cyber punk double issue and i think he comes close to what makes mark's fiction so distinctive here.

hooray!

Lawrence F. McCaffery Jr. (born May 13, 1946) is an American literary critic, editor, and retired professor of English and comparative literature at San Diego State University. His work and teaching focus on postmodern literature, contemporary fiction, and Bruce Spring-steen. He—not Mark, Charlie Rose, or Harmony PR staffers—is responsible for the following much-quoted words, which appeared as a blurb on the back cover of *My Cousin, My Gastroenterologist* in 1990: "Establishes Mark Leyner as the most intense and, in a certain sense, the most significant young prose writer in America."

EXCERPTS FROM
I SMELL ESTHER WILLIAMS

LAUNCH

I'VE GIVEN THE raft with the woman you've been waiting for a little push so you should be receiving her any day now. She has a very deep cleavage like liz taylor. You may have to thaw her out. She is dead like I am.

I am doing my impersonation of the new jersey shore. I, of course, am lying on my side and masturbating into a bedpan that I've banged into a likeness of deep cleavage. If the costa rican nurse touches my nipple, I tell her that the nipple is the living room of a run-down two-family house by the sea. If she puts her eiderdown electron-image tubes to both my nipples and only if she shows me her shiny gold molars and sings Tengo Cabanga Por Mi Patria, I tell her that two escaped convicts from the woman's house of detention are in the living room, pulling taffy and watching a television show with the sound off, and if she brings me seconds for lunch when chicken fried steak is served, I pretend that they are snorting thick lines of crystal speed, and I promise her jewelry. If she draws a picture of what she thinks the raft woman's ass would look like projected on a drive-in movie screen without lifting her pencil from the paper, I open the living room door and mr. and mrs. hogan, a couple from Philadelphia, enter and I pull her dress up over my head and we hypnotize each other and pretend that we have no control over what we say or do. If it is late at night, we pretend that we have lost the right to vote and that we have been sterilized by missionaries. We pretend that we have cut the moorings and let the raft drift away, that we are exiled on an island for savage morons.

The woman who I'm sending knows all about you. We have spent many nights reminiscing about you and laughing about your ingenuous kindnesses and social clumsiness. She is impressed by your poems and surmises that, as a child, you must have been force fed like farm poultry. Of course she is drifting very peaceably now right towards you. It's a fine sunny day. She and the raft look marvelous, rocking in the tide. She is doing her impersonation of an automobile showroom. You would enjoy it very much. She, of course, is lying on her back and the sun is glistening against all her automobiles, her sedans, her squared-off economy models, her red convertibles. If she draws a thin piece of kelp across the inner part of her thigh, like a bow across a violin string, you can hear all your favorite buddy holly songs. I, of course, am on my knees, peering through an antique vasco da gama spyglass, watching her revolve in momentary eddies. I too am enjoying her uncanny impersonation of an automobile showroom. If the nurse brings me a fat pungent-smelling costa rican cigar, I pretend that I am a newspaper boy in a vintage 1930s-style newspaper boy's cap. If she takes off her starched white nurse's cap, unfastens her bobby pins and lets her luxurious black tresses fall into my eyes, I enter the automobile showroom and yell, extra! extra! yeshiva boy slays showgirl whale swallows mob kingpin bald cure called hoax mets split! She in turn impersonates mrs. hogan. I think we want fifteen automobiles! she says. Look how fast my husband is! Mr. hogan runs from car to car spinning the plates he's balanced on each antenna. Of course she's drifting towards you now! She is coming to you of her own volition. Do not let that disturb you. It was, in large part, her idea. Oh, look. The raft has a nice teakwood desk. She is writing a letter. She will either put the letter in a bottle and throw it at me or save it for you. At the end of the letter, after recapitulating the ups and downs of her epically repressed life, she writes, p.s., I want the second movement of mozart's piano concerto in b flat major played at my funeral. She begins to lose weight. I enter a room where people are frantically pacing back and forth. Everyone thinks *I* look negro, I say. I am, of course, dying. I've placed two hundred dollars on furrowed brow in the sixth at aqueduct for you. She will be exhausted when she reaches you. She will be almost dead. My life is over. The nurse is doing her impersonation of an afternoon in bethesda, maryland. I pretend that I am a house. When she gives me a blow job, I tell her that someone in the house is doing yoga exercises and that someone is painting the maid's room institution-green. The woman I'm sending you has taken off her bathing suit top. You will like her breasts very much. She is doing her famous impression of someone who takes three hours to eat a teaspoon of potato salad. The nurse says that mr. hogan is in a deep trance. Now king me. Checkmate. Gin, he says. The bed is masquerading as the sauna at seton hall university. A young man named theo enters. Let's go down on each other, he says. My nurse is playing the role of a girl with very beautiful red pubic hair. You're not the most subtle guy in the world, she says. He bites her stomach. Yum! she says, Your whiskers are like porcupine quills. My father's pizzeria is the best in new jersey, he says. Oooooo! she says, You're clever, too! The costa rican nurse, who, admittedly, represents a repressed feral idealization of my mother, collapses to the floor and does her impersonation of a molting boa constrictor.

I am skipping smooth flattened stones in the direction of the drifting raft. I am trying to get the woman's attention. She is not a shape. A nude chiaroscuro set in relief against the horizon. I cup my hands and yell, I was sitting in the library when I first heard two members of the parnassian society whispering your name back and forth. Remember? There were only two books in the entire library that hadn't been taken out—Portable Power Tools by leo macdonnell and The Penicillin Man by john rowland, she calls out to me. I begin to weep because she has remembered. There are some things, she calls out, that a woman never forgets. I pretend that the cliff rising above the dark water is a lovers' leap. We jump. She is doing her impersonation of a woman who has jumped before. The raft is disappearing now.

My life is over. It has been over for months now. I am sending this woman to you partly because we have preyed on each other's consciences far too long, and partly because you are my only friend and this is the woman you have been waiting for, for so many years. She is dead like I am. You too will be dead soon. When she arrives, do not mince words. Do not pretend with her.

MEMORIA IN AETERNA

HOPING THAT ONE last slug of warm Schlitz would give him the courage to finally say to Patty, "I love your breasts, the way one breast presses against the U of your sweatshirt, the way the other presses against the A, making the S a spot where a man could lay his head in peace," Oscar tipped his airline cup to his lips. But the words wouldn't come and god Oscar wanted to slip his hand under that shirt and feel her warm bare back and kiss her freckled nose. "This is where I get off," he said, crestfallen, squeezing past Patty's knees and ambling up the aisle to the door of the plane. "Bye," he waved sheepishly; and he jumped. As he fell through the air, he looked up towards Patty's window and Patty was frantically waving his parachute in her hand, yelling "Oskie, you forgot this!" Oscar's descent, being the shortest path between two points, was swift. He hit the ground with an awful thud. I was the first to reach him. "Oscar, buddy, ol' pal of mine, say a few syllables," I said. His eyes seemed a bit glazed. "Someone just hit me in the head with a pillow," he said. "Oscar, Oscar," I keened, "you're seven-eighths dead, you're all busted up like a ceramic Buddha dropped from the

World Trade Center—do you have any last words?" I wet his lips with my italian ices. "All I ever wanted to do," he whispered, "was finish my novel…and drag a good Catholic girl through the mud a few times." "Ciao, old friend," I said. Randy, Normandi, Ray, Rachel, Wayne, and me—we'll never forget you.

THE BOAT SHOW

LOOK. I'VE JUST returned from a used bookstore. It's run on the honor system. You pay at the main store across the street. It's easy to steal the books. There are economics textbooks, volumes of Shakespeare filled with sophomoric underlining and marginalia, books that people probably purchased in drugstores and supermarkets before going on vacation, marriage manuals, and stacks and stacks of National Geographics. That's clear, isn't it? I've given a partial list in order to generally characterize the store's stock. Once I stole an art magazine from the place. I felt guilty. After all, it's commendable that someone has faith in other people these days, and it's commendable that someone is offering books at such cheap prices. More people should read, right? So this time I didn't steal anything. I simply went through a few piles of Modern Photography magazines and ripped out all the photographs of nude women I could find. When I got home, I tacked them up to the walls of my study. Are you following me so far? Now I am looking out the window of my study. I am going to try to make you see what I see. With me? O.K. A red car just drove by. A blue one. And then a white coupe with a black vinyl roof.

A man in a white v-neck undershirt just leaned out his door and took his mail out of the box. His house is painted a kind of olive-green color. The house to the right of his is a very muted salmon-pink. The house to the right of that is a deep scarlet with white trim. Now, what color is the house next to that? I'll give you a minute or two. While you think, I'll have a cigarette and look at my new photographs. There's one of a blond woman I particularly like. She looks like a girl named Sharon I knew in Boulder. I think Sharon's married now and lives up in Buffalo, New York. Anyway...O.K., time's up. How many of you wrote down, red brick with beige trim? Good. Alright, now you've got the hang of it. Again, I'm going to try to make you sense what I sense. Ready? Here we go. The electric heater in my study runs on a thermostat. So all day it turns itself on and off. Sometimes, though, it gets too hot. Let's say it's getting too hot now. Follow me? I'm taking off my flannel shirt. O.K. O.K. I'll take off my undershirt too. Now I'm bare-chested. And for the sake of argument, I'll tack a spare photograph of two nudes on horseback to my chest. Ouch...there. Nice horse, huh? Now I'm looking out the window. A dog is howling. Awwwooooo. Awwwooooooo. I hear a helicopter. I lean next to the window and check the sky. Very gray. A guy with a trainman's cap and ponytail just got out of a pickup truck and walked up the street carrying a clipboard. Did you see him take the pen out from behind his ear? Good. A group of about fifteen African diplomats just walked by. If I didn't know better, I'd say one of them is pointing right at me. Look at all the litter in the street. That's terrible. Whatever happened to "keep America beautiful"? Went out with hula hoops and swallowing fish, right? O.K. Look at the beer cans. I can make out Stroh's, Miller, a Michelob...and a Budweiser. Now I'm going to look directly beneath my window. I'm going to try to be very specific here. Next to the curb are two plastic trash barrels, green and red with black lids. Adjacent to the barrels is the neighbor's hedge...it's made up of some kind of perennial shrub (I'm squinting now and leaning way over), some kind of perennial shrub with prickly…prickly bipinnate leaves and tiny tiny pink flowers. You are enchanted by the tiny delicate pink petals. N'est-ce pas? You want to crush them with a mortar and pestle and massage them into your scalp. You are repeating the word "pestle" to yourself until it loses its meaning. Alright. Don't move. Do you see the reflection of my finger in the window? Do you see the reflection of my face? Am I pointing to a dimple, a pock mark, or a dueling scar? Yell out your answer! Now we are dancing. Are you inhaling as I exhale? In other words, have our gears meshed? Are you still lashed to the cross of my thoughts? Uh oh. I'm feeling light-headed. The right side of my brain is giving a blow job to the left side. You don't get a choice on this one—I'm going to do all four—I'm going to a. Smash my china to the music of Felix Mendelssohn, b. Drive the endless highway west, c. Collect the latex footprints that lead to this room, *and* d. Open my veins in a warm bath. Now where is my tweed jacket with a wedding band in every pocket? Where is my yiddish phrase book? My itinerary? That's the last one. You'll have to leave. I'm going to throw myself out the window. Put me in one of the plastic trash barrels. Tack a photograph of yourself to my forehead. Goodbye now. We part!

2

MY COUSIN, MY GASTROENTEROLOGIST (1990)

THE STORY SO FAR

1985–1986   Teaches as an adjunct at Jersey City State College and Brooklyn College

1986   Marries Arleen Portada

March 29, 1987   Hulk Hogan body-slams André the Giant at WrestleMania III

1987–1990   Works as copywriter at the Wyatt Company's Executive Compensation Service and then at the Falcone Agency, all the while working day and night on *My Cousin, My Gastroenterologist*

Meets Mercedes Pinto (who's working as a word processor at ECS)

1988   "I Was an Infinitely Hot and Dense Dot" appears in the *Mississippi Review*'s cyberpunk issue, edited by Larry McCaffery

1989   Michael Pietsch (then an editor at Harmony Books), having read "I Was an Infinitely Hot and Dense Dot" reprinted in the *Harper's Magazine* Readings section, calls Leyner up at Falcone and asks if he has other work and if he'd be willing to punctuate any of it. Leyner is like, If you ask nicely (Pietsch had)

1990   Publication of *My Cousin, My Gastroenterologist*

"IDYLL"

blue cheese & office equipment

Ben Dolnick

RECOMMENDING MARK LEYNER, I feel as if I'm walking up to knots of people at a party and thrusting before them samples of an unspeakably pungent blue cheese. Half—probably more than half—of the guests will mount a refusal so visceral and emphatic that it will verge on panic. The other half, though, will take a bite, close their eyes, and experience a pleasure so intense and complex that they will, for a few seconds, forget the party completely.

I count myself among the blue cheese savorers, but I understand the rejecters' position; part of me even shares it. This does not, I must at some level acknowledge, smell good. And yet…

Mark Leyner does something for me that no other writer does, something that no other writer even tries to do. I read him when my mind's plumbing needs not just snaking but also hydrojetting—an industrial-strength blast of hypervivid oddity. He's never created a character worth remembering, and I'm not sure I can recall a single scene he's written, but that's because characters and scenes aren't what he traffics in. He traffics in words—the angular, miraculous, multitudinous things themselves.

So let's look at those words.

But first, for the uninitiated: Mark Leyner belongs, taxonomically, somewhere in the lineage of Douglas Coupland, David Foster Wallace, and Robert Coover. Which is to say that he once had a goatee and that a certain Gen X aura of sunglasses and coffee-shop anticonsumerism trails him still. He wrote a handful of uncategorizably bizarre books in the '90s, took a break (during which—as if determined to live out one of his random-meaning-generator sentences—he cowrote the bestselling book of medical trivia *Why Do Men Have Nipples?*), and then, with 2012's *The Sugar Frosted Nutsack*, picked right back up where he left off.

His books are full of—they are delivery mechanisms for—spiky little word clusters of hypnotic weirdness: "larval psychotics," "shimmering, serrated monster," "epoxied chunks of chipmunk meat." He is, in other words, a poet—a poet whose vocabulary derives not from nature but from infomercials, action movies, and Saturday morning cartoons. It's therefore tempting to dismiss him as a bit of historic cultural flotsam, the literary equivalent of an MTV veejay—until you sit down and read him. His idiosyncratic brilliance is no more of the '90s than Emily Dickinson's was of the 1870s. His books will be—or anyway should be—read as long as there are people silently staring at pieces of paper for fun.

The book to start with is *My Cousin, My Gastroenterologist*, his 1992 collection of short stories (or short somethings). Here, in its entirety, is the story "Idyll":

> I was reading an article that contained the words "vineyards, orchards, and fields bountiful with fruits and vegetables; sheep and goats graze on hillsides of lush greenery"

and I realized that in five months none of these things would exist and I realized that as the last sheep on earth is skinned, boned, filleted, and flash-frozen, Arleen and I would probably be making love for the last time, mingling—for the last time—the sweet smell of her flesh which is like hyacinths and narcissus with the virile tang of my own which is like pond scum and headcheese and then I realized that the only thing that would distinguish me in the eyes of posterity from—for instance—those three sullen Chinese yuppies slumped over in their bentwood chairs at the most elegant McDonald's in the world is that I wrote the ads that go: "Suddenly There's Vancouver!"

The first thing to notice about this sentence is that it's a sentence. The second thing is that it sounds sensible. In its music, its shapeliness, its sinuous journey toward its exclamatory end, it resembles the English prose that you might find in a book-club pick, maybe something by Franzen or Egan. There's nothing in its form that would snap the drowsing Audible listener awake.

But its content is, of course, insane—and insane in the particular electrified, self-responsive way that characterizes Leyner's best work. Fiction writers are perpetually asking themselves, What is the most interesting thing I could do here? By "here," they mean: in this chapter, in this section, in this character's arc. Leyner operates at a different frame rate: he scans for the maximally interesting possibility numerous times per sentence.

The first forty words of "Idyll" cohere; they could be the opening of a novel about an impending enviro-apocalypse.

I was reading an article that contained the words "vineyards, orchards, and fields bountiful with fruits and vegetables; sheep and goats graze on hillsides of lush greenery" and I realized that in five months none of these things would exist

Okay, we think. Maybe a nuclear blast is coming. So far, so

parse-able. But then we come to the last sheep on earth and its uncomfortably dwelt-upon demise.

and I realized that as the last sheep on earth is skinned, boned, filleted, and flash-frozen

Flash-frozen is, for me, the moment when this sentence surrenders its Ordinary Prose membership card. The logic of enviro-apocalypse has departed, and the logic of food prep has set in. That list of verbs (skinned, boned, filleted) has acted as an incantation upon our poor suggestible narrator, and it has carried him, apparently, into the realm of fast-food commercials.

But there's hope, because here comes Arleen and the order-restoring pull of lovemaking. Sex with a beloved is the sort of thing that might happen in a doomsday literary novel, right? Surely this will get us back on track.

Arleen and I would probably be making love for the last time, mingling—for the last time

Nice rhythmic repetition! Emphasizing the lastness of this last time is just what we hoped tender, sex-treasuring prose would do.

—the sweet smell of her flesh which is like hyacinths and narcissus

Well, our narrator has briefly been bashed over the head with a romance novel, but no matter: we're describing smells; we're creating parallels.

with the virile tang of my own which is like pond scum and headcheese

And we're off the tracks again. He has fallen into the mine shaft of smell description (just as he previously fell into the mine shaft of sheep dismemberment) and forgotten entirely the loving, poignant business in which he was engaged.

But anyway, the sex is finished. The narrator's eyes, pained by the brightness of apocalypse, softened by the affections of Arleen, are turning now toward eternity.

and then I realized that the only thing that would distinguish me in the eyes of posterity from—for instance—those three sullen Chinese yuppies slumped over in their bentwood chairs

This is sounding a bit specific to be a "for instance," but yes, go on.

at the most elegant McDonald's in the world

Okay. Whatever. Just tell us what it is that distinguishes you. We can see the end of the sentence—not to mention the story and the world—approaching. Take us home.

is that I wrote the ads that go: "Suddenly There's Vancouver!"

This finale, with its exultant exclamation point, is the literary equivalent of stamping hard on a stair that turns out to be a landing—and it is the moment that always, no matter how many times I read it, makes me smile in baffled admiration. Here Leyner has led us, by the grammar and "logic" of the sentence, to expect a triumphant bugle blast—and instead he's produced the sort of tagline, perfectly calibrated in its banality, that we've all found ourselves staring at in irritable torpor (Who writes these things?) on empty train platforms.

And now he's bowing.

Because what he's actually done here—in the guise of delivering a lyrical account of one man's attempt at reckoning with the apocalypse—is engage us in a kind of highbrow game. We have no choice, as well-trained readers, but to seek coherence, to provide necessary set decoration, to translate sound into imagery. Leyner is one of the shockingly few writers who recognize the comic potential in this state of affairs. Presented with the fragile, expensive office equipment that is our language-comprehension machinery, most writers type up solemn memos and set about mastering the communications system. Leyner makes Xeroxes of his own butt.

Ben Dolnick is the author of a handful of novels, including *At the Bottom of Everything* and *The Ghost Notebooks*. He lives with his wife and daughter in Brooklyn.

EXCERPTS FROM
MY COUSIN, MY GASTROENTEROLOGIST

I WAS AN INFINITELY HOT AND DENSE DOT

I WAS DRIVING to Las Vegas to tell my sister that I'd had Mother's respirator unplugged. Four bald men in the convertible in front of me were picking the scabs off their sunburnt heads and flicking them onto the road. I had to swerve to avoid riding over one of the oozy crusts of blood and going into an uncontrollable skid. I maneuvered the best I could in my boxy Korean import but my mind was elsewhere. I hadn't eaten for days. I was famished. Suddenly as I reached the crest of a hill, emerging from the fog, there was a bright neon sign flashing on and off that read: FOIS GRAS AND HARICOTS VERTS NEXT EXIT. I checked the guidebook and it said: *Excellent food, malevolent ambience.* I'd been habitually abusing an illegal growth hormone extracted from the pituitary glands of human corpses and I felt as if I were drowning in excremental filthiness but the prospect of having something good to eat cheered me up. I asked the waitress about the soup du jour and she said that it was primordial soup—which is ammonia and methane mixed with ocean water in the presence of lightning. Oh I'll take a tureen of that embryonic broth, I say, constraint giving way to exuberance—but as soon as

28

she vanishes my spirit immediately sags because the ambience is so malevolent. The bouncers are hassling some youngsters who want drinks—instead of simply carding the kids, they give them radio-carbon tests, using traces of carbon 14 to determine how old they are—and also there's a young wise guy from Texas A&M at a table near mine who asks for freshly ground Rolaids on his fettuccine and two waiters viciously work him over with heavy bludgeon-sized pepper mills, so I get right back into my car and narcissistically comb my thick jet-black hair in the rearview mirror and I check the guidebook. There's an inn nearby—it's called Little Bo Peep's—its habitués are shepherds. And after a long day of herding, shear-ing, panpipe playing, muse invoking, and conversing in eclogues, it's Miller time, and Bo Peep's is packed with rustic swains who've left their flocks and sunlit, idealized arcadia behind for the more pungent charms of hard-core social intercourse. Everyone's favorite waitress is Kikugoro. She wears a pale-blue silk kimono and a bro-cade obi of gold and silver chrysanthemums with a small fan tucked into its folds, her face is painted and powdered to a porcelain white. A cowboy from south of the border orders a "Biggu Makku." But Kikugoro says, "This is not Makudonarudo." She takes a long cylin-der of gallium arsenide crystal and slices him a thin wafer which she serves with soy sauce, wasabi, pickled ginger, and daikon. "Conducts electrons ten times faster than silicon…taste good, gaucho-*san*, you eat," she says, bowing.

My sister is the beautiful day. Oh beautiful day, my sister, wipe my nose, swaddle me in fresh-smelling garments. I nurse at the adamantine nipple of the beautiful day, I quaff the milk of the beau-tiful day, and for the first time since 1956, I cheese on the shoul-der of the beautiful day. Oh beautiful day, wash me in your lake of cloudless azure. I have overdosed on television, I am unrespon-sive and cyanotic, revive me in your shower of gelid light and walk me through your piazza which is made of elegant slabs of time. Oh beautiful day, kiss me. Your mouth is like Columbus Day. You are the menthol of autumn. My lungs cannot quench their thirst for you. Resuscitate me — I will never exhale your tonic gasses. Inflate me so that I may rise into the sky and mourn the monotonous topography of my life. Oh beautiful day, my sister, wipe my nose and adorn me in your finery. Let us lunch alfresco. Your club sandwiches are made of mulch and wind perfumed with newsprint. Your frilly toothpicks are the deciduous trees of school days.

I was an infinitely hot and dense dot. So begins the autobiography of a feral child who was raised by huge and lurid puppets. An autobiography written wearing wrist weights. It ends with these words: A car drives through a puddle of sperm, sweat, and contraceptive jelly, splattering the great, chopsocky vigilante from Hong Kong. Inside, two acephalic sardines in mustard sauce are asleep in the rank darkness of their tin container. Suddenly, the swinging doors burst open and a mesomorphic cyborg walks in and whips out a 35-lb. phallus made of corrosion-resistant nickel-base alloy and he begins to stroke it sullenly, his eyes half shut. It's got a metal-oxide membrane for absolute submicron filtration of petrochemical fluids. It can ejaculate herbicides, sulfuric acid, tar glue, you name it. At the end of the bar, a woman whose album-length poem about temporomandibular joint dysfunction (TMJ) had won a Grammy for best spoken word recording is gently slowly ritually rubbing copper hexafluoroacetylacetone into her clitoris as she watches the hunk with the non-Euclidian features shoot a glob of dehydrogenated ethylbenzene 3,900 miles towards the Arctic archipelago, eventually raining down upon a fiord on Baffin Bay. Outside, a basketball plunges from the sky, killing a dog. At a county fair, a huge and hairy man in mud-caked blue overalls, surrounded by a crowd of retarded teenagers, swings a sledgehammer above his head with brawny keloidal arms and then brings it down with all his brute force on a tofu-burger on a flowery paper plate. A lizard licks the dew from the stamen of a stunted crocus. Rivets and girders float above the telekinetic construction workers. The testicular voice of Barry

White emanates from some occult source within the laundry room. As I chugalug a glass of tap water milky with contaminants, I realize that my mind is being drained of its contents and refilled with the beliefs of the most mission-oriented, can-do feral child ever raised by huge and lurid puppets. I am the voice...the voice from beyond and the voice from within—can you hear me? Yes. I speak to you and you only—is that clear? Yes, master. To whom do I speak? To me and me only. Is "happy" the appropriate epithet for someone who experiences each moment as if he were being alternately flayed alive and tickled to death? No, master.

In addition to the growth hormone extracted from the glands of human corpses, I was using anabolic steroids, tissue regeneration compounds, granulocyte-macrophage colony-stimulating factor (GM-CSF)—a substance used to stimulate growth of certain vital blood cells in radiation victims—and a nasal spray of neuropeptides that accelerates the release of pituitary hormones and I was getting larger and larger and my food bills were becoming enormous. So I went on a TV game show in the hopes of raising cash. This was my question, for $250,000 in cash and prizes: If the Pacific Ocean were filled with gin, what would be, in terms of proportionate volume, the proper lake of vermouth necessary to achieve a dry martini? I said Lake Ontario—but the answer was the Caspian Sea which is called a sea but is a lake by definition. I had failed. I had humiliated my family and disgraced the kung fu masters of the Shaolin temple. I stared balefully out into the studio audience which was chanting something that sounded like "dork." I'm in my car. I'm high on Sinutab. And I'm driving anywhere. The vector of my movement from a given point is isotropic—meaning that all possible directions are equally probable. I end up at a squalid little dive somewhere in Vegas maybe Reno maybe Tahoe. I don't know...but there she is. I can't tell if she's a human or a fifth-generation gynemorphic android and I don't care. I crack open an ampule of mating pheromone and let it waft across the bar, as I sip my drink, a methyl isocyanate on the rocks—methyl isocyanate is the substance which killed more than 2,000 people when it leaked in Bhopal, India, but thanks to my weight training, aerobic workouts, and a low-fat fiber-rich diet, the stuff has no effect on me. Sure enough she strolls over and occupies the stool next to mine. After a few moments of silence, I make the first move: We're all larval psychotics and have been since the age of two, I say, spitting an ice cube back into my glass. She moves closer to me. At this range, the downy cilia-like hairs that trickle from her navel remind me of the fractal ferns produced by injecting dyed water into an aqueous polymer solution, and I tell her so. She looks into my eyes: You have the glibness, superficial charm, grandiosity, lack of guilt, shallow feelings, impulsiveness, and lack of realistic long-term plans that excite me right now, she says, moving even closer. We feed on the same prey species, I growl. My lips are now one angstrom unit from her lips, which is one ten-billionth of a meter. I begin to kiss her but she turns her head away. Don't good little boys who finish all their vegetables get dessert? I ask. I can't kiss you, we're monozygotic replicants—we share 100% of our genetic material. My head spins. You are the beautiful day, I exclaim, your breath is a zephyr of eucalyptus that does a pas de bourrée across the Sea of Galilee. Thanks, she says, but we can't go back to my house and make love because monozygotic incest is forbidden by the elders. What if I said I could change all that….What if I said that I had a miniature shotgun that blasts gene fragments into the cells of living organisms, altering their genetic matrices so that a monozygotic replicant would no longer be a monozygotic replicant and she could then make love to a muscleman without transgressing the incest taboo, I say, opening my shirt and exposing the device which I had stuck in the waistband of my black jeans. How'd you get that thing? she gasps, ogling its thick fiber-reinforced plastic barrel and the Uzi-Biotech logo embossed on the magazine which held two cartridges of gelated recombinant DNA. I got it for

Christmas....Do you have any last words before I scramble your chromosomes, I say, taking aim. Yes, she says, you first. I put the barrel to my heart. These are my last words: When I emerged from my mother's uterus I was the size of a chicken bouillon cube and Father said to the obstetrician: I realize that at this stage it's difficult to prognosticate his chances for a productive future, but if he's going to remain six-sided and 0.4 grams for the rest of his life, then euthanasia's our best bet. But Mother, who only milliseconds before was in the very throes of labor, had already slipped on her muumuu and espadrilles and was puffing on a Marlboro: No pimple-faced simp two months out of Guadalajara is going to dissolve this helpless little hexahedron in a mug of boiling water, she said, as a nurse managed with acrobatic desperation to slide a suture basin under the long ash of her cigarette which she'd consumed in one furiously deep drag. These are my last words: My fear of being bullied and humiliated stems from an incident that occurred many years ago in a diner. A 500-lb. man seated next to me at the counter was proving that one particular paper towel was more absorbent than another brand. His face was swollen and covered with patches of hectic red. He spilled my glass of chocolate milk on the counter and then sopped it up with one paper towel and then with the other. With each wipe of the counter the sweep of his huge dimpled arm became wider and wider until he was repeatedly smashing his flattened hand and the saturated towel into my chest. There was an interminable cadence to the blows I endured. And instead of assistance from other patrons at the counter, I received their derision, their sneering laughter. But now look at me! I am a terrible god. When I enter the forest the mightiest oaks blanch and tremble. All rustling, chirping, growling, and buzzing cease, purling brooks become still. This is all because of my tremendous muscularity...which is the result of the hours of hard work that I put in at the gym and the strict dietary regimen to which I adhere. When I enter the forest the birds become incontinent with fear so there's this torrential downpour of shit from the trees. And I stride through—my whistle is like an earsplitting fife being played by a lunatic with a bloody bandage around his head. And the sunlight, rent into an incoherence of blazing vectors, illuminates me: a shimmering, serrated monster!

ENTER THE SQUIRREL

HE'D NEVER SHOT a woman before. He'd shot men, plenty of them. Shot them, bludgeoned them, garroted them, drowned them, poisoned them, he'd even pushed some poor slob out of a 747 as he crapped in his pants and pleaded for his life. But he'd never shot a woman before. No, wait a minute. He had shot a woman before. There was that dance therapist in Fort Lauderdale. He'd filled her with so much lead you could have sharpened her head and done a crossword puzzle with her. He'd shot women before but never anyone as beautiful as this. He'd never shot a beautiful woman before, that's it. And this one was beautiful, wow. Long legs, long long hairy prehensile toes. An ape-woman. Square peg teeth, hairy floppy ears, a bridgeless nose with wide flattened nostrils. He'd never shot an ape-woman before. Well, come to think of it, he had shot an ape-woman. Back in '63 in Reno. But he'd never shot an ape-woman this beautiful. Nope.

...Where was I? muses Big Squirrel, reloading his pistol. Oh yeah...don't forget, put plenty of duck sauce on the egg rolls. One of the kids in the audience stands up. Big Squirrel, you forgot to put the egg rolls in the microwave. All the kids in the audience start to giggle. Big Squirrel, you're so silly, they chime, hysterical with giggles, you're a big silly, you can't eat egg rolls when they're frozen! Big Squirrel fires a warning shot in the air. It's time for yoga! he says. Yea! yea! go the kids. OK, how many of you have accumulated mucus in your lower bowel? Yea! yea! Yogi Vithaldas, come out here. The organist plays a few bars of snake charmer music. Kids, give Yogi Vithaldas a nice Big Squirrel hello. Howdy, Yogi Vithaldas, they chime. Hello, kids. Yogi Vithaldas, tell the kids out there a little bit about yourself. Well, I just got married, Bill. Did you hear that, kids?! Yea! yea! Yup…my beautiful wife is a psychic who specializes in mediumistic psychotherapy — say you're in the middle of psychoanalysis and your analyst dies — you don't want to have to forage through upper Manhattan for someone new and start all over again at square one in the uterus — so my wife will conduct a séance and contact your late-lamented analyst in the spirit world: knock once for libido fixation, twice for obsessive-compulsion neurosis. And my brother-in-law is a movie star — y'know that Japanese film *In the Realm of the Senses* where the woman cuts off her lover's penis and walks around Tokyo for four days with it in her pocket — well, my brother-in-law played the penis. And the three of us are honeymooning at the beautiful Beijing Buena Vista Motel where we'll play mah-jongg with Madame Jiang Qing and toast the memory of Mao Zedong with hundred-year-old egg creams. Yea! Mazel tov, Yogi Vithaldas, now what do you have for us today? Today I have a yogic bowel cleansing exercise that can save you kids a lot of big gastroenterologist bills. Yogi Vithaldas assumes the graceful lotus pose. Without warning, Big Squirrel screams, It's kung fu time! and leaping high into the air delivers an explosive roundhouse kick upside Yogi Vithaldas's head that sends his right eyeball flying into a Styrofoam coffee cup. Olé! go the kids. OK, kids, today we have rare footage of lions eating a Christian taken by an amateur photographer at the Colosseum in 290 A.D. As the grainy, flickering footage appears on the studio monitor, Big Squirrel comes backstage to towel off. I approach Big Squirrel at the Pepsi machine. Big Squirrel, you are the world's most formidable master of Tiger and Crane style kung fu. Walid Jumblatt's Druse Militiamen are heading for the U.S.A. We need your lethal and balletic Tiger and Crane style kung fu to defeat and slaughter Walid Jumblatt's Druse Militiamen. What is your answer? Big Squirrel stares mystically into his Pepsi. I hear the twang of a chest hair being plucked, he says. (What Big Squirrel say mean Big Squirrel help fight Walid Jumblatt's Druse Militiamen.)

I'm dialing numbers frantically, fingers flying over push buttons in a blur, in my ear a crazy cacophony of electronic beeps. I'm getting places like Wales, Sterling Colorado, Vladivostok, Altamont Speedway, Barnes & Noble Annex, Nuremberg, Braintree Mass., and Biafra. I'm stirring a pitcher of Tanqueray martinis with one hand and sliding a tray of frozen clams *oreganata* into the oven with my foot. I've got a dozen cigarettes going simultaneously in ashtrays all over the apartment. God, these Methedrine suppositories that Yogi Vithaldas gave me are good! As I iron a pair of tennis shorts I dictate a haiku into the tape recorder and then dash off to snake a clogged drain in the bathroom sink and then do three minutes on the speedbag before making an origami praying mantis and then reading an article in *High Fidelity* magazine as I stir the coq au vin. These Methedrine suppositories are fantastic! I'm spinning through the apartment like a whirling dervish, finishing things I'd put off for months, cleaning the Venetian blinds, defrosting the freezer, translating *The Ring of the Nibelung* into Black English, gluing a model aircraft carrier together for my little son. I'm writing to my congressman, doing push-ups, changing a light bulb as I floss my teeth and feed my fish with one hand, balance my checkbook with the other and scratch my borzoi's silky stomach with my big toe. The stimulatory effect of the suppositories is convulsive. I'm an exploding skeleton of kinetic vectors. I stand upon a peak in Darien like stout

Cortez shouting I write the songs! I rupture into afterimages like the nude descending a staircase. Holographic clones of myself appear all over the apartment smoking cigarettes and drinking martinis. Where are the women, they chuckle. Mona arrives to borrow a cup of sugar. Quaaludes. Clothes shed. Gang bang. Death. Ambulance. Police. Apartment a mess. Next morning call maid. Maid arrives, drinks martinis, swallows goldfish, and vomits on little son. I take a deep breath...

The omens are inauspicious. In my haunted closet, mothballs mysteriously assemble into a triangle like a rack of billiard balls, my pants wriggle from their hangers and dance the cancan. Each night I have the same dream: I'm sitting on the john in the men's room at Avery Fisher Hall—at the climax of Rimsky-Korsakov's *Scheherazade* a swordfish flies up out of the toilet water and buries itself in my rectum, but when I look down into the bowl I find that in actuality I've defecated the missing 18-minute section of Watergate tape. Each morning I wake up on the ledge of a tall building gripping the concrete with white fingernails. In kindergartens and pediatric waiting rooms, young children greet each other with handshakes and eerily formal salutations. Whales throw themselves on the decks of whaling ships with interminable Schopenhauerian suicide notes pinned to their dorsal fins. The Puerto Rico Day parade is the largest in history, it is visible even to the astronauts who point excitedly from the porthole of their orbiting space shuttle, but tragedy strikes when the parade's grand marshal Herman Badillo bludgeons himself to death with his own ceremonial scepter after learning that his mother's gynecologist was aboard the ill-fated Korean jetliner flight #007. My mother wanders around the house like a member of the Manson family, saying "Maalox is groovy," and when I ask her to explain she says that the mucilaginous remains of history's cannibalized explorers from Magellan to David Rockefeller have collected in her stomach like wads of undigested chewing gum, giving her terrific heartburn, she says that she has a huge hair ball in her stomach made of the exquisitely flaxen underarm hair of Amelia Earhart. Cupping my ear to a bowl of Rice Krispies I hear German V-2 rockets falling on London Bridge. Unemployed laboratory mice laid off after cuts in federal research funding huddle in skid row alleyways guzzling miniature bottles of airline whiskey. When the president finds out that the astronauts left a new popularized version of the Bible on the moon instead of leaving the King James he is outraged. He calls an emergency meeting of the Girl Scouts and the Teamsters Union. In that Bible, he fumes, Delilah uses Nair on Samson's head and Jesus Christ is crucified with Phillips-head screws and Krazy Glue. He makes the astronauts go back to the moon and switch Bibles. But there is another snafu and this time instead of leaving the King James Bible on the moon they leave Cecil Brown's novel, *The Life and Loves of Mr. Jiveass Nigger.* Two elderly chimpanzees who, in the heyday of television documentaries about primate speech capacity, required sumptuous private dressing rooms with stars on the doors, now sit dejectedly in a Miami Beach Laundromat using sign language to bemoan their dwindling pensions and persistent hemorrhoids. Moving men hoist a Soviet-made antiaircraft rocket launcher into the third-floor window of a Beirut brownstone. Put it right next to the chifforobe, says Wali Assam, coyly raising her veil. Wali Assam is Beirut's most celebrated sexual self-help authoress. Her latest volume, *Liquidating the Zionist Entity in the Nude,* is number one on the best-seller list. Please don't make me move the chifforobe, says one of the workmen. Which one of you grungy hunks has the biggest muscle, she says, undulating the ruby in her navel. Don't flirt with the workmen! bellows a stentorian voice that rattles the china. Who is that? demands Wali Assam. This is your kitchen drain speaking! Don't flirt with the workmen! An enormous Caucasian fat man in plaid Bermuda shorts spraying Windex on the front windshield of a Datsun 280-Z with a Playboy rabbit dangling from the rearview mirror gets a cramp and calls out, Grandma! Grandma! Vultures circle above. The scene is worse at Bergdorf Goodman's:

frenzied women in estrus writhe on their bellies in the aisles, moo-
ing, snorting, and ululating, clutching violently at their breasts
and loins. In an effort to quell the feral cravings of the super-horny
shoppers, Abolhassan Bengazzara, the reptilian sadist and Savak
alumnus who commands the notorious Bergdorf Goodman's internal security police, orders his men to load their weapons with darts
containing powerful doses of Librium and testosterone. Me and
Huck are trapped in a fitting room in the junior miss department.
Every time one of us pokes his head out a dart comes whizzing by.
You don't want to get hit with one of those darts, says Huck, they'll
make you sleepy and your balls'll swell up like muskmelons. During
a lull in the shooting Huck goes foraging for food and returns with
a bag of Famous Amos cookies, a pocketful of papaya jelly beans,
and a box of frozen tortellini. Later by the campfire Huck reclines
with his ukulele and sings love songs to his girlfriend in Hannibal.
When ten-story radiation-spawned mutant leviathans rise from the
bubbling slime of toxic cesspools, tossing their ophidian manes of
napalm-spouting lymph tubes, the U.S. Air Force will shower them
with hydrogen bombs but don't cry, little love bug, after the mushroom cloud clears we'll be eating cream of mushroom soup in Monte
Carlo, where the manhole covers are embossed with champagne
glasses & bubbles and the gendarmes are armed with party favors,
croons Huck. Huck is heavily into a Bertolt Brecht/Barbra Streisand
thing. Later we go to the Thalia and sit through a double feature of
Mother Courage and *Yentl*. During the climactic scene in *Yentl* where
Barbra Streisand eats 300 salted herrings to prove to the other rab-
binical students that she is macho, Huck weeps uncontrollably and
vomits.

That night Walid Jumblatt's Druse Militiamen roll into town,
gunning the engines of their Harley-Davidson 1200s, firing celebratory bursts from their Kalashnikov assault rifles into the sky,
their flamboyant phosphorescent nylon djellabas streaming behind
them like the wind-whipped ensigns of a buccaneer raiding ship as

teenage girls, roused from their slumber by the pungent pheromones that waft from the armpits of the hell-bent Moslems on wheels, emerge from between their crisply creased sheets and pastel quilts, insert their diaphragms and plugs of spermicide, garnish their faces with cherry-red lipstick and lavender eye shadow, slip into tight capri pants, flimsy halter tops, and gem-studded slave bracelets, and flock somnambulantly to the local bar as if bitten by vampires.

Over decaffeinated espresso in his tersely appointed Gramercy Park apartment-cum-atelier, I chatted with Big Squirrel as he packed his valise in preparation for battle with the Druse Militiamen. Ball-bearing swivel nunchaku. Check. Black vinyl zippered nunchaku carrying case. Check. Ninja hood. Check. Ninja throwing stars. Check. Long-handled broadsword. Check. Butterfly knives. Check. Protective groin cup. Check. Big Squirrel executed a reverse aerial somersault onto the coffee table, scissoring my head between his knees. I involuntarily spit a hot stream of decaffeinated espresso into his lap. Our eyes met. It was a moment of intense spiritual communion. I want you to promise that if anything happens to me you'll see that my wife gets this, Big Squirrel said, waving the protective groin cup in my face. Please repeat the aforementioned, Big Squirrel, the viselike grip of your knees is causing considerable static along my auditory nerve path in addition to cutting off the vital flow of blood to my cerebral cortex and thalamic receptor nodes. Big Squirrel relaxed his hold and reiterated his solemn request. Listen, man, I said, I love my country. And I swear to you, Big Squirrel, that if you fall in battle I will personally deliver this protective groin cup to your bereaved wife. Thank you, said Big Squirrel, it was given to me as a wedding present by my father-in-law, chief of the Poznaks — a moody and fiercely independent tribe which inhabits a coastal plateau of Northeastern Ethiopia. The tribal truss-maker fashioned it from the bony carapace of a mud turtle. The Poznaks are an ingeniously resourceful people who subsist entirely on hot dogs, using the frankfurter skins for clothing, mashing the minced filling along with manioc tubers to make the glutinous pulp which is the staple of their diet, decocting the juice of the frankfurter and using the psychotropic distillate in their shamanistic rituals, and dipping the sharpened points of ossified hot dogs in curare and shooting them from their blowguns. Their magnificent cave paintings of picnicking Poznaks, meticulously stippled in the red sticky sweat of hippopotami, anticipated the pointillism of Georges Seurat by thousands of years. The Poznaks taught me many esoteric and deadly styles of kung fu including the 5 Plum, the Phoenix Eye, and the Jade Claw, and also Deli Style kung fu. Big Squirrel sighed heavily and averted his eyes. When my wife left her people in Ethiopia and returned with me to the U.S.A. she was very homesick and cried for weeks and weeks. She was unable to acclimate herself to this culture. She became irritable and I often had to resort to my most powerful kung fu to subdue her tantrums. As time went on she became increasingly despondent, listless, and withdrawn. I'd come home and find her washing barbiturates down with tumblers full of whiskey. Her sadness was breaking my heart, it was murdering me. Finally, upon the advice of my cousin, chief of gastroenterology at Mount Sinai, I had my wife committed to the Chef Boy-Ar-Dee Institute of Psychiatry. There psychiatrists told me that it was essential that my wife eat tremendous amounts of Italian food if there was to be any hope of her ever leading a normal life. They said that since Mussolini's invasion of Ethiopia they'd seen this condition in many of their Ethiopian patients. Throughout their formative years their parents ceaselessly revile Italian people and culture. The children in time come to associate their parents' derogation of Italy with parental derogation of themselves, resulting in increasingly bitter episodes of masochistic self-appraisal and ultimately functional ego death. By gradually introducing small amounts of Italian food into the diet of an Ethiopian adult, the psychiatrists are exploiting precisely those crossed wires which are buried deeply in the associative processes of the patient who has a desperate subconscious need to eat and enjoy

Italian cuisine, thereby correspondingly revivifying his or her own sense of self-worth. Because of the severity of my wife's condition, doctors recommended a massive infusion of Italian food into her diet. Antipasto, pasta fagioli, and manicotti for breakfast. Ziti, ravioli, and chicken cacciatore for lunch. Fried calamari, stromboli, veal scaloppine, chicken parmigiana, and linguini in white clam sauce for dinner. And tremendous amounts of Chianti, Soave Bolla, espresso coffee, cannoli, and spumoni between meals. Tears welled in Big Squirrel's eyes and rolled down his cheeks. I held him in my arms as I'd never held a man before. Hush now, Big Squirrel, I said softly, I'll see that she gets the protective groin cup. I'll see that she gets the protective groin cup. I'll see that she gets the protective groin cup....

After Big Squirrel's nap we went to a place called the Coal Hole, a restaurant on the Upper West Side located in an old coal mine. You take an elevator car about 300 ft. underground to the dining room. It's pitch dark and everyone wears one of those hard hats with the attached spotlight. Most of the waiters have black lung disease. It was the last restaurant Mimi Sheraton reviewed before quitting the *Times* and having her jaw wired shut. The dining room was extremely warm. I ordered a Tab. Big Squirrel ordered a Pepsi. There was an extraterrestrial serenity in Big Squirrel's face as Dionne Warwick's "Do You Know the Way to San Jose" wafted over the PA system. Do you really love Tab? he asked. He didn't wait for a reply. I think Tab tastes like raw sewage, he said. Big Squirrel, when you go off on what may be your final mercenary operation, there'll be a lot of people pulling for you. Do you have any parting words of advice for all the kids out there? If you want to be successful in life, he said, everything you do must be an act of patricide. You must always kill the father. Every song you sing, every sentence you write, every leaf you rake must kill the father. Every act from the most august to the most banal must be patricidal if you hope to live freely and unencumbered. Even when shaving—each whisker you shave off is your father's head. And if you're using a twin blade—the first blade cuts off the father's head and as the father's neck snaps back it's cleanly lopped off by the second blade.

The heat in the dining room had become unbearable. My gauzy flesh billowed like loose fabric in the hot drafts. And Big Squirrel's tattoo ran in lurid rivulets down his chest.

THE SUGGESTIVENESS OF ONE STRAY HAIR IN AN OTHERWISE PERFECT COIFFURE

HE'S GOT A car bomb. He puts the key in the ignition and turns it—the car blows up. He gets out. He opens the hood and makes a cursory inspection. He closes the hood and gets back in. He turns the key in the ignition. The car blows up. He gets out and slams the door shut disgustedly. He kicks the tire. He takes off his jacket and shimmies under the chassis. He pokes around. He slides back out and wipes the grease off his shirt. He puts his jacket back on. He gets in. He turns the key in the ignition. The car blows up, sending debris into the air and shattering windows for blocks. He gets out and says, Damn it! He calls a tow truck. He gives them his AAA membership number. They tow the car to an Exxon station. The mechanic gets in and turns the key in the ignition. The car explodes, demolishing the gas pumps, the red-and-blue Exxon logo high atop its pole bursting like a balloon on a string. The mechanic steps out. You got a car bomb, he says. The man rolls his eyes. I know that, he says.

ODE TO AUTUMN

WHEN THE FORENSIC pathologists performed their autopsy on you
they cried, those hardened professionals,
because peeling the skin from your head
was like peeling the skin from an onion

the flesh between your breasts
was a thin and pasty dough
which yielded easily to their scalpels

and the forensic pathologists, those hardened professionals,
shook their fists at the photographs of the 10 most wanted men,
one of whom murdered you, and wept

oh amy, what threnody matters
in a world whose software
enables a crossword puzzle, orphaned by your death,
to ask, "who now will do me?"

i am not roller-skating through piles of brittle autumn leaves
i am roller-skating down the aisles at macy's in narcotic slow motion
    to the music of john philip sousa
i'm skating past every surveillance camera
i'm skating across every closed-circuit television screen
salesmen come and go, murmuring, "jerry lewis est mort...jerry
    lewis est mort"
if only i had the software to conjure one macy's salesgirl at the end
    of this endless corridor into whose arms i'd roller-skate deliri-
    ously to the optimistic cornets of john philip sousa
but i don't have the appropriate software
and it would be brainless to continue skating

IN THE KINGDOM OF BOREDOM, I WEAR THE ROYAL SWEATPANTS

I FINALLY LOST my patience and shrieked: Get out, get out, all of you! My little bedroom was filled with pilgrims, militants, hostages, clerics, extremists, dissidents, mediators, ideologues, pragmatists, and militiamen. If you're all not out of here in ten minutes, I'll have a light-infantry unit equipped with armored personnel carriers and artillery in here so fast it'll make your heads spin. Now out, move it! My ultimatum was punctuated by the *boom boom boom* of BM-13 multiple-rocket launchers and the whistling sound of rising missiles. I pointed to a bunch of jerks standing near my bookcases—these guys had really bugged me. They'd been continuously making derisive wisecracks at my expense. At night they noisily sucked on sour balls, making it impossible for me to sleep, and they were either actually selling crack to my little brother or attempting to induce my little brother to start using crack. I want you guys identified and then blindfolded and shackled and driven in buses to special interrogation centers—now! A burly fanatic committed suicide soon after he surrendered, biting into a cyanide capsule that had been hidden in a ring on his right hand. His friends leveled accusatory looks at me, as if I were somehow responsible for his death. I don't care, it was his choice, I don't have the patience for this shit anymore, everybody out! We can't leave, someone said. Why? There's a river between here (he pointed to a spot on the map) and our ancestral homeland, there (he pointed again), and the river is too deep to ford. Yes, yes, mumbled his compatriots, too deep to ford. You'll find portable pontoon bridges in my bureau in the second drawer from the bottom.... Take them and shove off. An old man with a gray beard edging his craggy face and a leather bandolier of ammunition around his shoulder was gesturing belligerently at another old man. What's the trouble? I asked. He took my AK-47 assault rifle. I walked up to the other old man and sure enough he had two AK-47s. Give him back his AK-47 and I want you both out of here, and be quiet when you pass my parents' room, I don't want them waking up, do you understand? Now we're getting somewhere, I said to myself as people starting clearing out. Okay, there's a 75-millimeter Chinese-made recoilless rifle and a Soviet-made ZU-23 antiaircraft gun in the hallway near the bathroom—whom do they belong to? A guy raised his hand: They belong to my paramilitary security force. All right, I want you, your paramilitary security force, the recoilless rifle, and the antiaircraft gun out of here, and be extremely careful taking the stuff downstairs—that's an antique walnut banister. A young Air Force cadet approached me, saluting. Sir, do you know where I can catch a B-1 bomber to New York, sir? What airport, cadet, there's Kennedy, LaGuardia, and Newark. Sir, LaGuardia, sir. Cadet, there are nuclear-armed B-1 bombers leaving every hour on the hour from Dyess Air Force Base in Texas, Ellsworth Air Force Base in South Dakota, Grand Forks Air Force Base in North Dakota, McConnell Air Force Base in Kansas, and Whiteman Air Force Base in Missouri. I want you out of here and on one of them by 0800 hours—do you comprehend the English language, cadet? Sir, yes, sir. Then why are you still standing here? Sir, a crazy thing happened last night, sir! What kind of crazy thing, cadet? Sir, we were getting ready to go to a party and while I was waiting for Arleen to finish getting dressed I was reading a John Donne poem entitled "Love's Diet," which opens with the lines, "To what a combersome unwieldiness / And burdenous corpulence my love had growne." So Arleen was finally ready, and I put the book down and we left the house, and we got in the car and took the Holland Tunnel into Manhattan, and we're driving up Sixth Avenue looking for a space, and plastered to a wall is a series of posters advertising a band that's playing somewhere and what do you think the band is called! Big Fat Love! I couldn't believe it…the eerie synchronicity, sir!

PSYCHOTECHNOLOGIES OF THE SOMBER WORKAHOLICS

EACH MAN LOVES his wife so very much   sometimes he hugs her with such ardor that it leaves her gasping for breath   he feels as if he wants to literally get inside her skin with her, to draw her flesh over them both as if it were a sheet or a quilt, to feel the palpitations and quivers of her internal organs warm and slick with their secretions against his nakedness   when she eats, he puts his ear to her cheek as she chews to better savor the music of her mandibles   he puts an ear to her stomach and enjoys the churning and gurgles of her digestion and an ear to her lower abdomen to note the sibilant rush of gas as it winds through her intestines, to the small of her back to hear each crack of her vertebrae, between her shoulder blades for the soft expansion and contraction of her lungs   at night, while she sleeps, he puts his ear against her scalp and listens for the almost inaudible rustling of her hair as it grows

in the old days they'd just throw you in a big iron caldron and boil you   now they put you in a teflon no-stick saucepan and they sauté

51

you for a while in walnut oil   i knew one guy who was poached   i know one guy who was fricasseed   i know one guy who was diced benihana style and stir-fried   i knew one guy—he was only in the steamer for three minutes and they said, take him out we'll eat him al dente   and they give these people varsity letters   my father took me to an endocrinologist and the endocrinologist said, he'll always be *eine kleine mensch,* don't send him to no state school 'cause see he's bite-size…he'll make a perfect hors d'oeuvre   that night my mother came up to my bedroom and she said, if you ever see one of them in a letter sweater or letter jacket you run as fast as you can unless you wanna end up with a frilly toothpick through your back or unless you wanna end up between two slices of wonder bread 'cause ain't no deus ex machina gonna swoop through the skylight and save your white ass   i never suspected you though, baby   you were so nice to me i took you back to your apartment   you poured me a nice cold heineken   i said, baby, i've been lonely for too long i got six years of pent-up rhapsodies in me   then i saw that fuckin' varsity ankle bracelet   i said, uh-uh, no way, and i tried to escape but you squirted me with bug spray and my legs went numb

the next thing i know i'm in the emergency room at the hospital and the doctor looks at me and says, "mah man, you dead"   he says, "i gotta help get your soul out of your body but it's gonna cost you a little extra"   "feel around in my pocket," says my eerie disembodied voice, "you can take my visa card"   "i'm gonna have to squeeze the soul out of your body by rolling you up like a tube of toothpaste…"

now, i am the sound of a playing card
ticking the spokes of a bicycle wheel

hello, mark   this is elizabeth hurlick   i'm one of trudy's friends from school   trudy asked me to call and tell you that when she gets home from work she's going to want to make love tout de suite and then eat 'cause she's got an early squash practice so she wants you to season the chicken with some basil and oregano and garlic and onion powder and paprika and put it in the oven at about 350° and then she wants you to run a hot bath and add some of the bayberry rum and spice bath beads which she says are in a silver crabtree and evelyn tin on the blue shelf next to the hair dryer and q-tips and she wants you to soak in the tub for a while   she says there's already a washcloth in there or you can use her loofah   and she said that while you're in the tub you should masturbate almost to the point of orgasm and stop and that way you'll have a more copious ejaculation later when you have sex with trudy because trudy says you have to propitiate the squash god and she says that the squash god is in the mood for a really super-copious ejaculation   and she said to tell you that when you get out of the tub you can daub some of your chanel pour homme cologne on your chest and in the hair on your belly and near your navel but she doesn't want you to use any deodorant under your arms because when you're having sex she wants your armpits to smell kind of macho sort of raunchy kind of ruggedly homo sapien kind of rural   and she wants you to wait for her wearing either the red or the white-and-gold kimono danny and kristen brought you from japan, whichever one you prefer   and you should wait by the window in the study, sort of voluptuously languidly posed like oscar wilde in the photograph by sarony, she said you'll know which one she means—it's in the montgomery hyde biography—and when she comes in through the door she wants you to say, i'm extremely utterly enervated from having spent all afternoon watching sparrows caper about the fire escape   and then you should nonchalantly let your kimono fall open so your meat sort of pokes out   and then she wants you to lift her skirt up and take her underpants off and she wants you to rub your knuckles up and down her perineum   if you're writing this down that's spelled p-e-r-i-n-e-u-m   it's the area between her anus and her genitals   and she said to tell you that while you're fucking you should try to keep an eye on the clock so the chicken doesn't burn   i hope you don't mind me leaving this sort of intimate personal message on your answering machine but i'm a really really good friend of trudy's and trudy's told me all about you and i hope we can all get together sometime maybe for burritos and a video on the vcr or something   trudy says you're creepy in a sort of attractive way and that sounds fun

THE SERENITY OF OBJECTS

I WAS DOING curls with a barbell and I became so sweaty and muscular that I couldn't stop fondling myself and thinking to myself, What a little savage you're becoming, and I ran into the kitchen to get the olive oil because I wanted to coat myself with it and somewhere in the back of my mind I wanted to be blinded and then pull the pillars of the temple down...and you were sleeping...and I remember lying down next to you and the almost inaudible splash of a gnat diving into the pool of perspiration that had formed in my navel must have frightened you because you jumped up in the bed and began screaming something about how two of America's most beloved screen stars, Hume Cronyn and Jessica Tandy, had been killed in a tragic accident. While filming Dino de Laurentiis's production of T. S. Eliot's "The Love Song of J. Alfred Prufrock," directed by John Landis who's known for his spectacular special effects, the huge metal robotic women who come and go talking of Michelangelo collapsed—crushing the aging Oscar winners.

3

ET TU, BABE (1992)

THE STORY SO FAR

June 10, 1990   Trish Hall's article about Leyner, "The Making of a College Cult," appears in the *New York Times*

1990–1992   Leyner begins drinking his own Kool-Aid (i.e., believing his own press). He conducts a series of experiments on himself, akin to those conducted by Dr. Jekyll, that will result in *Et Tu, Babe*

    Meets Martha Stewart, whom he will befriend and accompany to miscellaneous events over the next couple of years

August 1991   Leyner and Mercedes attend Stewart's fiftieth birthday party in East Hampton

1992   Leyner and Arleen Portada divorce

1992   Publication of *Et Tu, Babe*

THERE'S NO SUCH THING AS POSTMODERNISM

*Even Some of Its Best-Known Practitioners
Were Confused About It*

Curtis White

MY FIRST PUBLISHED fiction in fifteen years came out this week. Whether it is well or poorly received, I plan on enjoying it. That's as it should be, because given the grim nature of the times, it is a book out of season—it is my "Ode to Joy." It is a book about nothing much more than its own happy self-development. No Trump, no pedophiles, no climate change. It is, as the French say (and I have to say it as the French say it because English has no equivalent, sadly, revealingly), a jeu d'esprit, a play of the spirit.

The only thing I've dreaded about this book is the possibility that reviewers will say it is just an example of that tired thing, that dead thing, postmodernism. The reason I've dreaded this is simple: there is not now nor was there ever something called postmodernism.

Even some of the best-known practitioners of postmodern fiction were confused about it, especially David Foster Wallace.

David came to Illinois State University, joining me and John O'Brien of Dalkey Archive Press, in 1995, just a year before the publication of *Infinite Jest*. One of the first serious conversations he and I had was about Mark Leyner, with whom I had directed the Fiction Collective in the 1980s (with Ronald Sukenick and Raymond Federman). David's ordinarily open, inquisitive face suddenly scrunched into a little knot of conviction. I did not know it, but he was already on record as saying that Leyner was everything that was wrong with postmodernism: the art of puerile game playing and yukking it up in a moral vacuum so far as human interests were concerned. He was a little annoyed to learn that Mark was a friend and someone I respected.

Leyner, famously, was mystified. "Who is this man and why is he saying these horrible things about me?" But—publicity savant that he is—I think he also knew that it was good to be on the public mind of the publishing world's newest new thing, DFW. So as far as I know, he didn't really mind David's criticism.

I said to David, "I know what you mean, but I think *My Cousin, My Gastroenterologist* is a much better book than you allow and… have you actually read *Et Tu, Babe?*"

He scowled, grumbled, and turned his bandannaed head away, as if to say, "Don't make me reconsider my firm prejudices."

Of course, Wallace was using Leyner as a way of marking his own difference from American postmodernism, never mind that his early work and even *Jest* scream "Pynchon! Barth!" He had a classic case of "anxiety of influence," and attacking Mark was a way for him to deny the association.

T. S. Eliot once observed of Henry James that he had a mind no idea could violate; David seemed to think something similar about Leyner with regard to human feelings. But Mark's chief virtue was (and is) his openness to the energy of play. And the desire for play—the freedom of play, the loving way that play calls us to the things of the world—is a fundamental human "feeling," inexact though that word is. It is human feeling brought close to the spirit, and it is perhaps the most important ethical idea given to us by the literary tradition that stretches from Rabelais to Laurence Sterne, Friedrich Schlegel, Romanticism, and all the great art movements of the ensuing two centuries, including the '60s counterculture and its literature, so-called postmodernism.

And that's my point and the point David missed: Mark didn't care about postmodernism. He never gave it a thought. Of course, he probably didn't care about Rabelais, either, but he didn't have to. He only had to be awake to the tradition of literary play and love of story that Rabelais inaugurated.

Mark's work has always had a subtle ethical character, a generosity, in its constant invitation to possibility and to play. As Schlegel would have put it, Mark is a "transcendental buffoon." His work is not merely ironic because he does not call attention to his playfulness — he just plays. He tries to become the world he wants, and he refuses the world of the disenchanted real. He is not showing off; he is showing the reader what it might be like to have a certain kind of happiness and freedom. Mark asks the essential literary question of the last two centuries: Having been shown how false the world is, and having been shown your own freedom, can you return to that false world after having read this book? (I would go so far as to say that this is the essential question for all art since Mozart, since Blake, and since Delacroix and Turner.)

Et Tu, Babe is a self-knowing whole. It is one of Leyner's many "Odes to Joy."

Here's an anecdote that says something about the Leynerian drama of play. Sometime just before the appearance of *My Cousin* (1989, say), Mark came to town to do a reading and a few workshops and to hang out with me and my wife, Georganne Rundblad. We played racquetball, drove around town listening to John Lee Hooker (Stomp Boogie: "Now dig my feets!"), and laughed a lot. My one mistake during his visit was taking him to a departmental banquet where some comp-rhet dullard held forth for half an hour over gummy cheesecake. At one point, I glanced over at him to see how he was taking it. I expected to be amused, but what I saw was actually a little scary. His face was stricken. He was not capable of enduring this with a good-natured smile of resignation. It was as if I'd brought him to the scene of an atrocity. His sense of the dreadfulness, the deadliness of that inconsequential affair was existential for him: it was like Jean-Paul Sartre's Roquentin, in *Nausea,* sitting on a bus while watching the seats melt away into nothingness. Actually, I envied the purity of his disdain. And it's not as if he was wrong. Oh, no — far from it.

But then the next afternoon, for a lark, we got some coffee and big oatmeal cookies and went to watch a high school baseball game at a nearby park. It was what you might expect of a high school game — the cookies were more interesting...until the last inning. The home team trailed by a run. Two men were on, first and second, with two outs. The next batter, a right-hander, drilled, killed, ripped a line drive over the second baseman's head. It hit the wall in right-center on one bounce. The batter ended up on third, a triple, and both runners scored. The game was over.

With the crack of the bat, Mark and I leaped to our feet, thrust our hands in the air, spilled coffee, and screamed in happiness at the dramatic satisfaction of the moment.

It was a beautiful thing. It was the "yes" side of Mark's "philosophy" of life against death.

It was very pure.

Curtis White is the author of many books, including the acclaimed *The Science Delusion: Asking the Big Questions in a Culture of Easy Answers* and *We, Robots: Staying Human in the Age of Big Data,* both from Melville House. His newest novel is *Lacking Character.*

EXCERPTS FROM
ET TU, BABE

PREFACE

June 6, 1993
Hoboken

Dear Peter Guzzardi,

As you know, I am not your average author. I dress like an off-duty cop: leather blazer, silk turtleneck, tight sharply creased slacks, Italian loafers, pinky-ring. I drive a candy-apple red Jaguar with a loaded 9-mm semiautomatic pistol in the glove compartment. When I walk into a party I'm like this: my head is bobbing to music that only exists in my mind. For our seventh anniversary, I gave my wife, Arleen Portada, a rotating diamond-impregnated drill bit—the kind that German and Russian geologists use in their deep drilling programs—programs that produce ultradeep holes with depths of up to 15 kilometers. But that's just the kind of guy I am. Dynamic. Robust. No nonsense. A steak and chops man. Double scotch rocks. A man who makes things happen. Big hairy hands. A powerful fist that comes down on a conference table with peremptory authority. Then there's stunning Arleen Portada. Mystic. Sensualist. Why is she covered with centipede stings?

If you spent all day on a sun-baked prairie wearing a sizzling orange minidress supervising a platoon of beefy workmen as they paint immense grain silos vibrant yellow and fuchsia, you'd be covered with centipede stings, too.

My whole life has been one long ultraviolent hyperkinetic nightmare. But yes, I am an author. (And a dog trainer— Peter, I taught my puppy Carmella to drink scalding-hot black coffee out of her bowl on the floor!) The other day, I imagined that it was the year 2187—a dozen people were gathered at the grave site of porn star John Holmes to commemorate the 200th anniversary of his death. Well, Peter, I want to be remembered by more people than that. I don't know…perhaps that's why I write.

The unwashed armpits of the most beautiful women in the world…a urinal with chunks of fresh watermelon in it…a retarded guy whining "Eddie, Eddie, get me an Ovaltine"—almost anything inspires me. Immediately after finishing *MY COUSIN, MY GASTROENTEROLOGIST*, I outlined a new book about people with trichotillomania— people who compulsively pull out their hair. There are 2 million to 4 million Americans who have trichotillomania. That's a lot of books! (That's a lot of hair, too!) I abandoned that idea though—that's not the kind of book that Harmony wants from a Mark Leyner, right? Well, I'm confident that, after perusing the following excerpts, you'll agree that the novel I hereby propose is indeed the kind of book that Harmony wants from a Mark Leyner.

ET TU, BABE—a master jam of relentless humor and indeterminate trajectories—teeming with creatures and the burlesque of their virulent lives—will undoubtedly be, page by page and line by line, the most entertaining book that Harmony has ever published.

EXCERPTS FROM **ET TU, BABE**

The four-foot hermaphroditic organism from a distant solar system twitched in my arms as I soul-kissed it. The laboratory director would have killed me if he'd known that I'd snuck into the Galactic Lifeform Chamber with a bottle of wine, a cassette player, and an eclectic selection of tapes (Felix Mendelssohn, Steppenwolf, Barbara Mandrell) for a clandestine tryst with the cylindrical being whom the lab technicians had christened "Kitty Lafontaine." I pipetted a few drops of 1982 Napa Valley Zinfandel into its alimentary aperture. Its synesthetic sensory apparatus was distributed evenly across the entirety of its shiny outer sheath so it could see, hear, smell, touch, precognize, etc., from any point on its body. To say that holding Kitty Lafontaine in my arms was like nestling a large holiday beef log from Hickory Farms would certainly not convey the spine-tingling xenophilic libidinous awe I felt, but it would accurately convey the shape, mass, and weight of this fascinating creature who would irrevocably change all our lives that summer.

//////// ////////

Dear Science Editor of the *Times*,

Frequently the counterman at a sandwich shop will ask "Do you want everything on it?" Well, what if you had a sandwich with literally "everything" on it? In other words, how large a sandwich roll would you need to accommodate all matter in the universe? And, as a corollary, imagine an inconceivably immense being capable of eating this almost infinitely capacious submarine sandwich. If this colossal creature began eating at the instant of the Big Bang, by what century would he be able to consume, digest, metabolize, and excrete the hypothetical hoagie? And would not this meal, by its very nature, exhaust time itself?

//////// ////////

Dear Editors at *Swank*,

Your article on the sensitive areolas of large-breasted women was excellent. Also, thanks for the recipe for paella valenciana that you published in the October *Swank*. I'm no gourmet chef, but I made the dish for my girlfriend and after dinner she couldn't keep her prosthetic hands off my veiny nine-inch chorizo.

//////// ////////

I had once intended to write an entire novel while having to urinate very badly. I wanted to see how that need affected the style and tempo of my work. I had found, for instance, that when I'm writing about a character who's in a Ph.D. program and I don't have to urinate badly, I'll have him do a regular three- or four-year program. But if I'm writing a novel and I have to urinate very very badly, then I'll push the character through an accelerated Ph.D. program in perhaps only two years, maybe even a year.

//////// ////////

In 1987, I enrolled in a 12-step program for people who pistol-whip their tailors. First I had to admit to myself that pistol-whipping my tailor was, in fact, a problem. Today I take life one day at a time. Each day that passes without my having pistol-whipped my tailor is a victory…a solid step toward recovery.

//////// ////////

-Do you believe in God?

-Yes, sir.

-Do you believe in an anthropomorphic, vengeful, capricious God who can look down on one man and give him fabulous riches and look down on another and say "you're history" and give him a cerebral hemorrhage?

-Yes, sir.

-You may take the stand. What is your full name?

-I am General Ramon Humberto Regaldo Rosa Cordoba Lopez.

-General Lopez, you are descended from a very illustrious family, is that not true?

-Yes, sir. My great-great-great-great-grandfather was a nobleman in Spain in the fifteenth century and it was he who first discovered that the atomized saliva of hunchbacks enhances the growth of flowers. He, in fact, retained a large staff of hunchbacks to sneeze on his tulips.

-General, are those your real nails?

-Sir?

-Are those your real fingernails?

-Yes, sir.

-General, you are a fucking liar!

-Objection, Your Honor!

-Your Honor, I can see, defense counsel can see, and the ladies and gentlemen of the jury can see that the General is wearing Lee Press-On Nails.

-Objection overruled. Continue.

-General, under direct examination you were asked to describe events that took place on the morning of April 26, 1987. You testified, and I quote: "I was a short thickset man with a fleshy, brutal face. I felt bad. I had been drinking heavily the previous night and the heat bothered me. My wife was sleeping. 'Wake up, stupid,' I snarled. I shook her and I kissed her savagely. 'You stink,' she sneered. 'Your breath smells like the steam that rises off fresh vomit.' I jabbed a syringe full of methamphetamine into her ass, which was covered with boils the size of potato pancakes." Is that still an accurate account to the best of your knowledge?

-Yes, sir.

-General, it strikes me as exceedingly odd that, asked to describe a particular morning on a particular day, you would say, "I was a short, thickset man with a fleshy, brutal face." Are we to understand by this that you were a short, thickset man with a fleshy, brutal face only on April 26, 1987?

-Objection, Your Honor. This kind of semantic nitpicking is an obvious form of harassment. The district attorney knows full well that the General was a short, thickset man with a fleshy, brutal face prior to April 26, 1987, that he was a short, thickset man with a fleshy, brutal face during April 26, 1987, and that he continues to be a short, thickset man with a fleshy, brutal face subsequent to April 26, 1987.

-Sustained.

-General, that afternoon, did you receive a call at the office from your wife?

-Yes, sir.

-What did she say?

-She said that she thought she'd been on her liquid formula diet long enough…that she was so light that the static electricity from the television set was pulling her across the floor toward the screen.

-And she called one more time later that afternoon?

-Yes, sir.

-And what did she say?

-She said that she didn't have much time to talk, that she was tied to the railroad tracks and the Bullet Train was coming.

-And that was the last time you ever spoke to her?

-Yes, sir.

-General, one final question. Do you have any tattoos?

-Yes, sir.

-On what part of your body and of what?

-I have $E = nhf$ (Max Planck's formula for the energy in radiation) tattooed on my penile glans.

-General, you are a pathological fucking liar!!

-Objection!!

-Overruled.

-General, I'd like you to look at your penile glans and read to the court what's tattooed on it.

-It says: $d = 16t^2$.

-Not $E = nhf$?

-No, sir.

-And what's the significance of $d = 16t^2$?

-It's Galileo's formula for the distance an object falls from its starting point as time elapses from the instant it's dropped.

-Your Honor, I have no further questions.

-General Lopez, you may step down.

////////////////////

The giant awoke, got high on drugs, masturbated, and then went into town to forage for a human-flesh breakfast. He stopped at an intersection where his eye was caught by the puffy orange Day-Glo parka of a postmenopausal crossing guard. He knelt down and plucked up the screaming crossing guard in his fingers and dropped her into a gunnysack slung across his back. He surveyed the town until he discerned the bright orange regalia of another prey whom he captured and then on to the next intersection and then on to the next and the next and the next until his gunnysack was filled with squirming crossing guards. He returned home and laid the gunnysack on the counter. He urinated and then he put some music on the stereo; it was a kind of music I'd never heard before—a single high-pitched oscillating tone.

The giant *peeled* the crossing guards. After his breakfast, the floor was littered with puffy orange Day-Glo parkas.

Why crossing guards? Japanese scientists speculate that their conspicuous puffy orange Day-Glo parkas make them particularly attractive prey. Why postmenopausal women? Japanese scientists point to reduced estrogen levels. They think that estrogen is bitter to the tongue of the giant and that he simply finds the low-estrogen women tastier. But there's an even more intriguing explanation. Estrogen deficiencies in postmenopausal women cause osteoporosis, which is characterized by brittle bones. In other words, postmenopausal women are crunchier.

//////// ////////

Well, Peter, how does that sound to you? I'm ready for it, babe—I'm massaging IQ-enhancing balm into my temples and I'm loading up on Winstrol, the steroid that got sprinter Ben Johnson disqualified from the 1988 Olympic Games in Seoul.

It's a forty-minute hydrofoil ride from Hong Kong to Macao. Look out toward the horizon. There's big Arleen rising up out of the water. Her white gown is fluttering violently in the wind, her lace veil is congested with sea spume. Isn't she beautiful? isn't she just fucking absolutely beautiful?

Oh, one last question, Peter. My agent has a supernumerary nipple below and slightly medial to her right breast. The nipple produces approximately one watt of heat, about the same as that given off by a miniature Christmas tree bulb. Is this a standard energy output?

Yours very truly,
Mark Leyner

Q: If you could offer the young people of today one piece of advice, what would it be?

A: When I was eight, I was sent to live on the melon farm of an uncle...

WHEN I WAS eight, I was sent to live on the melon farm of an uncle—a sixth-grade dropout who attributed his IQ of 70 to sniffing gasoline and glue from the age of five, and whose manner of compulsively clawing at the skin behind his neck was a characteristic sign of amphetamine toxicity. One morning he served me a cereal that consisted of sweetened corn puffs and marshmallow, hook-nosed, bearded "Jews." I asked him never to serve that cereal to me again. The next morning, he set a heaping bowl of the same cereal on my place mat. I killed him with a 12-gauge shotgun blast before lunch. That night I buried him in the cyclone cellar. I stole his pickup truck and drove out to a huge diesel-run electric turbine plant near the outskirts of the city and I had my first sexual experience. Afterward, I lit a cigarette and looked up into the sky—there was God, wearing a pink polo shirt, khaki pants, and brown Top-Siders with no socks, his blond hair blowing in the powerful wind of charged particles and intense ultraviolet radiation from the galactic center. I hated him. And he hated me.

I have spent the majority of my 36 years in orphanages, reformatories, prisons, and mental institutions. I had four oboe teachers and each one fell into an irrigation sluice and drowned. I'd tried explaining to my social workers that I hated double-reed mouthpieces. I pleaded with them not to make me take lessons on any instrument in the oboe family, which also includes the English horn, the bassoon, and the double bassoon. But nobody listened.

I hated the other children. Especially the ones whose parents could afford to provide proper orthodontic care. I had to gnaw constantly. My incisors grew four to five inches a year: if I'd stopped gnawing, my lower incisors would have eventually grown until they pushed up into my brain, killing me. Over the years, I was treated for a slew of psychiatric and behavioral problems: dyslexia, depression, excessive anxiety, obsessive-compulsive disorder, alcoholism, illicit drug abuse, obesity, eating disorders, exhibitionism, persistent aggressive and violent behavior, and hyperactivity combined with severe attention deficits. Yet there was a voice within me that said: Someday you will be considered the most intense and, in a certain sense, the most significant young prose writer in America. And I listened.

Today I live in a lemon-yellow stucco mansion with sweeping views of the bay. Each morning, I nibble iced raw turtle eggs and chocolate-dipped strawberries in a garden ablaze with hibiscus and bougainvillea — a far cry from the antisemitic breakfast cereal forced upon me by my half-witted uncle on his squalid melon farm.

My advice to the young people of today? I'm tempted to say: Surround yourself with flunkies and yes-men and have naked slaves, perfumed with musk, fan you with plastic fronds as you write. Because that's what's worked for me. But what does history teach us?

The 83rd President of the United States, Hallux Valgus, had no mouth or gastrointestinal tract. How did this Christian Scientist who refused intravenous nourishment survive? Only during the autopsy following President Valgus's assassination were scientists given the opportunity to solve this riddle. After painstaking dissection and analysis, pathologists found that Valgus was nourished from within by symbiotic bacteria. Their research revealed that the "tissue" of his trophosome, a large body structure which comprised half of Valgus's torso and which Valgus kept concealed beneath his ubiquitous spandex unitard, was composed of closely packed bacteria — over 100 billion per ounce of tissue. They found that his blood, deep red from a rich supply of hemoglobin, absorbed oxygen, carbon dioxide, and sulfur dioxide from the polluted atmosphere and transported it to the trophosome. Thus ensured a rich supply of chemical resources, the bacteria living inside Valgus produced carbohydrates and proteins, which Valgus then metabolized. Hallux Valgus, the 83rd President of the United States. The first occupant of the Oval Office to depend on symbiotic chemoautotrophic bacteria living within him. (His long and detailed *Memoirs* provide a unique picture of the personalities and politics of his times.)

Be petulant, narcissistic, and charismatic. That's what President Valgus would have exhorted today's young men and women, had not a hit-squad of gnat-sized robots filed stealthily into his ear and mined his brain with plastic explosive. And love. Love with extreme lucidity and barbaric ferocity. One of my foster mothers couldn't wait to shove me onto the school bus each morning so that she could get inside, doff her frowzy terry cloth robe and greasy housedress, squeeze into her edible lingerie, and await the arrival of the electrician, plumber, UPS delivery man, cable TV installer, exterminator — whichever beefy workman was fortunate enough to ring the doorbell first. That's not what I mean by "love." When I use the word *love*, I'm thinking about the witty, urbane, wasp-waisted Arleen Portada.

They were the heady, idealistic days of the early Valgus administration. Congress had just officially designated Bernard Herrmann's shrieking score for strings composed for the shower murder scene in *Psycho* as the national anthem. The Look that year was "postcoital" — tousled hair, runny mascara, smeared lipstick. Scientists working on the Human Genome Initiative announced identification of the specific gene that not only predisposes a person to take dancing lessons, but that actually determines his or her dance predilection: ballet, jazz, tap, or ballroom. It had been an exceptionally rainy spring, and indeed on the day we met, the sun was out for the first time in weeks...

I was climbing trees that afternoon and Arleen happened to be below stalking live subjects for a research project she was doing as part of her MSW program at Fordham University. She shot me with air-rifle darts full of tranquilizer. I lost muscle control gradually — one hand missing its grip, then the other — and fell into a net Arleen held outspread below. She carried me tenderly back to the lab for processing and measurements: total length, arm length, chest diameter, testicle length and width. "Look at the lunch-pack on this guy," she said, appreciating my scrotum. I hadn't really been planning to "get involved," but how could I resist the subtle, sophisticated blandishments of this young and beautiful psychotherapist?

Winning your place in the hierarchy is a basic part of primate life and each day is a savage, pitiless battle for dominance — so don't expect everyone to like you. Today I *am* the most intense, and in a certain sense, the most significant young prose writer in America. And I have the body of a grotesquely swollen steroid freak. Yet, I have many enemies. And these enemies will hurt me, unless I hurt them first, ergo the punji sticks and claymore mines that riddle the grounds surrounding my headquarters. Ergo my phalanx of bodyguards: seven formerly frail, arthritic nonagenarian widows with heart disease selected from a nearby nursing home. Arleen and I took them in, treated them as members of our own family, administered large doses of synthetic human growth hormone and testosterone to each woman, and replaced her atrophied musculature with powerful artificial muscles made out of polymer gels that contract when electricity is applied and expand when the current is turned off. Do you want to see carnage unparalleled in the annals of internecine strife? Try laying a finger on me, Arleen, my dog Carmella, or one of my fans.

* * *

It was determined at an October 17th meeting—attended by my literary agent Binky Urban, editor Peter Guzzardi, publicist Susan Magrino, and lecture agent George Greenfield—that I disguise my appearance before entering the Hyatt Self-Surgery Clinic in New Brunswick, New Jersey. Although the dimpled, clean-shaven face framed by blond-flecked chestnut tresses combed back into an undulating pompadour had become an instant icon to millions of fans who clipped photos from the pages of *Rolling Stone, Creem,* the *New York Times,* and the *Asbury Park Press* and pasted them to dormitory walls and three-ring binders, sometime in early November, a makeup artist was summoned to Team Leyner headquarters and instructed to execute a temporary new Look. The Look was Hezbollah—Party of God—closely cropped black hair, black beard, white button-down shirt, black pants.

The Hyatt Self-Surgery Clinic? Self-surgery clinics were the medical equivalent of U-Hauls or rental rug shampooers. Clinics provided a private operating room, instruments, monitoring devices, drugs, and instructional videocassettes for any procedure that could be performed solo, under local anesthetic, on any part of your anatomy that you could reach easily with *both* hands. As I pulled into the parking lot of the recently renovated Hyatt, I realized that I'd left my copy of Edmund Spenser's *The Faerie Queene* in the Mercury Capri XR2 that I'd test-driven for *Gentleman's Quarterly.* All my notes on the 132-hp turbocharged roadster were scrawled in the margins of the Elizabethan poet's magnum opus. I called Casale Lincoln Mercury on my cellular car phone and asked for Joe Casale, showroom manager. My heart went out to Joe—tiny misshapen "pinhead," flipper-like forearms.

"Joe Casale."

"Joe, this is Mark Leyner. I was in about an hour ago to test-drive the new Capri and I think I left a book on the passenger seat. Can you have someone check and see if it's there?"

"No problem, Mr. Leyner. Just hold for a couple of seconds."

"Thanks, babe."

A minute or two passed and Casale returned to the line.

"Mr. Leyner, I'm sorry but the Capri you drove is out on the road again. Where are you now?"

"I'm at the Hyatt Self-Surgery Clinic in New Brunswick."

"I'll tell you what, Mr. Leyner, why don't I drop the book off at the clinic later this evening."

"It's not out of your way?"

"It's no problem, Mr. Leyner."

"Thanks, babe."

I parked, slung my overnight bag over my shoulder, and went in to register. The clerk at the front desk keyed my name and American Express number into the computer.

"Mr. Leyner, what procedure will you be performing on yourself?"

I hesitated for a moment before responding. It seemed injudicious to divulge to this woman that a deceased rodent was impacted between my prostate gland and urethra and that the surgical procedure I intended to perform was a radical gerbilectomy.

"Appendectomy," I lied.

"Mr. Leyner, do you have a preference with regard to O.R. accommodations?"

"Well, where do the real players stay?"

"The 'real players,' sir?"

I pushed my sunglasses down the bridge of my nose and superciliously eyeballed the desk clerk over the blue mirrored lenses.

"The players...the Stephen Kings, the Louis L'Amours, the Jeffrey Archers, and Ken Folletts and James Clavells."

"Mr. L'Amour was in last month to perform his own cold-fusion blepharoplasty and he stayed in...let me check...ah yes, the Tivoli Suite."

"I would like the Tivoli Suite, then."

"Very good, sir."

* * *

It's 10:30 p.m. I'm in the Tivoli Suite and I've just self-administered a spinal block leaving my lower torso insensible to pain. I'm about to make my first incision when I hear the doorknob turn.

"*¿Quién es?*" I ask. "Who is it?"

With the exception of my instrument tray and my lower abdomen, which are illuminated by high-powered halogen lamps, the room is pitch dark. I tilt a lamp toward the door and discern a figure with a tiny head and a copy of Edmund Spenser's *The Faerie Queene* tucked under his flipper.

"Joe?" I inquire.

"It was right on the passenger seat where you left it, Mr. Leyner!"

"Thanks, babe."

Joe turns to leave.

"Joe, wait a minute. How'd you like to come work for me?"

"Work for you, Mr. Leyner?"

"Yeah. Move into headquarters, coordinate the staff, oversee the bodyguards, y'know, do a little of this, a little of that—you'd be my adjutant, my aide-de-camp. It's a great group of people, you get free medical treatment from Dr. Larry Werther—my cousin, my gastroenterologist—and basically I think you'd do a great job and I think you'd have a ball. What do you say?"

"Mr. Leyner...I think you have yourself an aide-de-camp," Joe says, extending a flipper.

"Welcome aboard, babe."

You enter the pink-and-yellow-splashed foyer and you're swept quickly toward the inner sanctum. Flashbulbs pop as svelte spokesmodel and media liaison Baby Lago pours the Moët. Out of the corner of your eye, you see Arleen ravaging a french-fried yam. She's wearing a short, provocative strapless dress by Emanuel Ungaro that's candy-box pink and pale green. The dress is so provocative that you want to approach Arleen and perhaps caress the nape of her neck. But you dare not. Because there I am. Even more heavily muscled than you'd expected. More frightening and yet somehow more alluring than you'd imagined. My crisp white shirt is by Georges Marciano and costs about $88. My suede jeans—Ender Murat, $550—are rolled up, exposing calves that make you realize for perhaps the first time in your life how beautiful the human calf can actually be—when it's pumped up almost beyond recognition. I'm being interviewed by a reporter from *Allure*, the new Condé Nast beauty magazine.

"I have a way of being noticed and being mysterious at once," I'm saying, "like a gazelle that is there one second and then disappears."

Joe Casale comes running in. "Mr. Leyner, Mr. Leyner—Marla's on *20/20*. You said I should let you know."

"OK, babe, thanks. Everybody quiet down! Joe, turn it up."

"Today Marla Maples, the twenty-six-year-old model-actress who first achieved notoriety as the 'other woman' in the Donald and Ivana Trump divorce, sits on death row at San Quentin as her attorneys exhaust their final appeals in an apparently futile attempt to save the blond serial killer from the gas chamber. Implicated in the deaths of Leonard Bernstein, Malcolm Forbes, Grace Kelly, Billy Martin,

Muppet-creator Jim Henson, and reggae singer Peter Tosh, Maples has devoted her final weeks to a letter-writing campaign in support of a congressional bill that will require television sets manufactured after July 1997 to be equipped with a computer chip that provides caption service for the deaf.

"Marla, you're young, you're leggy, you're busty—yet in a matter of days, the State of California is going to put you in a metal room and fill it with sodium cyanide gas. Do you have any advice for other leggy, busty, young women who might be experiencing peer pressure to experiment with serial killing and who might be watching tonight?"

"That's enough, Joe. Turn the TV off, OK? Thanks, babe."
I apologize to the *Allure* reporter.
"Now…where were we?"
"I was asking you how you got started as a writer, and, more specifically, how you got started writing liner notes for albums."
"When I was six, I came home from school one day and I went down into the basement to look for a bicycle pump and I found the dead bodies of my parents. They were each hanging from a noose, naked. All their fingers had been cut off and arranged in a pentagram under their dangling feet and in the center of this pentagram of bloody fingers was a note and the note said: 'Dear Mark, You did this to us.'

"A year later, I took a job as a bookkeeper at an insurance agency that was located in an old two-story brick building not far from here. And on my first day of work, a few of my colleagues took me out to lunch. After a long silence, one of them finally said that there was something very important that they needed to tell me. He said that about thirty or forty years ago, our office building had been owned by a very wealthy man. And this man was a chronic philanderer. And his wife knew about his affairs. And she decided that the only way to end his infidelity and to preserve their marriage was to get pregnant again, to have a 'change-of-life baby.' So she stopped using contraceptives and, sure enough, she got pregnant. The baby was born, a boy. And he was horribly deformed. He had neurofibromatosis — Elephant Man's disease. The couple kept the child shackled in a storeroom in the husband's commercial property. He was never brought to the couple's home, but kept for his entire childhood in a dark, windowless storage room in the very building that this insurance company now occupies. The child, the monster child, did nothing to stop the husband's philandering. In fact, if anything, the tragedy of this birth, of having to go every day to the storage room and find this chained horror writhing in its own excrement, simply deepened the husband's despair and inflamed his bitter compulsion to betray his wife. All of this finally drove the wife over the edge and one night, while the husband was working in the office building, she set it on fire. The husband's charred body was found, but somehow the deformity escaped. And although he's never been seen, it's rumored that on his birthday he goes foraging for a special meal of human flesh.

"At this point, my colleagues looked at me beseechingly and confided their suspicion that the monster child returns at night to the building. 'We're begging you,' they said, 'don't stay late. If there's extra work to be done, take it home. But there's danger — we feel it, we feel that he comes back.'

"It was soon Christmas season. And one of my responsibilities was to close out the books for the year. It was a very hectic time for us and one night I was asked by the president of the company to stay late, finish some work, and then lock up. That night I worked on the books until almost two in the morning — the building, of course, completely empty except for me. I finished up, turned out the lights, armed the building's security system, locked the door, and exited. I walked through the parking lot to my car, opened the front door, and got in. There was a smell…a smell of rotting flowers, of putrid water from a neglected vase…and the stench of decaying flesh. I felt

83

something on my neck...not fingers, but stumps...finger stumps caressing my neck. I turned around and there were the corpses of my parents seated in the back, and they were gazing at me with wide eyes and horrible grins on their faces. I was ice-cold and nauseous with terror. I opened the car door, rolled to the ground, and ran back to the building. Fumbling frantically with the keys, I finally got the door open. I took a few trembling steps into the dark hallway, when I felt something brush against my leg and then do a series of...are you familiar with classical ballet steps?"

The *Allure* reporter nods. "Somewhat."

"Well, it did a series of *brisés volés*. This is a flying *brisé* where you finish on one foot after the beat and the other is crossed in back...it's basically a *fouetté* movement with a *jeté battu*. And then it landed in the middle of the reception area in an *arabesque à la hauteur*—that's an *arabesque* where the working leg is raised at a right angle to the hip, one arm curved over the head, the other extended to the side. It was the monster child! And he had a birthday hat on his head! To my astonishment—especially after everything I'd heard—he wasn't such a malevolent creature after all. We talked for quite a while—touching on a wide range of issues—and then he said that he had a friend who was in trouble and he asked me if I could help her. I said I'd try. I followed him deep into the woods, maybe two or three miles until we stopped. And there seated against a tree, sobbing inconsolably, was Julianne Phillips.

"'What's wrong?' I asked her.

"She said that Bruce Springsteen had just left her for Patti Scialfa.

"'Listen, I've got a car,' I said. 'Is there somewhere I could take you?'

"'P-P-Paula's.'

"Well, it turned out that Paula was Paula Abdul. And we became very close. And it was through Paula that I met Elton and then Axl and Queen Latifah. And that's basically how I got started writing liner notes."

"Thank you very much, Mr. Leyner, that was absolutely fascinating!" the *Allure* reporter gushes. "And good luck on your new book."

"Thanks, it was a pleasure chatting."

I'm frequently asked that question about how I got started writing liner notes and I have to admit that it's become somewhat tedious explaining it over and over again. So I feel a bit pooped and sneak off to the bedroom for a quick nap. There's an open book on my pillow. This is one of Arleen's modes of communicating with me. She'll leave a certain book, opened to a certain page and passage, on my pillow, and I'll deduce from the text what Arleen is trying to tell me. Perhaps a passage from Wordsworth's *The Prelude*, indicating that she'd like to spend more time in pristine, rural environments. Or an issue of *Vogue*, hinting that a new blouse or pair of shoes might be appreciated. Or maybe a chapter from Greenberg and Johnson's *Emotionally Focused Therapy for Couples*, implying that we're not "connecting" as Arleen feels we should be. So I take the volume—a weighty anthropology textbook—from the pillow and read the indicated passage:

> When the men have retired to the "sulk house" to sulk, the youngsters run exuberantly to the river. In they wade, and with playful boasts, attempt to snare recyclable refuse— everything from broken chunks of polyvinyl chloride buoys to foil packets of ketchup—from the swift current. The women, who have been watching from either the menstrual gazebos or the song stalls where they flatten manioc cakes between their hands to rhythmic doggerel, shout praise at the boys and heap derision on the ensconced brooding men, impugning their scavenging prowess and disparaging their virility. The men sulk for usually an hour, when a preset timer resounds in the sulk house and, depending on whether the men have planned a hunting raid or just want to watch television and drink, prepare themselves accordingly.

If TV and drinking comprise the agenda, the men change from their dark, cowled sulking robes into gym shorts and flip-flops and undo their topknots, letting their long orange hair fall casually down their backs. They then make exaggerated exhibitions of pride about their hair, tossing their heads and narcissistically flipping their tresses about with the backs of their hands. Although these displays of extravagant, almost effeminate vanity usually culminate in gales of laughter, this is a crucial, highly ritualized transition activity that psychologically enables the men to shift from sulking to watching television and drinking—a transition that is physically accomplished by walking through an underground passageway from the sulk house to the spirit house. Once in the spirit house, the remote control for the television—a device made out of black beeswax, paraná palm thatch, jaguar bone, and toucan feather tassels and featuring power, mute, volume, and channel buttons—can only be operated by the "kakarum" (powerful one). To be acknowledged as a kakarum, a man must have killed at least several persons. It is considered a feat of overwhelming courage and strength to kill a kakarum and wrest from him jurisdiction over the remote control—but this rarely happens, and in fact none of the elder informants can remember a remote control ever being taken from a kakarum. Kakarums are believed to possess supernatural power derived from the souls of the men they have killed. The prospect of acquiring this power by killing a kakarum and usurping his remote control rights is often too enticing for ambitious young men to resist. But conflicts over the remote control almost invariably end with the violent death of the young challenger, whose body is then dumped down a metal chute that delivers it into a pit located between the menstrual gazebos and the song stalls where the victim is prepared for burial by his matrilineal grandmother or mother-in-law. The kakarum then chooses a TV program and signals the commencement of drinking by announcing, "Let us drink until we vomit" and "Drink quickly so that you may be drunk soon." The beverage that's consumed—and consumed in staggering quantities—is a beer made from masticated pupunha mash and sugar cane extract. It's produced in two versions: regular and lite, which is less filling. The first man to vomit is known as "wetcówe" (vomiting one) and it is he who goes outside the spirit house and makes a loud, dramatic display of vomiting in order to signal to the women to come join the men and "utcíwaiwa" (party). The women, having been signaled by the wetcówe, change from the drab clothes they'd been wearing in the menstrual gazebos or the song stalls into short, back-strapped sequined dresses, and they dance single file toward the spirit house chanting, "utcíwaiwa wetcówe! utcíwaiwa wetcówe!"

Having read the preceding selection, I'm initially at a loss to determine what message Arleen has intended to convey. Could she be trying to say that we should go out dancing more? Or that I have a drinking problem? Or that I'm dictatorial about what we watch on television? Or that I'm moody and sulk too much? Perhaps she's suggesting that I kill someone to enhance my supernatural powers. Or maybe—just maybe—she's trying to say that I need to get away from the rarefied and glamorous world of my headquarters. Maybe Arleen, in all her psychotherapeutic wisdom, is trying to tell me to return to my roots, to re-stomp the rough-and-tumble stomping grounds of my youth.

So the next day, I went back to the old neighborhood to look up Rocco Trezza.

"Hey, man, where's Trezz? You seen Trezz around?" I asked a guy who used to hang out with Rocco and me.

The guy dismissed the question with a wave of his hand.

"Trezza's been bakin' doughnuts," he said disdainfully.

I hadn't been back to the old neighborhood for some twenty years and obviously I was no longer fluent in the local patois. But I didn't want to ask what "bakin' doughnuts" meant and seem like some kind of hick, so I just shook my head and rolled my eyes and said, "Bakin' doughnuts...oh man." I bid the guy adieu and walked down the street, trying to figure out what he meant — "bakin' doughnuts"? Maybe it meant he was doing nothing — cooking up a big zero every day. Maybe he was doing a lot of crack — blowing smoke rings through his mind. Or maybe he was pimping — maybe "doughnuts" stood for vaginas and "bake" meant control, exploit — taking the raw dough of young girls and parlaying it into lucrative pastry. Or maybe Rocco had hit it big — maybe "doughnuts" stood for the fat round digits in a seven-figure income. Then I thought maybe it meant that he was wasting his life away masturbating...maybe "doughnut" stood for the round configuration of fingers and thumb around the penis and "bakin'" was a literal reference to the heat caused by the friction of hand against dick or a figurative reference to the passion of autoeroticism.

I was so lost in thought as I rounded the corner of the street that I barreled right into a guy — didn't even see him coming. As I helped him up off the ground, I suddenly recognized him and I was so stunned that I let go and he fell back on the sidewalk.

It was Rocco. Rocco Trezza. He was older. A bit heavier in the gut. His hair had thinned out. But he was unmistakably Trezz. Same inimitable style: the thigh-high jackboots, the black latex jockstrap, the Prussian spiked helmet strapped under the chin.

"Trezz, I can't believe it...after all these years."

Trezz hugged me. "How's it goin', man?" he asked.

"I'm good. I'm good. I got a hit book out, my wife got $35,000 because a ceiling fell on her head while she was watching the Academy Awards, and we got a dog named Carmella."

"Carmella?"

"Yeah, Carmella...Trezz, it's really good to see you, babe."

"Likewise. I been reading about you."

"Hey, Trezz, I want to ask you about something."

"Ask."

"Trezz, I hear you been..."

I hesitated for a moment, wondering whether I should pursue it or not.

"Trezz, I hear you been bakin' doughnuts."

Rocco stared at me and I could see the fury just boiling up within him.

"Bakin' doughnuts? Bakin' doughnuts? You heard I was fuckin' bakin' doughnuts?!!"

He wrestled me down and pinned me to the sidewalk. His breath hit my face in hot gusts.

"After all these years...after all we've been through...after every fuckin' thing you and me have been through—you think that I would possibly fuckin' end up bakin' doughnuts?!! Huh?!!"

I threw him off me and we both looked at each other, sitting there on the sidewalk. I still had no idea what it meant—"bakin' doughnuts."

"Trezz," I said, "I didn't believe it...OK? I knew it was a fuckin' lie."

"It is a fuckin' lie," he said, helping me up.

I put my arm around him, and me and Trezz walked down the street. And it was just like the old days.

I'm sitting by my pool, which is encircled by the eight-foot, four-ton basaltic bluestone pillars from Stonehenge's inner circle that I bought with a portion of my latest advance from Harmony Books, when Baby Lago brings me a fax that's just come in. It's from Stu Gallenkamp, V.P. Marketing, Columbia Records, re: the liner notes I'd written for George Michael's *Listen Without Prejudice, Vol. 1*. It says:

Dear Mr. L., I just got off the phone with George. He loves the liner notes and in fact called them the most intense and, in a certain sense, the most significant liner notes he'd ever read. But he agrees with me on the advisability of deleting the following paragraph: "The teenage baby-sitters are slathering me with Ben-Gay. I'm eleven. I've got this erotic fascination with the girls' armpits—it's completely unfocused; I don't know quite what I want to 'do' to or with their armpits, but I'm locked into their brunette stubble. The two girls shut my bedroom door, lock it, and turn out the lights. They take the warm pink wads of bubblegum from their mouths and affix them to special acupressure points on my body. They remove their tampons and smear menstrual blood on my eyelids. They shave their armpits and rinse their razors in a basin and we drink the hairy water and we chant—their Marlboros glowing in the crepuscular shadows. Then one of them—I think it was Felice—puts my face into her freshly shaven armpit, which smells slightly but deliciously of teeny-bopper b.o., and she says 'count backwards from 100' and the next thing I remember is waking up and it's Rosh Hashanah, U.S.A., in the 1990s."

At breakfast the next morning, Baby Lago informed me that we were out of turtle eggs and strawberries. I felt like driving her new Porsche 911 Turbo, so I offered to fetch the groceries myself, and she tossed me the keys and her flame-resistant driving gloves. I negotiated the concrete antiterrorist road barriers in first gear, the tachometer needle climbing toward the 6800-rpm redline. I brought the car to a complete stop where the headquarters access road meets the highway. I looked at myself in the rearview mirror...nice. And then I stomped on the gas, tore through the gearbox, and hit 60 mph in 4.8 seconds.

Approximately four miles west of Exit 16, outside of Wenton's Mill, I began following a 1983 light-blue Chevy Impala, Tennessee plates, traveling west on Rte. 70. My initial observation was of a male caucasian driver approximately 25–30 years of age and two passengers, a female caucasian and a female Hispanic, both approximately 25–30 years of age. As I followed the vehicle, I observed its occupants engage in almost continuous sex. The male driver was being fellated by the female caucasian, who was propped on hands and knees in the middle of the front seat. She, in turn, was enjoying vigorous cunnilingus courtesy of the female Hispanic who was supine in the passenger seat, her bare feet dangling out the window. Near Fannington, at the junction of Rte. 70 and the interstate, I observed a rearrangement within the moving vehicle: the female Hispanic climbed across the front seat and took over the wheel, the male caucasian slid to the middle, and the female caucasian repositioned to the passenger seat, and the sex resumed immediately. The male caucasian lay on his side, sucking the female Hispanic driver's nipples through her T-shirt and stimulating her clitoris with his hand, his legs scissored open, presenting his genitals to the seated female caucasian, who initiated uninhibited fellatio. I observed three subsequent realignments within the moving vehicle with only momentary hiatuses in sexual activity. Approaching Exit 3, outside of Knoll, I decided to pull the vehicle over. I attached my flashing red light to the roof of my car, and the vehicle slowed, pulling onto the shoulder of the highway. I got out of my car, approached the Impala, and gestured to the driver—at the time it was the female caucasian—to roll down her window. She did. The smell of sweat, semen, and vaginal mucus was overpowering. Half-eaten chicken wings and drumsticks, Juicy Fruit gum wrappers, crushed Marlboro packs, and empty beer cans were strewn all over the car. The occupants wore no trousers or underpants. Their pubic hair was full of potato chip crumbs.

"I'm charging you all with public lewdness," I said, and I looked at my watch in order to log the correct time on my report. It was 10:45 A.M.

The occupants looked at me and began to speak. But they didn't use words. A soft crackling sound, a kind of modulated static, issued from their mouths. I looked at my watch again. Incredibly, it was almost 12:45. Somehow two hours had passed.

The female Hispanic proffered a stick of fluorescent chewing gum. I chewed it....

When I came to, I was in a hospital room. Four days had passed. Dr. Larry Werther, Baby Lago, Joe Casale, Rocco Trezza, and Carmella were pacing around my bed. I had a severe headache.

"Where are the bodyguards?" I asked.

"They're out in the hall, Mr. Leyner," Joe Casale said, as he worked the remote control on a television set cantilevered from the wall opposite my bed.

"What about Arleen?"

"She's got clients till ten, then I'll pick her up and bring her over."

"Larry, what was in that chewing gum?"

"When they pumped your stomach, Baby Lago took samples and analyzed them in the lab back at headquarters. Gas chromatography, mass spectrometry, nuclear magnetic resonance—she did the works. It was ibotenic acid. A powerful neurotoxin—destroys nerve cells in the brain. It's a good thing Joe Casale had tailed you."

I gave Joe the thumbs-up. "Thanks, babe."

Joe turned his gaze momentarily from the TV and gestured with his flipper. "No problem, Mr. Leyner."

"Joe also found this stuffed in your mouth."

Larry handed me an ivory mah-jongg tile with the words *Vote for Iron Man Wang* engraved on one side.

"Damn..."

"Forget about it, man, that's Hong Kong," Trezza said, taking my hand in his. "You can't worry about that shit now. You've got your books and your liner notes to write—that's your life, man.

Not chasing Iron Man Wang and his posse of hotwired sex freaks around the world. That's chump shit, man."

That's why I loved Trezz. He always knew exactly what to say to make me feel better. I playfully snapped the elastic waistband of his black latex jockstrap.

"Trezz, y'know if you ever decide to stop bakin' dough—"

Trezz's eyes flared instantly.

"...if you ever decide to stop doing whatever it is that you're doing, I'd love to have you come work for us over at headquarters. And that's a serious offer."

Trezz was about to respond when Joe Casale interrupted from across the room.

"Hey, Mr. Leyner!" he said, gesturing at the TV with the remote control. "Look at this—"

The Brazilian actress Sonia Braga, Elle MacPherson, two Victoria's Secret models, and Claudia Schiffer, the German model featured in Guess? jeans ads, were sitting around talking about what kind of man turns them on the most.

"I like a guy about five-seven," said MacPherson.

"Yeah," said Braga in husky, heavily accented English, "five-seven and about a hundred and thirty pounds."

One of the Victoria's Secret models, a voluptuous redhead in burnished gold satin and black lace demi-cup bra and bikini, was staring into space as she conjured her ultimate turn-on. "Light brown hair...and balding."

"Oooooh yeah...balding!" enthused the other Victoria's Secret model breathily. She sported a black velvet bustier and leather miniskirt.

"My *Liebchen* must have some broken blood vessels on his nose and he must be bowlegged," said the pouting Guess? jeans model, squirming a bit in her chair as she spoke.

MacPherson was distractedly tracing abstract figures in the rug when she looked up and announced: "To really turn me on so that I just melt, a man must have an irritable colon and epaulet-like patches of hair on his shoulders."

"A muscular upper body, skinny legs, and really small feet—about a size seven," Braga asserted.

The German cover girl vigorously nodded her assent. "And hazel eyes and a mole in the right eyebrow," she added.

The others swooned in unison. "Oh yes, a mole in the right eyebrow!"

The auburn-maned Victoria's Secret model had shut her eyes. Her hands were crossed over her breasts as she swayed from side to side. "I can even picture what he's wearing," she whispered. "He's got a leather blazer on over an Oakland A's T-shirt, black jeans…"

"…and snakeskin boots!" MacPherson growled.

"Yes! Yes! Yes!" squealed everyone.

MY INSIGNIA IS a guy surfing on an enormous wave of lava—it's an avalanche of this lurid molten spume with this glowering chiseled commando in baggy polka-dotted trunks on an iridescent board careering across the precipice of this incredible fuming tsunami of lava—and there's an erupting volcano in the distance in the upper right-hand corner. It's excellent.

I have it tattooed on my heart. And I don't mean on the skin of my chest over my heart. I mean tattooed on the organ itself. It's illegal in the States—I had to go to Mexico. It's called visceral tattooing. They have to open you up. They use an ink that contains a radioactive isotope so that the tattoo shows up on X-rays and CAT scans.

Do you want to get sick to your stomach—I'll describe the fetid, vermin-infested office of the "physician" who did my first visceral tattoo: Dr. José Fleischman. I went to sit down on what I thought was a couch in his waiting room…it wasn't a couch. It was thousands—tens of thousands—of cockroaches that had gathered in a mass that was the shape of a couch. The same thing happened with what I thought was a magazine. I reached for what I thought was the latest issue of *Sports Illustrated* and it moved. It wasn't a magazine at all, but a rectangular swarm of centipedes with a cluster of silverfish lying near the upper edge, and I guess from a distance, and in the dim light, the silverfish against the dark background of centipedes looked as if they formed the words *Sports Illustrated.* There was no receptionist and there were no other clients.

Finally, Fleischman emerged from the back room. The lenses of his eyeglasses were the thickest I'd ever seen. They actually bulged several inches out from the frames. It was as if he were wearing two of those snow-filled glass paperweights on his face. His clothes were soaked through with sweat. I explained that I wanted a surfer on a wave of molten lava tattooed on my heart and I handed him a color Xerox of my insignia. He lit a cigarette and studied the rendering from various angles, holding his head askew and squinting through the smoke.

"My friend," he said, speaking for the first time, "what chamber?"

"Chamber?" I asked.

He pointed with his cigarette to a yellowing diagram on the wall.

"The two atria are thin-walled. The ventricles are thick-walled. I recommend the ventricles. Either one—it's your call, *amigo.*"

I scrutinized the diagram for a few seconds.

"The left ventricle," I announced.

"Bueno," said Fleischman. "Today, we gonna put you out, open you up, and I'm gonna just do the outlines, then I sew you up. Then in two weeks, we open again, we fill in the colors, and sew up, all finished."

I was still looking over the diagram.

"Say, Fleischman, while you got me on the table, could you do 'Mom' on my pulmonary artery?"

"What kind of calligraphy you like? You like somethin' like this?"

He showed me an X-ray of someone's thyroid gland with the

word *Mother* done in what he called "Florentine style"—a very serpentine, filigreed style of lettering.

"That's very nice." I nodded.

Those were my first visceral tattoos. I've had many since. A tip to the guys out there—visceral tattoos really turn on female medical technicians and nurses. I've had numerous hot relationships start because a med-tech or a nurse saw one of my X-rays and went nuts over all the tattoos. They know that any wimp can go out and get "Winona Forever" stenciled on his arm—but it takes real balls to have yourself put under general anesthesia, sliced open, have a vital organ etched with radioactive isotope ink, and then get sewn up again every time you want to commemorate that special lady.

Next, I want to have the words *Desert Storm*—*Thunder and Lightning* tattooed on my left frontal cortex. But I don't know where I'm going to go for that one. Brain tattooing is illegal even in Mexico. Someone told me maybe Malaysia.

AAH!

He's just arrived, apparently having come straight from the gym. The iconic proliferation of his face and body in magazines and newspapers and posters across the country has ironically inured us to the real majesty of his physical presence. Only when confronted by him in person, his face flushed, his hair slicked back, his torso veiny, topographical with muscle, visibly hot from the tremendous workout that professional bodybuilders have called kamikaze-like in its intensity, do we apprehend—with a spine-tingling frisson that I can only compare to my experience as an adolescent of seeing a huge lathery stallion and then a dirigible in rapid succession—how gorgeous he really is. It's almost impossible to conceive that this is the body of an acclaimed writer. And not just an acclaimed writer, but perhaps the most influential writer at work today, certainly the writer who single-handedly brought a generation of young people flocking back to the bookstores after they had purportedly abandoned literature for good. Between mouthfuls of fennel-flavored monkfish, he chats amiably with a group of admirers who've surrounded him. His Ecuadorian girlfriend, wearing a lavender bustier and short chiffon skirt, gazes at him lovingly...

— *Martha Stewart*

It came as something of a surprise to discover that Martha Stewart's August 3rd birthday/housewarming party in East Hampton was merely a pretense to meet me — and not simply to meet me, but to gather material for her adoring profile entitled "Totally Brilliant... Totally Buff" which appeared in the September issue of Condé Nast's *Traveler*, and from which the foregoing is excerpted. After all, I'm a ruthless, corrupt, self-indulgent hypocrite; an opportunist, compulsive womanizer, liar, bully, and amphetamine addict. I approach fiction as a great ravenous lion might approach a helpless effete antelope who's lying in the grass stupidly licking the gelatin that oozes from her hooves. Yet sometimes fiction is such docile prey to my depredations that it sickens me, and I feel like abandoning it to the hyenas and focusing my creative powers exclusively on poetry.

I composed a very beautiful poem earlier this morning when I was in my garden, weed-whacking:

Why did best-selling author Martin Cruz Smith
testify before a secret Senate subcommittee
that superlawyer Alan Dershowitz has
continuously lactating breasts that could someday
produce up to 50 gallons of milk a day in space?
Legendary legal eagle F. Lee Bailey and
sf virtuoso Ray Bradbury debate the issue
that's tearing the American legal and dairy communities
apart.
Martha Stewart,
you awaken in me a new fury,

a new desperation to stun my enemies!
No family but fans!
I a hunk, a psycho!

It is rare that a poem so fully realized and of such complexity would arise spontaneously and intact, leaving me to merely rush to my laptop, the loam from my garden darkening the keyboard as I furiously type, verses beginning to fade from memory much as a dream dissipates upon awakening. Aah, if only one could apply a kind of oneiric fixative to dreams before they vanish...

FEELINGS

TODAY MY MARBLE citadel looms high above the asphalt, which is littered with the sun-bleached skeletons of my enemies. My dog Carmella wears a gold Rolex just above each of her four paws. I'm often seen dining at Spago, L.A.'s enduringly glamour-packed eatery, or strutting around Yemen in a full-length ermine coat, a hooker on each arm. Just yesterday, I was invited by ABC's *The American Sportsman* to go to Australia to hunt bandicoots with aboriginal boomerangs along with Ken Follett and Whitley Strieber. Bergdorf's is charging $3,500 for a hand-carved Baccarat crystal bottle of "Team Leyner," the perfume. (Forty million scent strips have been inserted in October and November issues of *Vogue, Harper's Bazaar, Elle, Vanity Fair, Mirabella, Glamour,* and *Mademoiselle.*)

What's a typical day like for Mark Leyner?

Yesterday, after a long afternoon of volunteer bereavement counseling and then reading to blind residents at a local nursing home, I go to Le Cirque. I drink something like 14 martinis. I get into a fight at the bar with the president of the Jersey City firefighters' union over a woman we're both trying to pick up. I kill him with a single roundhouse kick to the side of his head. I leave with the woman, who's cooing to me in a gravelly basso profundo voice. When we get to my apartment, I dump out the contents of her pocketbook: loaded jade-handled pistol, Quaaludes, Thai "golden eggs" (vibrating anal-stimulation balls), a packet of pharmaceutical-grade morphine, a little black book with the private phone numbers of Pentagon officials. I get up on the bed and dance to the electronic music they use to drive fleas and cockroaches crazy, my hard-on glowing in the dark and keeping time like a metronome, and then we fuck until dawn, strangling each other almost to the point of unconsciousness with kimono sashes each time we climax.

The next morning, I prepare a Jerusalem artichoke and spinach salad, stewed rabbit in white wine, and a pureed chestnut and chocolate layer cake, and I bring it over to Sister Norberta for the homeless shelter she runs at the church. I write for the rest of the day—extended, lyrical, almost psalm-like meditations on the redemptiveness of love.

Will I ever reconcile my inner contradictions? Is it so terribly wrong to live the way I do?

4

TOOTH IMPRINTS ON A CORN DOG (1995)

THE STORY SO FAR

September 13, 1992   Appears on the cover of the *New York Times Magazine*—"The Ridiculous Vision of Mark Leyner: America's Best-Built Comic Novelist"

1992   In Los Angeles, on book tour for *Et Tu, Babe,* Leyner encounters a very ripped Sigourney Weaver in the gym at the Chateau Marmont hotel. It's an omen. The very next morning he receives a phone call from Mercedes informing him that she's pregnant

Appears on *Today* to chat with Bryant Gumbel about *Et Tu, Babe*

June 26, 1993   Gaby Leyner is born—delicately plucked from Mercedes Pinto, like one matryoshka doll from another

December 17, 1993   Leyner and Mercedes are married

1993–1996   Makes appearances on the *Late Show with David Letterman, Late Night with Conan O'Brien, The Jon Stewart Show* (MTV), *Politically Incorrect,* etc., etc.
    Contributes essays and articles to *The New Yorker, Time, The New Republic, George, Travel & Leisure, Elle, GQ, Spin, Playboy, Maximum Golf,* etc.

1994–1995   Writes *The Fractals* for Brillstein-Grey Entertainment

1994   Leyner and Mercedes stay at the Hotel Excelsior on the Via Vittorio Veneto, in Rome, promoting the Italian translation of *Et Tu, Babe*. Appearing on the Italian equivalent of *The Tonight Show,*

Leyner sits nuzzled next to a beautiful Sri Lankan translator whose warm breath in his ear makes the entire evening a complete hallucination from which he fails to ever fully emerge

1995 Publication of *Tooth Imprints on a Corn Dog*

1996 "Human Bomb" appears on *Liquid Television* on MTV

MARK LEYNER'S HYPER TEXT

Andrew Hultkrans

I inhabit vast pavilions whose emptiness
is set ablaze by the vermilion sunset.
My menagerie of shaved animals is not open to the
    public.
But you may go to the special room
where every object is coated with Vaseline
and you may put something up your ass.
I will be down in half an hour.
Presently I am drugged and supine in my lichen-covered
    bathtub,
dazedly eating lychee-nut fondue
from a chafing dish of gurgling white chocolate at tub-
    side,
as a succession of anatomical freaks mount a klieg-lit
    proscenium
and perform for my entertainment.
A scorched breeze conveys the acridity of spent rocket fuel
    from
a launched garbage barge heading for the vast necropolis
    on Pluto,

loaded with the compacted corpses of executed insurgents.
It doesn't get much better than this.

—Mark Leyner, *Tooth Imprints on a Corn Dog, 1995*

AS YOU KNOW, I'm not your average critic. Tina Brown regularly plies me with Armani suits, Hermès tie-of-the-month memberships, and supplicant, leggy supermodels. Terrence Rafferty and James Wolcott respectively clean my bathroom (a brutal, thankless task) and do my laundry—including the weekly forklift runs to the dry cleaners. These and other sycophants attempt to curry favor with me, coveting, along with the entire literate English-speaking populace, the nuggets of blinding brilliance that explode from my swollen and, frankly, chemically enhanced cerebral cortex. You've seen that American Express ad with Martha Stewart slavishly laboring over a flawless swimming-pool mosaic of Botticelli's *Venus,* rendered entirely from cut-up credit cards? That's my pool. That's my Martha.

The annual ABA conference has become a bacchanalian festival of payola engineered to make me feel like a god. You wouldn't think that the fusty, hopelessly nineteenth-century publishing industry could command such resources, but boyee, you should see the spread they lay out for me—the ultraswank, cybernetically enhanced "smart" hotel rooms that anticipate my every need; the surgically sculpted, freakishly flexible, sexually insatiable escorts; and the smorgasbord of experimental designer drugs, including the soul-stroking aphrodisiacs resulting from the fusion of anabolic steroids with phenylethylamines such as MDMA. Any novelist, artist, filmmaker, or musician who might foolishly attempt retaliation for one of my career-ending critical eviscerations is dispatched with elegantly discreet efficiency by my crack squad of Elektra assassins—stunningly gorgeous Amazons who can kill with a playing card in fifteen blazingly unique ways.

From my perch atop the Mount Olympus of clout, few mortals are visible. One figure, however, towers above the rest of the flea circus like the colossus of rogues. He is Mark Leyner—author, bodybuilder, martial artist, media magnet. According to his own PR, he is "the most intense, and, in a certain sense, the most significant young prose writer in America." I quote this accolade not from his press kit (my only use for press kits is as tank lining for my Gila monster) but from his fiction itself. Indeed, such absurdly inflated blather takes the place of characterization and plot in his novels; it is the fabric that holds his monstrous mediagenic personality together.

Leyner began publishing his compressed narratives for the "eMpTV" generation in 1983, when his first novel, *I Smell Esther Williams,* established him as a purveyor of old-school metafiction, a literary heir to Donald Barthelme. It was not until seven years later that he resurfaced as the megalomaniac steroid freak we have grown to love. A harbinger of later excesses, *My Cousin, My Gastroenterologist* bore the stamp of his day job as an advertising copywriter for arcane medical prostheses such as artificial saliva and biodegradable incontinence briefs. It also began Leyner's ongoing quest to create the most radically unhinged "about the author" blurb of all time, tracking his rake's progress from his birth as "an infinitely hot and dense dot" to his current profile as a "terrible god," a "shimmering, serrated monster" whose whistle evokes "an earsplitting fife being played by a lunatic with a bloody bandage around his head." Less thematically coherent than his later works, *My Cousin* hints at a growing fascination with the mesmerizing demagogic potential of the postmodern media. In a roiling sea of nonlinear micronarratives, Leyner's lucid self-awareness occasionally surfaces, as when he boasts of his "poetry" that "these spicy, violent, superbly plotted verses are perfect for television."

More precisely, Leyner's fiction is television—a literary kamikaze mission to challenge television's supremacy in the ratings war of our attention economy. Indeed, Leyner views writing as a game of Mortal Kombat for the hearts and minds of an oversaturated audience: "The energy in my writing comes from a feeling that writing is dying, or is at least under great threat from other media...when I sit down and write, it's as if I'm at war with ultimately superior forces. I'll go down in flames, and take literature with me." The original Short Attention Span Theater, Leyner's prose captures the latter-day frisson of channel surfing. Each sentence is a discrete sound bite of spurious technobabble and foaming megalomaniacal hokum. In toto, they constitute a miracle entertainment product that is somehow nonfat yet more filling. The difficulty of sustaining such rhetorical intensity accounts for the relatively short length of Leyner's books, yet this brevity is by strategy: "There's not going to be a single slack verbal moment—no empty transitional phrase or routine expository sentence anywhere. I won't settle for anything less than maximum, flat-out drug overkill, the misuse of power."

Such "misuse of power" is rarely the novelist's privilege, and it is precisely this tension between the traditional image of the writer as agoraphobic esthete and Leyner's vision of the writer as a "swollen steroid freak" who "makes more in a year from product endorsements than most people make in a lifetime" that creates the savagely absurd humor in his first fully realized work, *Et Tu, Babe*. An ode to literary megalomania, *Et Tu, Babe* is an ironic masturbatory fantasy of unlimited media clout. During the novel's gestation period, Leyner was told by an enthusiastic sales executive at Crown that he wasn't writing a novel but a marketing plan. That a publishing-industry big shot could be delighted by the central joke of the book, yet not get it, neatly demonstrates Leyner's gift as a double-edged satirist of our hype-driven culture. Indeed, in a literary marketplace where

Martin Amis's new teeth garner as much press as his new novel, it is entirely plausible that a publishing insider could consider *Et Tu, Babe* even-keeled neorealism.

Despite its passages of hypertechnical jargon and its unrepentantly '90s tabloid-TV sensibility, *Et Tu, Babe* is a classic tragedy, an irresponsibly overblown epic poem documenting the precipitous fall of an international multimedia celebrity. It's all there — the unfettered hubris, the feminine temptation, the inevitable treachery, and the final heroic exile, which, for a media persona, spells death. Leyner's disappearance leaves a PR void that the novel's final chapter fills with the words of fellow celebrities — Clarence Thomas to Joan Jett — as they reminisce about their last moments with the literary demigod on *Larry King Live* and *A Current Affair.* A fitting wake for a media-constructed cyborg personality.

> We will all pretend to be who we are, we'll all be actors and actresses. Then, at some juncture, one of us who's, say, pretending to be fat, will decide to actually become fat in order to more effectively play that role. This will engender a mass movement from the simulacrum back to the real. This is sometimes called the "De Niro-ization" of culture. These migratory shifts back and forth from the real to the simulacrum will calibrate the rest of history.
>
> —Mark Leyner, *Tooth Imprints on a Corn Dog*

In the three years since the publication of *Et Tu, Babe,* the Brandeis-educated Jersey resident Mark Leyner and the "shimmering, serrated" literary Übermensch Mark Leyner have begun to merge. Whether the result of an irresponsible practice of Method Writing or merely of an inevitable commodification by our spectacular society, Leyner's media persona is now at least somewhat commensurate with his actual renown as a writer. Besides the steady flow of work for *The New Yorker, Esquire,* and *The New Republic,* there are the *New York Times* op-ed pieces, the *David Letterman* appearances, the Sunday *New York Times Magazine* covers, the paparazzi shots capturing Mark tripping the light fantastic with Martha Stewart. All this has become fodder for Leyner's latest book, *Tooth Imprints on a Corn Dog,* a scrapbook of magazine work, new pieces (including the inevitable "The Making of 'Tooth Imprints on a Corn Dog'"), and a play entitled *Young Bergdorf Goodman Brown.*

Tooth Imprints is the portrait of the artist as a young media darling "slashing a path through the rank vegetation of American popular culture with the warped machete of [his] mind," a series of postcards from the top. Attempted by another writer, this closet-cleaning collection would be seen as a cheap marketing scam, like yet another Smiths compilation. But Leyner's fiction has always been modeled on dense sound bites and celebrity-rag puff pieces, so the warmed-over status of more than half the book is consistent with the author's project. *Tooth Imprints* is the kind of book the Mark Leyner of *Et Tu, Babe* would release every other month, just to keep the cash flowing and the media buzzing. No longer in need of that cartoonish, steroid-fueled alter ego, the arrived Mark Leyner eases gracefully into his new role as authority on all things from bodybuilding chic to senatorial tattoos. In one piece, "Great Pretenders," he breaks a childhood vow never to use French poststructuralist terms like *simulacrum* and meditates on manufactured identity in our world of "surrogates, poseurs, impersonators, double agents, undercover cops, placebos, body-snatchers, and Stepford spouses." To counter the professional actors who bamboozle us daily with their "nimble artifice," Leyner exhorts us to shed our "plodding authenticity" and to "fight dissimulation with dissimulation. Go faux to faux!" And in a Borgesian gag ending, he shows us how, bringing us (and him) full circle, from the simulacrum to the real and back again: "You play the sophisticated, erudite reader—prosperous, well-traveled, tanned, and fit—whose esemplastic apprehension of the text is an art form in and of itself. I'll play the elegant, mordantly witty belletrist whose writing combines the delicacy and voluptuousness of poetry with the rigor of science and the vivacity of jai alai....Now from the top...."

Having succeeded in reifying what was once an ironic self-delusion, Leyner is the first novelist retrofitted for a digital bully pulpit. In the five-hundred-channel Valhalla of the near future, a sophisticated artificial intelligence modeled on his downloaded consciousness will lead the innocent channel surfer through the lurid boulevards of LeynerWorld for three dollars per minute. See you there. I'll be wearing an Armani blazer, an Hermès tie, and elegantly tapered silk pants with famous writers clutching at my three-quarter-inch cuffs.

Andrew Hultkrans is an author and the former editor in chief of *Bookforum*. His writing has appeared in *Wired, Salon, Filmmaker, Tin House,* and *Artforum*.

EXCERPTS FROM
TOOTH IMPRINTS ON A CORN DOG

TO MERCI PINTO LEYNER

WHEN MERCI WAS wheeled into the operating room to undergo the C-section that extricated our daughter, Gabrielle, from the umbilical knot she'd tied around her leg, the doctors set up this curtain that divided Merci into two sectors: the upper part for nonparticipants—Merci and me—and the business end, which apparently was for M.D.s and R.N.s only. Now, I *love* surgery—so as soon as I deduced that they were about to make the first incision, I got up and started to walk around to where the action was, because I couldn't see a damn thing up at Merci's head, and by this point she was sufficiently anesthetized and tranquilized that I figured she didn't need my "moral support" anymore, plus the fact that, in order to be allowed into the operating room, I'd scrubbed with hexachlorophene and donned full surgical regalia—gown, cap, mask, and gloves. Now, putting me in surgical garb is like putting a drag queen in an Yves Saint Laurent evening gown—I just light up. (Often I feel like a surgeon trapped in a writer's body.)

Anyway, as soon as the doctors see me coming, they get very peremptory and very territorial about Merci's uterus: "Mr. Leyner, please! You're to remain on that side of the curtain or you're going to have to wait outside."

Merci hears this, lifts her head up, and says in her sweet little voice, frayed only slightly by some 30 hours of labor: "Doctors, it's perfectly OK for him to assist—he watches a lot of medical programming on cable TV on Sundays."

The logic of this statement is so cogent and irrefutable that the doctors all just shrug their shoulders as if to say: "Well, that's about equivalent to the training we have, so welcome aboard, c'mon down, have a hemostat, grab a retractor, etc."

This incident exemplifies Merci—her sense of humor and sang-froid in the midst of difficult circumstances, her bracing pragmatism articulated in her dulcet Ecuadorian Tinker Bell voice. One of the coolest things about Merci is the way she talks. I need only slightly amend Michael Kimmelman's description of art historian Meyer Schapiro's writing to characterize Merci's discourse. Something like: "Her chirpy-timbred buoyant palaver, while uncompromising, dense, and dizzying in its references, is without cant or pomp."

People have said about me "unfettered imagination, nice arms," but she's got a pretty unfettered imagination herself. It's probably just as likely for her to say, just out of the blue, something like "bioluminescent acne" as it would be for me.

Don't you find it really revolting when an author thanks his wife by saying: "Only a woman with so-and-so's understanding and patience would have endured my manic highs and sloughs of despond, my chilly remoteness and insularity, and, alternately, my infantile need to be burped and changed, my obsessive philandering, my inexplicable need to fuck every woman in her step class, my having squandered her Christmas Club money on my methamphetamine habit, the Charivari sprees, the cognac binges with the inevitable vomiting and weeping, my paranoia, my hypochondria, my loss of interest in personal grooming and hygiene, and a recent compulsion to titillate myself by putting larvae in her food—all of which, rightly or wrongly, I felt was necessary to get through this long creative night. Her editorial acumen and rigor, her wise encouragement and enabling love, etc. etc."? This is your basic "I'm so complex and difficult, and my wife is so simple and forbearing" (a.k.a. "simpering imbecile puts up with anything overweening dickhead dishes out") formula.

Well, interestingly enough, a perfectly inverse equation underlies life at the Pinto-Leyner household. Merci is the complex one, and she's delightful to live with. (In an article for the Neapolitan textile-design fanzine *Bistecca,* I think I said that she had "close to optimal interpersonal ergonomics.") How easily one pictures her researching Montessori schools in an ecru mohair tank top and peppering her conversation with Vivienne Westwood this and Benazir Bhutto that. Y'know what I'm saying?

On the other hand, I'm simple, but extremely difficult to live with. And it's not like I'm racked with self-reproach about it either. I'm just the cream-soda-swilling, crotch-scratching, irascible, coughing-up-indigestible-bits-of-grizzle-from-some-meat-on-a-stick, surly, greasy overalls-over-candy-colored-latex-minikimono (my work uniform when I'm in the throes of a novel or a play), don't-bother-me-till-halftime kind of guy that society has made me. So hey, what the fuck? I'm not apologizing for who I am. I'm just trying to say that Merci is more complex, OK?

I'll give you an example: the gullibility ruse. Merci will feign gullibility in order to reveal and then revel in my own misreading of her apprehension. It's the sort of "you must *really* be naive if you think I'm that naive" game that she plays with such cunning. Here are several examples of "fun facts" that I've casually purveyed, only to find out weeks, sometimes months, later that, notwithstanding her feigned credulity, Merci had immediately dismissed as patently erroneous:

- Stephen Foster, the American songwriter and composer responsible for such enduring favorites as "Oh!

Susannah" and "Camptown Races," had jet-black hair growing from one armpit and bright red hair growing from the other—a genetic anomaly that occurs in only one out of 5 million people.

• Neville Chamberlain, the British statesman whose controversial policy of appeasing Adolf Hitler resulted in the 1938 Munich pact, refused to keep his contact lenses in the customary plastic storage case, preferring instead two rain-filled hoofprints.

• In the future, supermarkets may be able to keep their produce sections so cold that temperatures will approach 700 nanokelvins, or somewhat less than one millionth of a degree above absolute zero—minus 459 degrees Fahrenheit. (At this temperature, atoms merge with each other to become what are known as Bose-Einstein condensates—a hypothetical superatomic state of matter that may never have existed anywhere before.)

• In recent laboratory experiments, McDonald's has produced brewed coffee that is 6,000 kelvins, or 10,300 degrees Fahrenheit—the approximate surface temperature of the sun.

• As a young man, while studying songwriting with Oscar Hammerstein II, Stephen Sondheim decapitated a defrocked priest who propositioned him in a men's room at a Manhattan furniture showroom. The headless torso remained ambulatory for some 15 seconds, tottering out of the lavatory and collapsing finally on a sectional sofa. Charges against Sondheim were never filed and he went on to become one of Broadway's most esteemed composers and lyricists.

• While candy-striping at a veteran's hospital in Akron, Ohio, 15-year-old Dorothy Hamill was caught putting objects in the rectums of anesthetized patients as they lay unconscious in postoperative recovery. (The impounded objects are now on display in a vitrine in the hospital's lobby.) Thanks to the intercession of her father, a Kiwanis officer and alderman, Hamill was allowed to quietly plead nolo contendere and avoid the publicity of a trial. Hamill's gold medal for figure skating in the 1976 Winter Olympics captivated the country and her perky, blunt-cut hairdo became the coif du jour in salons across America.

- Boxer Sonny Liston so despised the taste and smell of buckwheat groats that his trainer would have a kasha effigy of his opponent brought to his dressing room minutes before a fight.

- During the Cuban missile crisis, President Kennedy was so adamant that his advisors remain available at every moment that he ordered them to wear diapers so that they wouldn't need to go to the bathroom. When the fastidious Secretary of State Dean Rusk demurred, he was briefly jailed.

- Martin Van Buren, the eighth president of the United States, had no bones or cartilage in his face. As a result of this abnormality, his face had the consistency of soft clay. This meant that it would become misshapen if kissed too roughly or handled at all. Sheet marks would last until his face was smoothed. If he slept on one side all night, he would wake up with that side of his face completely flattened. A sculptor was retained by the White House to remold Van Buren's face every day. But despite the efforts of the facial sculptor, his physiognomy varied wildly from day to day, as evidenced by portraits that show him with a bulbous nose on one day and a long aquiline nose on another, with high cheekbones and glinting blue eyes on one and a sloping forehead and rheumy, protruding eyes under a single continuous brow on another.

As I complete this dedication, I can't help but think back to a time some seven years ago. It was only a few weeks after I'd met Merci. I was in a paramilitary writers' colony in Idaho. One day we were on a 50-kilometer march with full pack and "composition intervals"—we were required to compose a poem at 15 km, an essay or short story at 25 km, and a novel outline and first chapter at 40 km.

There I was at the first interval, and all I'd produced was:

The pilot of a skywriting plane
suffers a fatal cerebral hemorrhage.
The aircraft falls,
scoring the immaculate azure
with a valedictory parabola of Dickinsonian dashes.

I knew this wouldn't be enough to satisfy my commanding officer, a sadistic taskmaster who considered anything under four or five stanzas a personal insult. I doffed my helmet and looked at a photograph of Merci that I'd taped inside. And there—in the first of by now innumerable occasions on which mere reference to her visage would inflame my imagination—gripping my legal pad and pen tightly against the backwash from helicopter rotors, I scrawled the full work:

The pilot of a skywriting plane
suffers a fatal cerebral hemorrhage.
The aircraft falls,
scoring the immaculate azure
with a valedictory parabola of Dickinsonian dashes.

Meanwhile, at the bar of a posh restaurant in Brentwood,
three couples without dinner reservations
wait so long for a table
that the women experience
synchronization of their ovulatory cycles.

Me, I'm just another prematurely wizened geek-savant.
Plucking a tiny stringed instrument
made out of a ring binder and orthodontic rubber bands,
I lie in a bath of hairy milk
and sing my lonesome blues.

[The fourth stanza has been redacted
because it doesn't fall within the scope of this poem.
And the time of the gentleman has expired.]

And so, Merci, I dedicate this *Corn Dog*, this red, sweating sausage sheathed in cornmeal batter and impaled on a honed stick, and each *Tooth Imprint*—each incisal pit and molar ridge—to you.

I know, sweetie, that you're not crazy about me taking this benthic pied-à-terre/atelier eleven kilometers below the surface of the Pacific Ocean in the Mariana Trench, some 320 kilometers southeast of Guam. But it's the only way I thought I'd be able to get enough peace and quiet and enough distance from the whole New York *scene* to be able to complete the next two books I'm under contract for.

The place is pretty swanky considering that it has to withstand about 16,000 pounds per square inch of pressure. When I need to shop, I travel back and forth to the supply ship on the surface in a brand-new 1996 ceramic-hull one-man submersible with a silver-zinc fuel cell, joystick navigation, voice- and video-transmitting fiber-optic microcable, taupe leather interior, roof rack, 5-disc carousel CD player, 150-watt Bose speakers. My only complaint is that it's a bit sluggish. And when you're down here eleven kilometers from the mother ship and you realize that you're out of coffee filters or those fabric softener dryer sheets—it's a long trip back up at five knots max. But work is going extremely well. Do you remember reading my proposal for a book called *The Tetherballs of Bougainville*? Do you remember how enthusiastic I was because I thought that not only would it be the first novel to really capture the febrile excitement of international tetherball competition but also the first novel to analyze tetherball as a kind of deep metaphor for fin de siècle gender relations? Does any of this sound familiar? There's a character named Colonel Alebua, Bougainville's despotic junta leader, a wild aficionado of American pop culture who names his daughter Kojacqueline. Ring a bell? Well, anyway, the novel's coming along marvelously, I think. And as soon as it's done, I'm contemplating a book-length meditation on the Edgar Winter song "Frankenstein." I don't know of another instrumental that speaks more powerfully to that strain of the American male psyche which yearns to grossly transform one's own body, swagger down an illuminated runway in a slaughterhouse-turned-disco thronged with Dionysian suburban housewives ululating with libidinal excess, and then launch oneself on a hallucinogen-fueled, out-of-body ascent that culminates in an orgasmic merge with a creature who manifests all the faces of the Dionysian housewives, but is in reality the huge throbbing cosmogonic placenta that was expelled nanoseconds after the birth of the universe.

But I've been thinking—that sort of describes almost *every* song. So I guess I'm not really sure about the second book yet.

On the off chance that anything fatal happens to me down here, I need to leave you with a couple of financial instructions. Do you remember the plot of land in Azerbaijan we won at that raffle in Montauk a couple of summers ago? Well, it may be a good time to sell. A consortium of oil companies including British Petroleum,

Amoco, and Pennzoil just bought oil fields in the Baku region of the Caspian Sea, and they're planning on running a pipeline into Turkey, which means—if my map is accurate—that they're going to have to come right through our property. I'm sure that Binky knows a realtor over there, but if not, there's probably a Century 21 or a Coldwell Banker in Azerbaijan that can help you.

A few years ago I bought stock in a soft-drink company by the name of Emerald Beverage. The stock hasn't performed particularly well (I bought it at $6 a share and it closed yesterday at $2.25), so you might be tempted to unload it before it drops any further. Try to hold on to it for a bit. The company recently switched ad agencies and they're about to launch a new campaign with a television commercial featuring a coterie of female office workers gathered at a window, mouths agape, leering at a chain gang along the road—the beefy convicts, stripped to the waist in a brutal sun, hack at stones with sledgehammers as sadistic guards guzzle Emerald Diet Cola and occasionally jab the prisoners with rifle butts. The ad's a winner and I think it gives Emerald Beverage stock good upside potential.

Anyway, Merci, I don't want to end with such morbid practicalities. I feel quite safe and I'm doing well. The apartment's slammin'. I'm really enjoying tooling around in the submersible. I get "Frankenstein" cranked up on the system and—sweetie, you'll get a kick out of this—even though it's absolutely desolate down here except for the occasional shrimp or anemone who's strayed from his hydrothermal vent, I put a bumper sticker on the aft ballast tank that says: How's My Driving?

I miss you and Gaby very much. I adore you both. And I'll be home soon.

Feb. 15, 1995
Challenger Deep,
Mariana Trench

JUST HAPPY TO SEE YOU, CHULA

MERCEDES IS IN the store exchanging one nursing bra for another and I'm waiting for her in the car.

My waiting game works like this:

I have to think of three foods with military ranks in their names before Merci comes out with the new nursing bra.

(The original nursing bra opened at the shoulder straps. My sister Chase told Merci that a nursing bra that opens between the breasts better facilitates public suckling. Ergo, Merci is exchanging the side-snap nursing bra for the center-clasp nursing bra at a maternity emporium called *Mothercare*.)

Merci's been in the store for five minutes and all I've thought of so far is: *General Tso's Chicken* and *Cap'n Crunch Cereal*.

I glance into the store and Merci's on line at the register.

This is a lucky break for me. Apparently there's a price difference between the side-snap nursing bra and the center-clasp nursing bra requiring Merci to either pay the difference or get cash back. Whatever the situation is, it affords me more time to come up with a third food with a military rank in its name.

Unfortunately, so far, I haven't been able to parlay this extra time into a third food. I've come up with *Beef Wellington* and *Caesar Salad*, but *Wellington* and *Caesar* are not military ranks but the names of historical military figures. I've also thought of *Kaiser Roll* and *Chicken à la King*—but again, no good—*Kaiser* and *King* are not military ranks but ranks of nobility.

Glancing back into the store, I see that Merci is now at the register. There's almost no time left and I'm very pessimistic about coming up with a third food. She's handing the cashier money. The cashier is refolding the center-clasp nursing bra into a fresh plastic bag emblazoned with the name *Mothercare*.

Who truly understands how the mind works?

Cognition is still something of a black box to neurobiologists.

What transpired along the neuronal circuitry of my prefrontal cortex? Just what happened within the network of excitatory and inhibitory synapses enabling neurotransmitters to alter the way that my pyramidal neurons integrated cortical signals across thousands of spines in their dendrites—so that suddenly (as Merci pushed through the revolving door and headed for my car) the words *Admiral Salt-Cod Fish Cakes* miraculously materialized in my consciousness?

Who will ever know?

Exquisitely sensitive to nuances in my verbal environment, per-haps hearing a child saying "Mira, mira" to his mother provided me with the phoneme that precipitated an instantaneous concatenation of lexical processing that resulted in *Ad-mi-ral* and then, in a cog-nitive flash, *Admiral Salt-Cod Fish Cakes* (a dish I once sampled at a diner in Gloucester, Massachusetts)—the third food with a military rank in its name, seconds before Merci's hand reached the car door.

Exulting, I pound the dashboard with my fist.

Merci looks at me like: What the hell?

And I'm like: Just happy to see you, chula.

THE MAKING OF "TOOTH IMPRINTS ON A CORN DOG"

I'VE BEEN COMMISSIONED by *Der Gummiknüppel* ("the German equivalent of *Martha Stewart Living* but with more nudity and grisly crime") to compose a poem for their ten-year anniversary issue. As I reported in the premiere issue of *Esquire Gentleman,* my first assignment for *Der Gummiknüppel* was to conduct a series of conjugal visits with Amy Fisher at the Bedford Hills Correctional Facility and to chronicle same.

The editors of *Der Gummiknüppel* have custom-ordered their poem with unusual specificity. The contract received by my agents at ICM stipulates "1,000 lines of free verse in the *poète maudit* tradition of Arthur Rimbaud, but infused with the ebullience and joie de vivre that made ABBA so popular in the 1970s." Not only are the stylistic requirements severe, but the deadline's a killer: They need the completed poem faxed to their offices in Baden-Baden in less than 35 hours.

This assignment, albeit lucrative, is no stroll through the park.

It's not something I can bang out amidst the domestic maelstrom of pregnant girlfriends, ex-wives, codependent dogs, etc.

So I catch the red-eye to L.A.

I will hole up at the venerable Chateau Marmont in Hollywood—the hotel where the great Billy Wilder bivouacked in his youth—and I will confect my verse under ideal laboratory conditions.

What follows is 24 hours of the postmodern writer in vitro.

[Room 25, Chateau Marmont, 8221 Sunset Boulevard, Hollywood, California]…

I have programmed the television in my bedroom to awaken me, and at six o'clock I'm roused by CNN. I mute the news and telephone room service for a sweetbreads burrito and a thermos of black coffee.

Several lines of verse have emerged intact from my hypnopompic state, and I scrawl them on a pad before they can evaporate:

> In a dressing room at Armani Kids,
> I found the dead body of a policewoman.
> I sucked her toe and she came to life.

There are also two fragments. The neo-Keatsian

> Beads of mercury dribble from
> the mouths of hemorrhaging androids…

and the evocative

> Tooth imprints on a corn dog.

After momentarily considering revising the initial lines to read: "At a counterfeit hair-care products lab, / I found the dead body of a policewoman. / I sucked her toe and she came to life," and then not (there's something so much more febrile and chthonic

126

about discovering this sleeping-beauty-in-blue at a juvenile cou-
turier), I decide against incorporating any of this material into the
poem. "From the Mouths of Hemorrhaging Androids" and "Tooth
Imprints on a Corn Dog" have possibilities as titles, though. (I also
make a note to pitch the "comatose policewoman found in dressing room—protagonist sucks toe—policewoman's miraculously
revived—becomes indebted to protagonist, who turns out to be
the Vitiligo Killer" idea to a couple of movie producers while I'm in
town.)

I stash the material that I've generated thus far in a safe in the
bedroom closet. (I've taken rather elaborate security measures to
ensure that no one plagiarizes my verse or disturbs me while I'm
composing. The "workmen" who appear to busy themselves with
maintenance and repairs in and around my suite are actually undercover security agents. For example, the "plumber" crouched beneath
the kitchen sink, with the pants hanging low in the rear, exposing
a good 2–3 inches of butt crack—he's one of my most highly dec-
orated counterinsurgency operatives. The exposed area between the
cheeks of his buttocks is actually *bugged* with hypersensitive micro-
phones, a microcomponent electroencephalography device, a Dop-
pler ultrasound transducer, and a remote telemetric sphygmoscope
and galvanic skin response sensor so that he can record the voices,
monitor the brain waves, image the internal organs, and evaluate the
veracity of any person or persons who come within a two-mile radius
of my hotel suite.)

Ravaging the sweetbreads burrito like a starved animal, I set
up my Apple Macintosh PowerBook 180 on the dining room table,
and I invoke my muse...my sullen muse in strapless black-lace bra,
black-velvet short-shorts trimmed in fur, black fishnet stockings,
quilted clogs and black *ET TU, BABE* cap.

And like the celebratory automatic-weapons fire of an anarchic mob, my neurons set the synaptic sky ablaze with electrical
discharge....

9:30 A.M.

Inner thoughts:

What a remarkable journey my life has been. I was born one of craniopagus quintuplets — five infants connected at the head, our bodies extending radially like flower petals. I was the only sibling to survive the surgery that separated us. My father was an imposing and remote figure, very much the martial patriarch who valued certainty and implacable resolve above all other attributes. (Father was particularly fastidious about language. I was with him on a plane once when he turned around in his seat and slapped a complete stranger across the face for mispronouncing the word *putsch*.) Mother, albeit not an intellectual — she was incapable of naming four American presidents, making change for $20, or reading a menu — was certainly a more empathetic and tender parent. But her influence was effectively muted by Father's strident and unyielding decrees. As a child, I was absolutely forbidden to express or inwardly harbor self-doubt. Soon after Mother's mysterious suicide, Father hired a telepathic governess from a Soviet parapsychology institute. If, in the sanctuary of my own bedroom, I had thoughts that even remotely hinted at irresolution or trepidation, the woman — an affectless martinet with an intricate circuitry of braids enveloping the back of her skull — would suddenly materialize to flay my bared buttocks with a heavy Cyrillic ruler, chiding in her eerie monotone: "Dun't sink negatif!"

After leaving home in 1972, I supported myself by doing odd jobs. For twenty dollars, I'd arrange the cash in your wallet, President-side up in increasing denominations. That was standard. Specials included alphabetical arrangement by last name of Secretary of the Treasury, by ascending or descending serial number, etc. I did a job for a lady who liked her wallet arranged with wrinkled bills up front and crispy bills toward the back. A transit cop once hired me to arrange his bills by shade; this is called "the fade" — bright cash up front, bleached cash to the rear. *Chacun à son goût.* Specials were extra, of course. You'd be amazed at the things that people won't do for themselves, or can't do because they have their weird little phobias. A guy once called me—a young guy, I'd say about twenty-five—and he wanted me to cut up his expired credit cards. The guy had this morbid fear of credit cards once they've expired. Obviously there's some complex psychopathology involved here, but hey…When I arrived at the guy's house, there were two expired cards—an American Express and a Sunoco—lying in his bathtub where he'd flung them in a panic a week before. So acute was his aversion that he'd refused to go anywhere near the tub. I might add that the dude had cultivated quite a stench (which cost him an extra ten bucks; if you had really bad body odor, that would cost you an extra $10 no matter what I did for you). And when I picked up the cards and walked toward him, he recoiled in horror, weeping, falling to his knees, pleading with me not to come any closer. I diced the cards with a pair of shears from my tool belt, and, per our agreement, disposed of them in a landfill some ten miles out of town. I charged him $60—the regular $50 for cutting cards, plus the $10 surcharge because he stank so bad. Ironically, he paid with a Visa card—active, I assume. I also killed pets. (Pet "hits" were a lucrative portion of my business. A lot of people wanted their pets dead because they'd become too much trouble, but they couldn't bring themselves to do it because they'd become so emotionally attached or for religious reasons or whatever—so, for a fee, I'd do it.) My first job, I garrotted an incontinent Schnauzer for a guy in Englewood, New Jersey. It got easier and easier after that. A woman once contracted me to kill her turtle. The lady's got something called purulent erythema serpens, which makes your skin look like Roquefort cheese, and she thinks she caught the disease somehow from the turtle, so she hates the turtle and wants it dead, and she wants to *see* it die. So I devise a nice little car bomb for the turtle—a matchbox pickup truck with a piece of lettuce in it and a cherry bomb under it. The turtle waddles onto the toy truck to eat the lettuce, I light the fuse, and boom! Arrivederci, Michelangelo. But I did all sorts of other things, too. I'd help you take your cowboy boots off—that was $3 a boot. If you were straightening a painting on the wall and you needed someone to stand across the room and tell you if it was level—that was $7 per painting, and I'd do four paintings for only $25. And I'd charge ten bucks to smell your milk—y'know, if you couldn't decide whether it was spoiled or not.

And today here I am at the Chateau Marmont—all expenses paid by *Der Gummiknüppel*—improvising a couple of pages of verse for more money than most people make in a year...the Chateau Marmont, where Howard Hughes satisfied his cravings for baby peas and young girls, where Diahann Carroll and Sidney Poitier trysted while filming *Porgy and Bess*...

What a strange, fascinating life it's been....

12:10 P.M.

The elation of an hour ago has collapsed into severe depression. I am racked with doubts about "Tooth Imprints on a Corn Dog." Although I'm intellectually aware that this is a requisite pattern in my creative process—the alternating waves and troughs of euphoria and despair—the emotional pain is unmitigated. Convinced that the poem requires the inclusion of more anecdotal material, I comb my journals for suitable vignettes. I leaf through the battered diary that I kept during a period in my life when I suffered from canine acral lick dermatitis and spent my days licking, scratching, and biting at my own flanks. In stunted script interspersed with pictures, like some arcane rebus, I recorded in unflinching detail my descent, my season in hell. I drank anything containing alcohol. In fact, my bar was stocked with Sterno, Old Spice, Windex, Nyquil, Aqua Net, and Lysol. (Plus tonic, bitters, and pearl onions, of course.)

But this material is far too bleak and splenetic, and would vitiate the generally mirthful tone of the poem. Perhaps I can somehow incorporate one of the stories I didn't get a chance to tell during my recent appearance on David Letterman's *Late Show*, e.g., *I recently attend a garish tribute to the Italian fashion designer Gianni Versace (where I witness Diane von Furstenberg's left breast fully emerge from her blouse—an event which, I've subsequently been told, traditionally signals the advent of autumn), and during dinner I'm regaling my tablemates with stories about my prior incarnation as a medical advertising copywriter, and I'm talking about how I wrote ads for a product called artificial saliva which was developed for people who suffer from something called chronic dry mouth, and I'm describing how the ad's body copy touted the product's pleasant taste and realistic viscosity, and I'm explaining to them how disappointed I was when the headlines I'd come up with were rejected by the client simply because they'd already been used ("Artificial Saliva—Don't Leave Home Without It" and "Artificial Saliva—Mmmm, Mmmm, Good!"), when this stunning and extraordinarily elegant Austrian countess whom I'm seated next to and who's been ignoring me through most of the meal suddenly turns to me and says in this husky sotto voce: "I'm very rich...and very bored." A remark which leaves me completely dumbstruck. Although for some inexplicable reason, I finally respond with: "Can your inner child come out and play?" Etc. Etc.*

But this material strikes me as egregiously blithe, posing a risk to the poem's magisterial gravity.

I am about to lose all hope, when a breeze wafts in from the open window. Actually, one can't even call it a breeze. Imagine an asthmatic fruit fly trying to blow out a birthday candle. That's the intensity of this wisp of a sigh, which conveys such a minute and evanescent concentrate of fragrances—first daffodils, then hyacinths, and finally lilac—that it might be more accurate to say that what's conveyed are the Platonic ideals of each fragrance, rather than the scents themselves. And somehow this most subtle stimulation of my olfactory nerve cells hits me with a force akin to that of a nightstick to the forehead. And the verse begins flowing anew.

12:55 P.M.

The sky is perfectly white and veined with
    vermicular trails of purple SCUD exhaust.
In a go-go cage dangling from a 10-story construction crane,
I am naked except for a 7-Eleven "Big Gulp" container
    and a rubber band.
"Swing me!" I call to the crane operator.
I want what I've never wanted before:
    terrifying centrifugal torque!
"Swing me, gringo!"
I laugh mirthlessly, eyes rolling,
    never so profoundly convulsed.
"Thanks, hon!" I wail.

The air is rent by a cacophonous peal of imbecilic laughter as a group of rickshaw pullers drinking contaminated home-brewed liquor beneath my balcony react to the verse that I have just recited—the opening stanza of the seventeenth canto.

1:30 P.M.
I telephone room service and order the 14-course lunch, including quail soup and steamed piglet.

2:25 P.M.
Nap.

6:05 P.M.
Russia is so desperate to earn hard currency, preserve jobs, and resuscitate a moribund economy that it's begun selling arms and military technology on Home Shopping Network. Viewers who tune in, unaware of this latest twist in the global weapons bazaar, may be shocked to see a svelte model in evening gown, pearls, and

satin gloves caressing a Russian S-300 surface-to-air missile, as its price — $849.99 — flashes in the lower left-hand corner of the screen. On-the-air callers are giddy with the incredible savings they're getting on individual weapons and entire weapons systems that up until now had been completely out of their price ranges. A housewife from Tullig, Arizona: "I can't believe it. I have three boys who all just graduated — two from high school and my oldest from college — and I just bought each of them the Kilo-class diesel-powered submarines you had on a little while ago. And I just can't believe the savings! Those submarines used to go for about $250 million each, but thanks to Home Shopping Network and the collapse of the Soviet Union, I got all three for only $2,250! And I'm thinking of getting the MIG-31 fighter plane for my nephew, who's being confirmed this spring. And for my husband, who loves cars and trucks and tractors — anything with a motor — I'm thinking, with Christmas coming, either the BTR-60 armored personnel carrier or the T-72 main battle tank. The discounts are just unbelievable!" Other former Soviet republics including Ukraine and Georgia have also lined up with Home Shopping Network to sell advanced fighter-interceptors, SU-27 fighter-bombers, MI-17 troop transport helicopters, aircraft carriers, as well as low-tech weapons like rifles, artillery, and ammunition. Home Shopping Network vice president Beatrice Pinto told CNN correspondent Wolf Blitzer that their recent "Back-to-School Package," consisting of two shoulder-fired surface-to-air missiles, a dozen Kalashnikov assault rifles with five thousand rounds of ammunition, two antipersonnel cluster bombs, and a tank-piercing artillery shell, elicited the largest viewer call-in response in the network's history. "We liquidated our entire inventory on that particular offer in twelve minutes! People just seem to love the fact that they can purchase high-quality weapons and sophisticated delivery systems over the phone from the comfort of their own living rooms for outrageously low prices, without having to deal with shady arms brokers who ream you with exorbitant commissions and surcharges."

* * *

Luckily I'd programmed the television to awaken me at six, otherwise I might have slept through the night. What a succulent piglet! Kudos to Andre Balazs, Philip Truelove, and the entire staff here at the Marmont. I chase two 50-mg tablets of over-the-counter pseudoephedrine hydrochloride with a chilled Mountain Dew and return to my PowerBook upon which the embryonic final canto of "Tooth Imprints on a Corn Dog" glows in the Hollywood dusk.

7:30 P.M.
Inner thoughts:

This will not be the first occasion on which, shackled by inexorable time constraints and challenged to produce literature, I surface from the depths, Houdini-like, opus in hand. A number of years ago, pursuant to a large wager with noted publisher and incorrigible sporting woman Michelle Sidrane, I absconded to a villa at Roquebrune-Cap-Martin on the Côte d'Azur and, in a fortnight, completed a twelve-volume series of mystery novels collectively entitled *The Executioner's New Clothes,* which includes *The Executioner Wears a Leisure Suit, The Executioner Wears a Pinafore, The Executioner Wears a Habit, The Executioner Wears a Chemise, The Executioner Wears a Bikini, The Executioner Wears Jodhpurs,* and *The Executioner Wears an Iridescent Silk Chiffon Jeweled-Front Gown with Matching Cape.* You're probably familiar with the opening paragraphs from *The Executioner Wears a Truss,* as they've been widely anthologized. Note the cool, vibey sort of "Kansas afternoon" feel I achieve by juxtaposing madras, velvet, and terry:

The two murderers have been on the road for almost fifteen weeks without steak au poivre, in desperately cold weather, wearing only madras slacks and turquoise chambray workshirts.

Back in New York, the Executioner staggers drunk from the Four Seasons, lurching desultorily toward a white limousine. All postpunk ennui, he dives headfirst into the car as if into an empty pool. And he sleeps, paralyzed, face pressed against the velvet upholstery. Relentlessly, clumps of darkness devour him.

When he regains consciousness, he's in a hotel room in Lake Tahoe. His girlfriend, Lucia, who's just emerged from the sauna, turbaned and swathed in plush towels, is squeegeeing sweat from her face with the edge of a freckled forearm.

"Thirty thousand tons of New Zealand anthracite just don't vanish into thin air," she says.

"I'm not interested in New Zealand anthracite at the moment," the Executioner says, massaging his temples. "I want you to explain that dinner to me again—the one at your parents' house. You said it was some sort of ritual meal commemorating...what?"

"Many thousands of years ago, my people were forced to flee their homeland suddenly one morning. When they fled, all they had time to take with them were half-filled cups of cold black coffee, cheese danish, and the sports section of the newspaper. And they barely had time to get even one sock on. That's why each year, when we commemorate our exodus, we eat these ritual foods—the cold black coffee and the cheese danish—and we read from a special sports section, and we wear a single sock. On all other nights we wear a pair of socks, but on this night we wear only one."

"Oh yeah," says the Executioner, fidgeting with his genetically engineered superfeminine gerbils who stand on their hind legs and, grasping the bars of the cage with their front claws, bombastically shout "Egöiste!"

Meanwhile, two coruscating gold-capped buckteeth sprout from the holographic moon, as the tectonic throb of Hong Kong's subterranean synthetic drum machine rattles the city, and handsome triad gangsters who pomade their hair with their own semen and tote bowling bags containing the severed heads of their business adversaries sprawl in chic hotel-lobby banquettes made of molded whale intestine filled with thermostatically modulated runny Camembert.

10:45 P.M.

The final stanza of the final canto. It must be a concise, allusive, unifying summation of the disparate themes and leitmotifs of the poem, an intricate précis, an envoi; in structure — a perfect miniature of the work's massive architecture, in tone — an effervescent exaltation of life itself.

I'm working two veins simultaneously.

I've been exploring the notion of educational foods. Specifically, is it possible to utilize soup as a pedagogical tool? Essentially, what *is* soup? I ask myself. A liquid food with a meat, fish, or vegetable stock as a base and often containing pieces of solid food. And then it hits me — why, of course — soup is the ideal gastronomic medium for educating children about maritime disasters and naval battles. For example: Chicken broth with little macaroni *Titanic*s and macaroni icebergs. Or Hearty Home-Style Battle of Trafalgar Bisque with barley Lord Nelsons. Defeat of the Spanish Armada Gazpacho. Cream of *Andrea Doria*. Battle of Midway Miso Soup with tofu aircraft carriers and kamikaze crackers.

At the same time, I'm exploring the lyrical possibilities of the 900-number tête-a-tête:

"Describe yourself to me."
"I'm a peroxide-blond in a black velvet miniskirt, actually."
"Describe something sexy that you've done recently."

"Something that I did that someone else thought was sexy or something that I thought was sexy?"

"Something you did that you found sexy."

"I didn't lick all the potato salad off my spoon before using it to stir my tea."

"Oh…that's good. Say that again."

"I didn't lick all the—"

"Slower."

"I…didn't…lick…all…the…potato…salad…off…my…spoon…before…using…it…to…stir…my…tea."

Now, how to hybridize these two strains—the pedagogical soups and the erotic phone conversation—into the germ of a final stanza, that's the problem. And then it hits me—why, of course—a sex-talk breakfast cereal with male and female marshmallow bits each containing an edible, lactose-activated, voice-synthesizing microchip so that when you pour on the milk and put your ear close to the bowl, you hear, for instance, one marshmallow murmur: "Please say it. Since Clinton was impeached, it's the only way I can… function. Say it slowly." And then another marshmallow responds: "All right, baby. I…didn't…lick…all…the…potato…salad…off… my…spoon…before…using…it…to…stir…my…tea."

1:15 A.M.

I've decided to forgo incorporating this material into the final stanza of the final canto. There's too much pathos in pornographic breakfast cereal. Now I'm just thinking out loud here, but how about something like: *As cyanide pellets are dropped into the bowl of sulfuric acid beneath my chair, / I extend the middle fingers of both hands. / "Fuck you all," I sneer. / I inhale deeply, and then nonchalantly blow a series of thick, perfectly formed smoke rings of poison gas. / Then suddenly my attorney appears. / "Here is my Magic Legal Pad," he says. / "Stand on it and it will fly you wherever you want to go—the Maldives, Mauritius,*

Tortuga, wherever. / And it's sanitary—after each person uses it, he or she discards the top sheet, so the next user can stand on a completely clean page."

No...that's no good.

I need something august. Something resplendent. Something like:

I inhabit vast pavilions whose emptiness
is set ablaze by the vermilion sunset...

1:16 A.M.

I inhabit vast pavilions whose emptiness / is set ablaze by the vermilion sunset.

Hmmmmmmm.

I inhabit vast pavilions whose emptiness / is set ablaze by the vermilion sunset.

That works for me.

There's a majestic plenitude to it. A fanatical lucidity. A still, immaculate violence. A sort of ironic, elephantine, paradisiacal hegemony.

1:17 A.M

Deep sleep, with intermittent drooling and spasmodic leg movement, and incremental hair and nail growth....

8:00 A.M.

Call it divine afflatus. Call it esemplastic power. Cite Coleridge awakening from his deep reverie, the magical lines of "Kubla Khan" still limpid in his mind; or Shelley who, brooding in a wood that skirts the Arno near Florence, was inspired by tempestuous gusts to compose the interlacing tercets and couplets of "Ode to the West Wind." I was applying benzamycin gel to a rash I'd developed after attending The McLaughlin Group Inaugural Reception in Washington, when it came to me—the final stanza of the final canto—verbatim, end-stops and enjambments intact; the original two lines efflorescing spontaneously into sixteen:

I inhabit vast pavilions whose emptiness
is set ablaze by the vermilion sunset.
My menagerie of shaved animals is not open to the public.
But you may go to the special room
where every object is coated with Vaseline
and you may put something up your ass.
I will be down in half an hour.
Presently I am drugged and supine in my lichen-covered bathtub,
dazedly eating lichee-nut fondue
from a chafing dish of gurgling white chocolate at tub-side,
as a succession of anatomical freaks mount a klieg-lit proscenium
and perform for my entertainment.
A scorched breeze conveys the acridity of spent rocket fuel from
a launched garbage barge heading for the vast necropolis on Pluto,
loaded with the compacted corpses of executed insurgents.
It doesn't get much better than this.

9:15 A.M.
I've just faxed the 1,257 lines of "Tooth Imprints on a Corn Dog" to *Der Gummiknüppel* in Baden-Baden.

I'm in my customized, four-wheel-drive, All-Terrain Lincoln Town Car, heading west on Wilshire Boulevard into Beverly Hills, and I'm on the line with Irene Webb at ICM, and, as a peripheral slurry of pink and aquamarine flies by, I'm screaming into the car phone: "What do you mean De Niro won't get in the terrarium?!"

It doesn't get much better, indeed.

5

THE TETHERBALLS OF BOUGAINVILLE (1997)

THE STORY SO FAR

May 17, 1996 Appears on *Charlie Rose* with David Foster Wallace and Jonathan Franzen

1996–1997 Writes *Iggy Vile M.D.* for MTV

1996–1998 Writes Wild Kingdom column for *Esquire*

1997 Leyner, Mercedes, and Gaby enjoy Thanksgiving dinner at Martha Stewart's house in Westport, Connecticut

1997 Publication of *The Tetherballs of Bougainville*

AN INTERVIEW WITH MARK LEYNER, AUTHOR OF *MY COUSIN, MY GASTROENTEROLOGIST, ET TU, BABE,* AND THE NEW NOVEL, *THE TETHERBALLS OF BOUGAINVILLE*

Laura Miller

EVEN THE MOST seasoned literary journalist might feel some trep-
idation when heading out to interview Mark Leyner for the first
time. In his second novel, *Et Tu, Babe,* he describes himself as "not
your average author. I dress like an off-duty cop: leather blazer, silk
turtleneck, tight sharply creased slacks, Italian loafers, pinky-ring. I
drive a candy-apple-red Jaguar with a loaded 9-mm semiautomatic
pistol in the glove compartment." In *My Cousin, My Gastroenterologist,* his first book, he writes, "I am a terrible god" and claims that,
since he took up bodybuilding, small birds die of terror and drop
from the trees whenever he goes for a walk in the woods.

This turns out to be an exaggeration. Leyner is a pleasant, articulate fellow whose good temper remained untarnished even at the end of a long publicity tour to promote his most recent book, *The Tetherballs of Bougainville*. *Tetherballs*, like all Leyner's books, features its author as its main character — or rather a version of "Mark Leyner" who's like an unchained, unholy amalgam of raging id and grandiose ego, drunk on pop culture and capable of mimicking its many degraded voices at will. As dazzlingly hilarious as Leyner's other books, *Tetherballs* is also the closest to, as Leyner puts it, "a bona fide novel." Its first part describes the failed execution of the fictional thirteen-year-old Leyner's father ("My father is not an evil person. He just can't do PCP socially"), who is then resentenced to New Jersey State Discretionary Execution: the state lets him go but reserves the right to kill him at any moment. Unfazed, the adolescent Mark proceeds to seduce the glamorous female prison warden, despite the fact that he needs to write a screenplay overnight so that the next day he can accept the Vincent and Lenore DiGiacomo/ Oshimitsu Polymers America Award for best screenplay written by a student at Maplewood Junior High School (the prize being $250,000 a year for life). How did he win the award without actually submitting the screenplay first? "That's the advantage of having a powerful agent."

The rest of *Tetherballs of Bougainville* consists of the screenplay itself, which simply records Mark's druggy tryst with the warden in her office. Of course, the screenplay includes the reading aloud of a long review–plot synopsis of the as-yet-unmade *Tetherballs of Bougainville* movie, which takes young Mark to the Solomon Islands, where he sets up a PR agency for "dictators, warlords, corrupt corporations and criminal cartels from around the world" with his partner, Polo, a genetically altered bonobo with a secret identity. And that's the short version.

* * *

Tetherballs is supposed to be more of a novel than your previous books, although it's still pretty unconventional.

In fact I'm the one who said that, on something I wrote for some piece of marketing: a "bona fide novel." That was a bit of exuberance, but I'd call it a novel. It's the first book I've written with a continuous story, and with somewhat stable characters. To me that's a huge leap.

Were you responding to something? _Et Tu, Babe_ was your response to attaining a level of success.

And then the next book, _Tooth Imprints on a Corn Dog_, had a number of pieces about being a father. There were reviews of _Tooth Imprints on a Corn Dog_ that said, "Well, here we have Mark Leyner getting older. He's maturing and writing about his family, and there's more of an emotional range to these pieces in this book." For some reason that really irritated me, so I decided to do a book that was inimical to that. I couldn't think of a creature more diametrically opposed to the good father than a thirteen-year-old boy.

The thirteen-year-old Mark Leyner in this book has written a film review of the movie that's based on the screenplay in the book. The structure gets so complicated.

He keeps this review in his pocket, as a talisman. This kid has never written a screenplay, never written anything except this movie review. The most wonderful thing that he can imagine is sitting in the morning, drinking coffee, and reading a review of the movie he wrote. So he wrote the review instead of having to actually write the screenplay and get a movie made.

But if you think about it, the review, although it appears late in the book, was actually written before the execution. Yet it refers to Mark's scene with the warden, which he couldn't possibly have known was going to happen when he wrote the review. There's a Chinese puzzle quality to this seemingly wild, goofy story. This

book isn't just one damn thing after another. It has an interesting, elaborate construction.

Writing one entertaining bit after another—which is what I do—I think that the danger is that people don't notice other things in the book. The one damn thing after another stuff is hugely funny, and comedy tends to drown out other aspects. Humor is very loud. Which is okay. I mean, I can't dictate to people how they should read the book. But this is the first time that I've done something in which the playfulness of the macrostructure is equal to the playfulness of the microstructure. That's why I like to say it's my first novel, because in a way, that's what a novel is: a book that's as interesting in its overarching structure as it is sentence by sentence, paragraph by paragraph. The experience of reading one damn thing after another is not sufficient to me anymore to give you, as a reader, but people sometimes don't notice the formal intricacies that I do. I don't mean that in a pompous way. I just can't think of a less pompous word.

Did you start out doing one damn thing after another?

I started out thinking I was a poet, and I guess poetry is one damn thing after another. The first thing I wanted to do was concoct prose that was as eventful, image by image, and line by line, as poetry. I thought that would be a great thing. When I was eighteen, I came up with this. It was my mission.

Did you always intend to be funny?

No, I didn't. It's only recently that I have taken, with complete equanimity and pleasure, to the notion of writing comedies. When I started, I wanted to be thought of as tortured and seductive, not funny, but humor tends to be a reflexive part of a person's sensibility. It's an almost impossible thing to teach anyone, which leads me to believe that it's intuitive. I really enjoy entertaining people, and I've become more comfortable with that aspect of it and less apologetic about it.

If someone were to say to me that he wanted to write prose that was as intense, line for line, as poetry, the last thing I would also expect him to want to do is to be entertaining.

Right, but that always seemed to make perfect sense to me, perhaps because I was influenced by what I found entertaining and also very artful and moving. I was a great fan of Jean-Luc Godard. There is a lot of humor in his movies. The entertainment value of something and its integrity as a piece of art never seemed mutually exclusive to me. In fact, it seems important that writers and artists provide entertainment for people. It's just recently that being funny ghettoized someone and exposed an artist to a certain degree of—not derision, but if you are very funny, you are not taken as seriously.

You'll take a topic that people think of as being personal, or private, or serious, and interbreed it with something from pop culture.

Not necessarily pop culture, but interbreed it with the kind of language that we associate with a much more public sphere of our life. I'll take intimate things and talk about them in the ways we would discuss sports or politics or a public figure.

For example, you use a banal brochure to describe something as terrible and violent as the New Jersey State Discretionary Execution sentence. It's in a Q&A format with a really perky voice.

A lot of these things are funny because they're true and disturbing. We're often given horrible news in very cheerfully cold pronouncements, from doctors or nurses. You know—you go into the doctor, then you're suddenly diagnosed, and the next thing you know, you've been handed this brochure about how to deal with your pathetic remaining five years with some horrible illness. And of course the Q&A brochure has to be upbeat. It's probably been written and printed by a drug company whose drug you will be taking for the next few years.

I used to write those Q&A brochures when I wrote advertising copy for medical advertising agencies. I was intrigued by the form because it's ostensibly a dialogue between two people. That's why one of my favorite parts of that Q&A brochure in the book is where one of the questions says, "This is a change of subject," and asks a question about baseball, and the brochure has this long tangent in it, making fun of the premise that this is a real dialogue.

I recently had to get some tests, one of these imaging things, and I went to a place in Manhattan. And after you had whatever your various image was—MRI or CAT scan, they did all kinds of things there—the patients were told to go wait in this long row of dressing rooms, with tiny little stalls and to keep your smock on. The doctor would come out and tell you what the result was. There were maybe twenty of these stalls. If you looked out, you could see all the little white, knobby knees of all the old people, some of them with terrible things wrong with them. Absolutely no privacy. So a doctor would come out and talk to someone, in earshot of anyone sitting there. Sometimes they'd say, "Well, we found a huge mass somewhere," or sometimes they'd say, "I can't see anything." But sometimes terrible, dooming news to people, in the most cold, impersonal environment I can imagine. People frequently get profoundly bad, life-altering news in these ludicrous forms.

That brings a kind of savageness to your humor.

I don't walk around chuckling all the time. My outlook is very bleak. It's worse than bleak; it's apocalyptic. I always expect to be killed, honestly. I expect horrible things to happen to people I care about. I am always readying myself for various kinds of loss. So this comedy of mine comes out of that.

The narrative in this book is like a radio. Sometimes it's tuned to the brochure station. Sometimes it's tuned to the movie review station—which is a voice you get down perfectly.

That idiom is so much a part of our consciousness. I mean, how many movie reviews do people read in newspapers? I read almost all of them, which is a lot, if you add them up. So that came easily to me, that idiom, where you give the name of an actress and there's a little aside about her last movie: "rebounding from her tepid role as…Little Orphan Annie" and so on.

It was so much fun to read, and so equal opportunity in its satire. At one point the warden and Mark are talking about stereos, and it's like those horrible conversations between your college boy-friend and his roommate where they just go on and on about their stupid equipment, and you expect to die of boredom. Then immediately Mark starts describing his room in a style that seems lifted from the *New York Times Magazine*'s special Home issue.

This thirteen-year-old boy is asked to describe his room, and he goes off into the language of interior design: "A white room *must* be anchored by something dark, or it just floats away." The stereo thing deteriorates into a discussion of the towel he uses but in this very technical language. I was on the plane today, and these two businessmen were talking the same way, about guns and gunpowder with all the numbers and the jargon—"That's nice gunpowder." "It's a 58."

Like the birds in the wild, showing each other their feathers.

It's like flashing whatever glands male animals flash at one another, but there are so many different ways to do it. It intrigues me, the way that we select different kinds of language to communicate with people who we don't know. You look at someone and size them up a little and pick one. Maybe this is a guy I can talk sports to, or something else.

It is useful in a way, a lingua franca.

Because of the nature of the culture we live in there isn't one lingua franca. There's a balkanization. When people begin to talk to each other, they immediately, desperately, try to find one of these languages. Which may be another comment the book is making, that we are so inculcated with these ways of speaking that we tend to speak that way without realizing it. We're being spoken and not really speaking, you know what I mean?

It's like a concept from poststructuralist literary criticism.

Thank you. Don't ever say that to me again.

It *is* like something they would say, though. They would say, "We are spoken by the language, rather than speaking it."

Yes, and I'm not a professor, and I said that. Well, all right, that's the second pompous thing I've said this afternoon—but I'm tired.

I'm wondering if you've had strange encounters as a result of these fictional personas you've invented for yourself.

People really want to believe that there is no fiction. I think they find it much easier to imagine that novelists are writing memoirs, writing about their lives, because it's difficult to conceive that there's a great imaginary life in which you can participate. That's more difficult for people to cope with than that I might be this megalomaniacal monster. People want that. Yeah, they want that. And you could see it after *Et Tu, Babe*. They'd meet me and be crestfallen, and say, "You're smaller than I thought." And then they'd say, "You're nicer," with this real sense that I'd let them down.

Or eventually they'll talk to me about drugs: "You must take a lot of drugs to write the way you do." The assumption that you are somehow an embodiment, a parallel, of your fiction, or that you take lots of drugs in order to write it—is a little disheartening to me. I think people have little faith in the imagination.

Why do you think they might be afraid of that?

Because that's the difficulty; that's the labor. That's what separates me from them. I can do this. I mean, I hope that's what separates me from them. When someone finishes one of my books, I don't want the reader to say, "I could've done that—how great! And this guy's just like me, we're brethren." I want a reader to say, "My God, I could never have done that. It's amazing. It's something I never could have done in my life and never will be able to do." That's the response I want. But I think that's what's being resisted. To conceive of a piece of art as something that is a labor of a unique imagination is not as pleasant as the idea of someone simply transcribing their own life, or taking drugs and writing crazy stuff.

"If I had time…"

Yeah, like "If I had a lot of time like he did and a lot of drugs, I could…" I don't mean to sound self-serving, but I think it's true.

One of the really irritating things about being a writer is that everybody thinks that they can do it, too.

Listen, I can tell from about twenty yards away when someone has a manuscript for me. I can just tell—they have that look. And everyone eventually does, ultimately. It's this misconception that it's enough if you've had interesting things happen to you. Most of us have about the same mix of banality and intrigue in our lives, and it's meaningless. The challenge of writing something has little to do with subject matter, certainly very little to do with one's own experiences. But there's this notion that if you just transcribe all the wacky things that have happened to you, the funny things your wacky uncle said, you'll have something very entertaining. Or if we're talking about the traumatic things, you can make a very moving piece of art. You can't necessarily do either. It's a whole different operation.

Yet another source of humor in your work is just that kind of outlandish but very common fantasy of being successful at everything. I'm assuming that *Tetherballs* features some of the fantasies you had as a thirteen-year-old boy.

Certainly. I think it's a very honest book, based on things that I dread or desire. For instance, the part about other writers, where I make the stunning claim that they've written nothing. That I, as a thirteen-year-old with a chimpanzee...

No, no — a bonobo!

Yes, it is very different, as I know. I did *extensive* research on this. I went to Africa. I research these books like you wouldn't *believe*.

In the novel, you as a thirteen-year-old, with your partner, a genetically altered bonobo, write quite a few novels during your spare time. You use pseudonyms made from anagrams of the names of famous Bougainvillean...

...tetherball players. Although I used minor-league tetherball players, because some of the big ones were so famous. I didn't want people to figure it out, and certainly in Bougainville, it would be easy to figure it out. We didn't want to anagrammatize Off-Ramp Tivana Poo Poo, for example.

You came up with such names as Donna Tartt, Douglas Coupland, Elizabeth Wurtzel, and Martin Amis. Then when you come back to the States, you discover that impostors have claimed to be these mythical "hot" young novelists when actually, you wrote *all* those books. What inspired this particular joke?

From my difficulty in seeing any writer, other than myself, get any attention. Ever. I think every single writer, if they were honest, would admit this. When someone wins an award, or someone has a wonderful review in the *New York Times,* or someone has a big movie made, it's hard. I have to say that I admire myself for one thing in connection to this: I've always been playfully honest about it. In one of my books, I set up a writing workshop, and if anyone shows any promise, they are either beaten or eliminated, so they aren't in the competition. It's a playful way of dealing with my anxiety about being eclipsed at some point by a new batch of younger writers and no longer being the enfant terrible. You know, if you ask some very hip person who they read, I want to be the person on their tongue, and I know that is not always the case. Nor should it be.

One of those writers, the ones whose work you "claim" as your own, has written about your work. Have you read David Foster Wallace's essay about...

I haven't read the essay. I've certainly heard about it. Almost everywhere I go, people ask me about it. Sometimes people have it with them and they read it to me. It's hard to comment on it. I should just go read it; then I can have an answer to the question. I don't really take umbrage at any of it. I've said to David, "That's fine if you say these things." He referred to me as the Antichrist in the *New York Times Magazine,* and I think that after having been called the Antichrist, everything else seems sort of mild.

It's not that different from being a terrible god.

I put these books out with the expectation that people will have all sorts of opinions about them. I hope that they are mostly very, very enjoyable for people in a unique way. I hope they strike people as unlike anything else. Some of what David said, that my books merely ratify popular culture instead of offering a moral critique, I disagree with. But I'm not that interested in getting into an ongoing colloquy with any other writer about what I do. My participation is the next book. We'll see what David thinks of this book. His name was particularly difficult to turn into a Bougainvillean anagram, so I hope he is aware of how much I labored.

I thought perhaps you should have left him out, but on consideration it seemed sporting of you to include him with everybody else, not to single him out even by exclusion.

I thought about all of these things. I really think twenty-four hours a day about these books as I write them. I try to consider every possible ramification, certainly with the David issue. He should be in there, not more saliently than anyone else but certainly not eliminated from the bunch. I think I did precisely the right thing.

Laura Miller is a books and culture columnist at *Slate*. In 1995, she cofounded Salon.com and worked there as an editor and staff writer for twenty years. Her work has appeared in *The New Yorker, Harper's Magazine, The Guardian,* the *Los Angeles Times,* the *Wall Street Journal,* and many other publications, including the *New York Times Book Review,* where she wrote the Last Word column for two years. She is the editor of *The Salon.com Reader's Guide to Contemporary Authors* (Penguin, 2000). She lives in New York.

EXCERPTS FROM
THE TETHERBALLS OF BOUGAINVILLE

PREFACE

WHEN AN ASTRONOMER observes a galaxy in some distant realm of the universe, what he is actually seeing is light that has traveled incomprehensibly vast distances over vast periods of time before arriving at the lens of his telescope. In the present, this galaxy may no longer even exist. He is quite literally looking at the past.

Theoretically, if we could travel to a point many light-years from the earth and somehow view the light emanating from our planet with the resolution of, say, a spy satellite—advanced photoreconnaissance spacecraft are capable of reading the washing instructions on a black silk chemisette from 22,300 miles in geosynchronous orbit—we could actually observe ourselves in the past.

But until we can outrace light, until we can set up our hyper-resolution telescope on some planetoid 15, 20, 30 light-years from the earth and—by dint of its optical wizardry—watch our youth unfold, we must make do with our memories, our diaries and notebooks, our videotapes, microcassettes, floppy disks, our photo albums, our evocative souvenirs and bric-a-brac—all the various and sundry madeleines we use to goad our hippocampi into reverse-scan.

With only the crude armamentarium of the memoirist at our disposal, it is impossible to portray the past with anything approaching clinical accuracy. Cognitive neuroscientists frequently use the image of hooded convict-drones pumping pink fiberglass insulation into the attic of a sumptuous mansion whose mistress sprawls below caressing the soft down of her belly with a riding crop to describe the way we fill the lacunae in our memories with a meringue of utter fabrication. And we invariably litter the mise-en-scène of our past with the cultural props of our present—Mommy staggers to the table at a Pee Wee Football Awards dinner anachronistically accoutered in an Azzedine Alaïa mummy dress, Great-grandpa, five days out of a shtetl in Poland, washes down Pringles with a 40-ounce bottle of St. Ides malt liquor as he waits in line for an eye exam at Ellis Island.

Wary of these pitfalls, I have tried my best—in the following capsules—to provide an accurate chronicle of my past. And I have tried to confront unflinchingly what were once dirty little secrets buried in the databases of government statisticians, but are now acknowledged as the Three Fundamental Sociological Axioms, the demographic triple pillar upon which our culture stands:

- By the time most Americans have reached the age of 35, they have either killed someone or been accessory to a murder.
- Virtually every American adult habitually engages in some form of sexual depravity that results in the ritualistic sacrifice or mutilation of, or transmission of flesh-necrotizing bacteria to, his or her partner.
- The overwhelming majority of American physicians, surgeons, ICU nurses, air traffic controllers, airline pilots, and school-bus drivers spend their working days in an alcoholic haze, narcotic stupor, or hallucinogen-addled dreamworld.

As you read on, some of you may experience an eerie shock of recognition. You may bolt upright in bed, murmuring to yourself, "I think I actually *know* this guy." Some of you may even say, "Hey, I think I *dated* this guy." (For female readers who lived in the Dallas–Fort Worth metropolitan area in the mid-eighties — if the droll conversational icebreaker "I'd like to get you real high and eat your pussy for an afternoon" sounds familiar — yes, that was me.)

On the other hand, you may feel as if you're reading your *own* diary. If you feel dirty and ashamed and yet flushed with arousal as if you've been caught in an act of auto-voyeurism, peeping through the bedroom window of your own doppelgänger, or as if you're intoxicating yourself on your own body's fumes and detritus, huffing your own halitosis or snorting a line of your own dandruff from the page, because each page is like a mirror, and you've literally never seen yourself so closely and the pores of your nose have never seemed so gaping, like rabbit holes, and suddenly there's that terror of actually falling down one of them, that terror of interminable free-fall... Well, OK, that's cool, that was my intention. In a sense, I've tried to write *your* autobiography. Or perhaps induce you to write mine...

Because what I really want is for you to actually inhabit my body, to get into my musculature and fascia, my limbs and trunk and head, to envelop your brain with my brain. I want you to wear my parka of viscera, to string yourself with my organs like a suicide bomber festooned with explosives. I want you to know what it feels like to walk through a Foodtown encumbered by the twitching heft of my 140 pounds and then to try to read a USDA nutrition label on a can of kipper snacks as your mind thrashes against the vortical undertow of my ghastly memories.

I want you to experience what it's like to be four years old and summoned to the school neurologist's office and told that because of hypertrophic dendrite growth in your brain, your head can no longer be supported by your neck — to be told that it's like trying to support a bowling ball on a single strand of uncooked angel hair pasta—and to have to wear a specially built cervical flying but-tress—a doughnut-shaped base worn around the waist, from which four thick metal flanges rise up to pinion the front, sides, and back of the head. I want you to experience the instantaneousness with which the uproarious din of a Chuck E. Cheese is stilled when you walk in sporting that device. I want you to feel what it's like to be ten and, while the other kids are frolicking at summer camps in the Berkshires, you're immured in the recesses of a mildewed hovel, sub-sisting on cigarettes and black coffee and spending twenty hours a day shooting a perverse misanthropic video version of *Pippi Long-stocking* using tiny intricate marionettes made of cockroach car-apaces, chicken bones, rat vertebrae pried from traps, discarded condoms, foil ketchup packets—whatever you can scavenge from the garbage-strewn halls. I want you to feel what it's like to be in postproduction, your editing equipment darkened by the shadow of your huge head. And I want you to feel what it's like to be suddenly remanded into the custody of a so-called aunt—a bushy-haired, pockmarked woman with a lush mustache and tall rounded karakul hat who fills your head with paranoid conspiracies and crackpot the-ories, including the notion that Jack Ruby didn't intentionally kill Lee Harvey Oswald, that his death was accidental and occurred as the two had rough sex.

In order to wear this garment of a body, you'll need to take the bones out. Bones function essentially as hangers and shoe trees. So filet first, then get in.

Once you're in, I'm out.

My soul is released.

But don't worry. It's cool. This was my intention. It's why I wrote this book.

You see, the soul can outrace light. (They've clocked souls leav-ing bodies at somewhere around 190,000 miles per second.) So while you're trudging around in my body, my soul will be on that distant planetoid, sitting on a couch in front of the telescope's monitor, drinking a beer, eating a mortadella, prosciutto, and provolone hero—watching the reruns of my past. Laughing, crying, belching.

Some night, when you're all alone and feeling particularly alienated and forsaken, close your eyes and cup your hands to your ears. You'll hear a kind of muffled roar. That's the cumulative sound of 30 billion souls—one from each human body that's ever walked the earth; each now alone on its own individual tiny desolate planet, furnished with couch, telescope, minibar, and self-replenishing hoagie—laughing, crying, and belching as they watch their lives loop endlessly in universal syndication.

PART ONE:
THE VIVISECTION OF MIGHTY MOUSE

MY FATHER IS strapped to a gurney, about to die by lethal injection, when the phone rings. Everyone—warden, lawyers, rabbi, Dad—looks at the red wall phone. That's the one that rings when the governor calls to pardon a condemned convict. But when it rings a second time, they realize that it's not the old-fashioned tintinnabulation of a wall phone, but the high-pitched electronic chirp of a cellular. I reach into my jacket pocket and answer: "Hello? [It's my agent.] What's up?" Everyone's giving me this indignant glare like, "Hey, we got an execution here," which I deflect with the international sign for "Bear with me, please"—the upraised frontal palm (gesturally closer to the Hollywood Indian's gesticulated salutation than to the traffic cop's "Stop," which is more peremptory and thrust farther from the body). I'm nodding: "Uh-huh, uh-huh, uh-huh... That's great! OK, I'll talk to you later." I slip the phone back inside my jacket.

"Good news?" my father asks.

"Yeah, kind of," I reply. "It looks like I'm going to win the Vincent and Lenore DiGiacomo / Oshimitsu Polymers America Award."

"What's that?" the doctor says, retaping the cannula in my father's arm and sliding the IV drip stand closer to the gurney.

"It's a very prestigious, very generous award given every year for the best screenplay written by a student at Maplewood Junior High School—it's $250,000 a year for the rest of your life."

"Jesus fucking Christ!" Dad exclaims.

"Mazel tov," says the rabbi.

"Whoa…hold on, folks," I say. "There's one big problem here—there's no screenplay. I haven't written word one. I don't even have a title yet."

The warden—an absolutely stunning woman in a décolleté evening gown—eyes me dubiously. "How'd you win the award if there's no screenplay?"

"That's the advantage of having a powerful agent," I say.

Everyone nods in agreement.

"Trouble is—I gotta get this movie written soon….Shit, I could really use a title. I can't write without a title, y'know, I gotta be able to say to myself, I'm working on *Such and Such*."

"How does *Like Lemon-Lime Sports Drink for Carob Protein Bar* strike you?" the executioner asks.

"I thought of that myself," I say, "but it's a little too close to *Like Water for Chocolate*."

"Mark, what about *Double Life: The Shattering Affair Between Chief Judge Sol Wachtler and Socialite Joy Silverman*?" the warden suggests.

"Too long."

Dad pipes up. "I've got the title," he says decisively.

"What?"

"*Eventually, Even Mighty Mouse Is Vivisected by the Dour Bitch in a White Lab Coat*."

There's a long silence.

"I love it," the rabbi finally says. "It's haunting. It's archetypal. It speaks to the collective unconscious. Every culture has, if not a full-fledged myth, than a mythological motif involving the man/rodent—strong, honest, resolute in his convictions, striving diligently to excel in life—who, in the end, is confronted by the merciless, omnipotent giantess—a sort of postpartum, premenstrual proto-Streisand—with opulently manicured and fiendishly honed fingernails, who plucks him up and slices him open from his Adam's apple to his pubic bone. *Eventually, Even Mighty Mouse Is Vivisected by the Dour Bitch in a White Lab Coat*," he reprises, gesturing as if at a marquee.

"C'mon, that's much too long," I say.

"Bullshit," rebuts my father. "The length is irrelevant. Moviegoers condense titles regardless. They called *One Flew Over the Cuckoo's Nest 'Cuckoo's Nest.' Willy Wonka and the Chocolate Factory* became *'Willy Wonka.' Steroids Made My Friend Jorge Kill His Speech Therapist: An ABC Afterschool Special* was simply *'Steroids.'* So they'll call this *'Vivisected'* or *'Dour Bitch.'* But you want succinct? How about *No Exit Wound.* Sort of Jean-Paul Sartre meets Jean-Claude Van Damme. Or you want a real contemporary, John Singleton sort of feel? What about something like *Yo! You're My Dope Dealer Not My Thesis Adviser. If I Wanted Your Opinion About My Dissertation, I'd Have Asked for It, Motherfucker!*"

I'm starting to get a little impatient. I glance at my watch, a Tag Heuer chronograph. "Listen, I gotta get over to the library and try to come up with some ideas. Can we, uh…" I make the international sign for lethal injection: thumb, index, and middle fingers mime squeezing hypodermic and then head lolls to the side with tongue sticking out of mouth.

The executioner and operations officer check and recheck the IV line and make a final inspection of the delivery module, which is mounted on the wall and holds the three lethal doses in syringes, each of which is fitted beneath a weighted piston.

Everyone's being especially punctilious here because of an accident that occurred recently at an execution over in Missouri, where leaks in the octagonal gas chamber's supposedly airtight seals allowed cyanide gas to seep into the witness room, killing ten people, including members of the condemned criminal's victims' families. Only writer William T. Vollmann, who was covering the execution for *Spin* magazine, walked away unscathed.

Dad beckons me to come closer. "Here, son, I want you to have this," he says, handing me his ring, a flawless oval Burmese sapphire flanked by heart-shaped diamonds.

Something about the way he contorts his body against the leather restraints in order to remove the ring reminds me of my first memory of my parents naked. I must have been three or four—they'd just gotten out of the shower and were toweling each other off. My father's entire body was emblazoned with tattoos of Frank Lloyd Wright buildings.

"What's that, Daddy?" I remember asking.

"That's the Kaufmann house at Bear Run, Pennsylvania, that's Taliesin West in Phoenix, that's the Johnson Wax building in Racine, Wisconsin, and that's the Guggenheim," he explained, pointing, his head twisted backward over his shoulder.

"Why'd you get those?" I asked.

"I was drunk, I guess…" he shrugged.

My mom's buttocks were tattooed with an illustration of an 1,800-pound horned Red Brindle bull crashing through the front window of a Starbucks coffee bar and charging a guy who's sitting there sipping a cappuccino and reading M. Scott Peck's *The Road Less Traveled*. The caption reads: "Life's a Bitch and Then You're Gored to Death."

Lately I've been trying to fix Mom up with the lawyer Alan Dershowitz, who helped prepare an amicus-curiae brief in support of my father's last appeal. Mom spends most of her time these days dressed in black, fingering her rosary beads, sighing, daubing away tears with a black, lace-trimmed handkerchief, and doing Goldschläger shots—so I thought it might be a good idea for her to start getting out more. My dad's family is really pissed at me because they think Mom shouldn't start dating until after the execution, and they're also mad because I sold some nude photos of Dad to this bondage magazine and they claim to have a right to some of the proceeds, and my position is basically: I tied him up, I took the photographs, they're my property, profits from their sale belong to me, end of discussion.

It's time. The superintendent reads the death warrant.

Everyone turns to the wall phone, giving it one last opportunity to ring.

"If you think the governor's gonna call with a stay of execution, you're nuts," I say. "She's probably not even awake yet. It's only noon."

(They'd lowered the voting age to 15 in order to bring the highest-spending demographic sector into the electorate. This resulted in the election of a 17-year-old as governor. It's been a real joke. At her inauguration, the chief justice had to make her remove her Walkman and spit out a huge multicolored bolus of Skittles so she could hear and repeat the oath of office. And you know how barristers and judges in England wear those white powdered perukes? Our new governor signed an order requiring the lawyers and judges in New Jersey to wear these big-hair wigs—y'know like mall hair. You should have seen my father's trial—I'm telling you, it was a joke.)

My father is not an evil person. He just can't do PCP socially. At the risk of oversimplification, I think that's always been his basic problem. Some people are capable of being social phencyclidine users and some people are not, and my father unfortunately falls into the latter category. Normally Dad's a very sweet, patient, benevolent guy, but when he's dusted, he's a completely different person—belligerent, volatile, *extremely* violent.

I remember once he was helping me with some homework—I

was in the third grade, writing a report comparing the ritualistic sacrifice of prisoners of war during the Aztec festival Tlacaxipeual-iztli (the Feast of the Flaying of Men) with recent fraternity hazing deaths at the Fashion Institute of Technology—and Dad was being just extraordinarily helpful in terms of conceptualizing the theme of the report and then with the research and editing (he was a fastidi-ous grammarian), and at some point the doorbell rang and Dad went downstairs. Apparently it was some of his "dust buddies," because he disappeared for about a half hour and when he returned to my room, he was transformed. Sweating, drooling, constricted pupils, slurred speech—the whole profile.

We started working again, and all of a sudden Dad grabbed the mouse and highlighted a line on the computer screen, and he said, "That's a nonrestrictive modifier. It needs to be set off by commas."

I probably said something to the effect of, "It's not a big deal, Dad, let's just leave it."

At which point he went completely berserk. "It's a nonrestrictive adjectival phrase. It's not essential to the meaning of the sentence's main clause. It should be set off by commas. It *is* a big deal!"

And he grabbed a souvenir scrimshaw engraving tool, which I'd gotten at the New Bedford Whaling Museum gift shop several summers ago, and he plunged it into his left thigh, I'd say at least two to three inches deep.

"All right, I'll put the commas in," I said.

Dad evinced absolutely no sensation of pain, impervious as he was, thanks to the PCP. If anything, impaling his thigh with the scrimshaw graver seemed to mollify him. He certainly made no attempt nor manifested the slightest desire to remove it, and later, while we were trying to come up with a more colloquial way of say-ing "bound to the wheel of endless propitiation of an unloving and blood-hungry divinity," Dad absently twanged the embedded tool as he mused.

Another fascinating and potentially mitigating factor emerged during my father's trial for killing a security guard who'd apprehended him shoplifting a Cuisinart variable-speed hand blender and a Teflon-coated ice-cream scooper from a vendor's kiosk at an outlet in Secaucus. (The imposition of the death sentence in New Jersey requires "first-degree murder with heinous circumstances." In this case, it was determined that the weapons used in the commission of the homicide were the purloined implements themselves — the hand blender and the ice-cream scooper. The lower torso of the security guard, who'd pursued my father down into a subterranean parking garage, had been almost totally puréed, the upper torso rendered into almost a hundred neat balls.) Unbeknownst to me, Dad had an extremely rare hypersensitivity to minute levels of gamma radiation. An eminent astrohygienist from Bergen County Community College testified that once a day there's a 90-minute gamma-ray burst originating from colliding comets within the Milky Way. She was able to link each of my father's most violent episodes (including the grisly murder of the security guard) to a corresponding gamma-ray burst. My father's intolerance was so acute, she contended, that exposure to as little as 15 picorads of gamma radiation resulted in extreme neurological disturbances.

Unfortunately, the jury in its verdict and the judge in his sentence proved unsympathetic to this theory. In retrospect, I think that the spectacle of my father's attorneys in their big-hair mall wigs leading witnesses through hours of arcane testimony about Gamma-Ray Sensitivity Syndrome tended to damage his cause.

My father has always been a good provider. And in terms of a work ethic, he's been a wonderful role model. He taught me that every morning — no matter how you feel physically and no matter what mood you're in — you have to get yourself out of bed, shower, shave, put on a dark suit, hood your face in a black ski mask, and go out into the world and make some money.

Back when I was in the fifth grade, Dad had just come off one of his best years — he'd been swindling insurance companies by faking auto accidents and claiming nonexistent "soft-tissue" injuries, and also traveling around the country, using a high-voltage taser stun gun to rob Publishers Clearing House Sweepstakes winners—and we all moved to St.-Leonard-de-Noblat in the Limousin region of France. This was supposed to be a very chic place. In the late nineteenth century they'd flooded 50 acres of pasture to create a beautiful lake with three islands. So when Mom and Dad gave me some brochures and I read about the man-made lake, I thought whoa! excellent! swimming, water-skiing, fishing. But the neighborhood had really gone downhill lately. Several large ancien-régime families, all suffering from lead poisoning, had moved in recently. There were two contending explanations for their condition: one, that they'd been eating foie gras from pottery finished with lead glaze (goose liver soaks up lead like the proverbial sponge), and two (this is the one that I believed), that they suffered from congenital pica and had been nibbling away for generations at the peeling lead-based paint and plaster from their dilapidated chateaus. Whatever the cause, they exhibited all the classic symptoms: reduced IQ, impaired hearing, and trouble maintaining motor control and balance. But, worst of all, these lead-poisoned erstwhile aristocrats had developed the unfortunate custom of washing livestock, defecating, and dumping corpses in the lake. By the time we moved back to the States, the coliform bacteria count in the lake was nearly 700 times the permissible limit. (And bear in mind that the French, being far less squeamish than Americans, have much higher acceptable coliform bacteria levels than we do.)

I think that we tend to select certain emblematic images to store in our memories as visual icons representing each of the journeys and sojourns in our lives. And when I remember our year in St.-Leonard-de-Noblat, I think of the topless contessa and her boom box.

Every sunny afternoon I'd go down to the lake and watch the contessa, a voluptuous woman from one of the most severely lead-poisoned families, struggle for 45 minutes to mount her chaise longue and then endeavor spastically for another half hour to remove her bikini top. This finally accomplished, she'd pillow an ear against her huge radio, which was turned up so loud that it literally drowned out the dredging equipment that the sanitation department used to remove bodies from the turbid water.

There I'd loiter, leering, until I'd hear my mother's calls—her voice so shrill that it easily pierced the roar of the dredging equipment *and* the blare of the bare-breasted contessa's ghetto blaster. I'd reluctantly trudge home to find Mom on the veranda, draining her second pitcher of kamikazes.

"Get your steno pad," she'd bark, lighting a cigarette and singeing the ends of a platinum tress that had swung into the flame of her Zippo.

And so each afternoon my mother would dictate yet another revision of her "living will." And although all sorts of frivolous codicils were continuously appended—often to be nullified the following day—the gist of the will remained constant: "In the event that I ever become seriously ill and my ability to communicate is impaired, please honor the following requests. No matter how onerous a financial and emotional burden I become to my family and no matter what extraordinary means are necessary, I want to be kept going. I don't care about mental lucidity, dignity, or quality of life, I don't care how flat my EEG is or for how long, I don't care if I'm just half a lung and a few feet of bowel—I want to be kept alive."

"Do you understand?" she'd snarl.

"Yes, Mom," I'd nod.

I'd file the latest version in a strongbox in her lingerie drawer, and then scamper back to the lake, hoping that I'd hadn't missed the departure of the contessa, a sad and beautiful spectacle. Her lead-suffused flesh luridly burnished in the gloaming, she'd attempt to free herself from her folding chaise, which would have collapsed around her like a Venus' flytrap enclasping some engorged and lustrous bug.

The warden reads the death warrant. The doctor daubs my father's limbs and chest with conductive jelly and attaches five EKG electrodes. He then gives him a pre-injection of 10 cc of antihistamine to minimize spasming.

"Do you have a final statement you wish to make?" the warden asks.

"Yes. I'd like to direct my last words to my son.

"Mark...Mark?"

"Just a sec, Dad," I say, my head bowed, eyes glued to the Game Boy that glows in my hands. "I'm on the brink of achieving a new personal best here."

I'm playing a game called *Gianni Isotope*. It's pretty awesome. The ultimate object is to enable the hero, Gianni Isotope, to save as many rock stars as possible from being turned into edible breaded nuggets at a space-based processing plant in the Lwor Cluster. You earn the opportunity to attempt the Lwor rescue mission by scoring a requisite number of points on the two preceding levels.

First, before beginning play, you have to choose the outfit that Gianni Isotope wears throughout the game. I usually just put him in what I wear to junior high every day—no shirt, Versace leather pants, and Di Fabrizio boots.

In Level One, you manipulate Gianni Isotope as he flies a helicopter into a city whose skyline comprises cylindrical and rectilinear towers of deli meats and cheeses. You/Gianni have to fly upside down and, using the whirring rotor blades of the helicopter, slice these skyscrapers of bologna, salami, ham, liverwurst, American cheese, muenster, etc., as thinly as possible. The object is to slice the city's entire skyline down to ground level. Points are awarded based on speed and portion control. You need 5,000 points to advance.

In Level Two, Gianni Isotope works for a private investigator in Washington, D.C., who's compiling scurrilous information about Supreme Court justices. You/Gianni can pick any of the eight optional sitting justices, or you can play the default setting — Clarence Thomas. If you choose Justice Thomas, for instance, you're given the following five stories:

- Thomas's fascination with breast size is well established. But he is also intrigued by more-arcane aspects of the female anatomy. His standard interview queries — proffered to job applicants when he chaired the Equal Employment Opportunity Commission — were gynecological in their scope and specificity: 1. Objectively describe your urethral meatus. 2. Is your perineum very hairy? 3. How violent are the contractions of your bulbocavernosus and ischiocavernosus muscles when you experience sexual orgasm, and how might that affect your performance at the EEOC?

- Thomas delights in sharing his frisky frat-house humor with fellow Supreme Court Justices. Recently, while the high court was hearing arguments about the constitutionality of a statute regulating interstate commerce, Thomas was seen scribbling a note and passing it to Ruth Bader Ginsburg, who read it, became slightly red in the face, and then shrugged back at a grinning Thomas. Sources with access to several of Ginsburg's clerks contend that the note read: "How big was Felix's frankfurter?" — a reference, of course, to Felix Frankfurter, the distinguished Austrian-born jurist who was appointed to the Supreme Court by Franklin Delano Roosevelt, and who served as an associate justice from 1939 to 1962.

- Thomas's self-titillating fear of pubic hair has been immortalized in his legendary entreaty "Who has put pubic hair on my Coke?" Ever attentive to the requirements of politesse and protocol, Thomas can couch his scatological solecisms in more delicate terms when he deems it appropriate. At a recent Embassy Row cocktail party, Thomas was overheard asking his hostess, the patrician wife of an ambassador, "Who has put a tuft of epithelial cilia on my Chivas?"

- Seated in the first-class section of American Airlines Flight #3916 en route from O'Hare to Dulles, Thomas, thoroughly engrossed in Willa Cather's *My Antonia*, suddenly looks up and exclaims, "Antonia's gotta be at least a 34C"—speculating upon the bra size of the novel's plucky protagonist.

- As a college undergraduate, Thomas submitted a final term paper for his American Literature of the Nineteenth Century class which was titled, "Hester Prynne, Spitter or Swallower?"

You/Gianni Isotope have to track down leads, interview witnesses, and unearth documents that will corroborate these anecdotes before rival investigators from the tabloids and liberal media elite do it first.

Then an indignant Justice Thomas, black judicial robes billowing in his wake, pursues Gianni Isotope through an aquatic labyrinth on jet skis.

During the labyrinth chase, Thomas's and Gianni's energy supply can become low. To replenish, Gianni can buy Citicorp stock from surfing Saudi princes in matching madras trunks and kaffiyehs. Justice Thomas can refuel by snaring Big Gulp Cokes from vending machines on buoys. If either character's energy supply becomes too depleted, he is engulfed in a large cloud of greenish incandescent gas and can only jet-ski very, very slowly.

If you/Gianni Isotope are able to scoop the Fourth Estate with Supreme Court scandal, elude the avenging Justice through the aquatic labyrinth, and then, finally, negotiate with a creature with the upper torso of a Dallas Cowboy cheerleader and the lower torso of a coatimundi without being shredded by its claws, you advance to the ultimate level.

Welcome to the Lwor Cluster in the Goran H47 Helix.

Rock musician is the protein of choice for the typical Lwor creature. Certain parts of the musicians are considered delicacies. Their burst eardrums are eaten by Lwors like popcorn while they watch movies. Their alcohol-ravaged cirrhotic livers are especially delectable to the Lwor palate and are mashed into a paste and served on flat bread and Wheat Thins.

At a processing plant, the live musicians are emptied onto a conveyor belt that leads to a darkened room, where Lwor workers hang them upside down from U-shaped shackles on an assembly line. The rock stars are stunned with an electric shock, their throats slit by machine, and they move through boiling water to loosen their scalps and tight pants. Machines massage off the hair and trousers, eviscerate and wash the musicians inside and out, and slice them into pieces. Seventy rock stars a minute move down the line. Nothing is wasted. Studded jewelry, latex underwear, blood, internal organs, even the decocted tattoo ink is collected and sent to a Lwor rendering plant to become ingredients in cattle feed and pet food for export to other planets. Processed rock musician is Lwor's most lucrative commodity. They debone it, marinate it, cut it into pieces, press it into patties, roll it into nuggets, bread it, batter it, cook it, and freeze it.

You/Gianni Isotope attempt to save the likes of Dave Mustaine of Megadeth; AC/DC guitarist Angus Young; Def Leppard drummer Rick Allen; Tom Araya, the bassist from Slayer; Joe Perry of Aerosmith; Eddie Van Halen; Terence Trent D'Arby; Jon Bon Jovi; and, inexplicably, Val Kilmer. (The updated version, *Gianni Isotope II: The Final Dimension*, includes Pantera, Rivers Cuomo of Weezer, and David Roback of Mazzy Star.)

For each rock star you rescue from the processing plant, you're awarded 1,000 points.

The highest score I'd ever gotten was 30,000. I'm about to pluck Metallica frontman James Hetfield from the deboning machine—which would give me a record-shattering 40,000 points—when my father breaks my concentration. Hetfield's filleted and flipped into the fry-cooker and time runs out. Game over.

"Fuck!" I mutter, flicking off the Game Boy.

I take a deep breath.

"What is it, Dad?"

"Did you bring your camera?"

"Yeah, but they won't let me take any pictures in here."

"That's too bad. I thought you could get a shot of me dead on the gurney and sell it to Benetton and maybe they'd use it in an ad."

There's a pause.

"Are those your last words?" the warden asks.

"No, that was just an aside."

"OK. We don't want to start administering the drugs if you're not finished. Unfortunately, that's happened before."

"You've killed people in the middle of their last words?"

"Well, if a person pauses for an extended period of time, we might just assume that he's finished, and execute him. We had a guy recently who ranted for a while and then he sighed and said nothing for about a minute, so we administered the drugs. But then the next day, when we went back and read the transcript and parsed the sentence, we realized that, having finished this long string of subordinate clauses and prepositional phrases and appositives, he'd apparently just paused in anticipation of introducing the main clause. So, as it turns out, unfortunately, we did execute him in mid-sentence. In mid-ellipsis, actually. So if you could give us a general idea of what you're going to say and about how long you think it might take…"

"You mean like an outline?"

"No, just a rough idea of where you're going. And that'll make it much less likely that we kill you *in medias res*."

"Well, I don't know…I was thinking of maybe starting off with some maudlin and desultory reminiscing—that should only take a couple of minutes—and then I thought I'd tell a brief impressionistic anecdote about hair, and then I figured I'd finish off with some sort of spiritual or motivational aphorism for my son. I think we're looking at about four or five minutes, tops."

"Excellent," says the warden.

"It's very nice," says the rabbi.

"All right, let's take it from the top," says the executioner, gamely.

"When your mother was pregnant with you—"

"Hold it," interrupts the executioner. "Are you referring to *my* mother?"

"No, I'm talking to my son."

"Well then don't look at me, look at him. And, Mark, while your father's addressing his last words to you, why don't you hold his hand?"

I make a face.

"What's the problem?" asks the executioner. "Are you two uncomfortable touching each other? Is that an issue?"

"No," we both say, simultaneously defensive.

"Well, then, c'mon. Mark, slide your chair up next to the gurney and hold your dad's hand. Now, Dad, you look at Mark and talk to *him*."

I pull my chair up alongside the gurney next to the IV drip stand and grasp Dad's left hand, which is secured at the wrist with a supplementary nylon-webbed restraint with Velcro fastenings. Dad looks at me and begins again.

"When your mother was pregnant with you—"

"Much better!" the executioner says in a stage whisper.

"—I fell for this bank teller who used to keep her deposit slips in her cleavage. And I'd go down to the bank every day to watch her and it would just drive me fuckin' nuts. Unbeknownst to me at the time, she had this whole incredibly elaborate, idiosyncratic filing system—regular savings account withdrawal and deposit slips in her cleavage, money market deposit slips under her right bra strap, IRA and Keogh deposit slips under the left bra strap, payroll checks went in the front waistband of her panties, mortgage payments back panty waistband, Christmas club deposits gartered at the thighs, etc. All I knew is that I was completely sexually obsessed with this woman. All day, all night, it's all I'm thinking about. So I learn from a friend of a friend of a friend that this bank teller loves steak. And you know those ads in the back of *The New Yorker* for Omaha Steaks? Well, I start having four filet mignons packed in dry ice sent to her house every week accompanied by little romantic poems. Call me old-fashioned—but I still think there's no better way to say 'I want you' to a woman than sending her meat in the mail. So one day some idiot from Omaha Steaks calls and leaves a message on the answering machine about whether I'd like to include eight free 4-ounce burgers in my next delivery and your mother plays the message, finds out about the bank teller, and the next thing you know, I'm getting a call from her psychotherapist forbidding me to send any more meat to this woman because it's jeopardizing your mother's mental health, and I say, 'I'm *forbidden*? What is this, some kind of edict, are you issuing a fatwa?' and he says, 'Call it a fatwa if you wish,' and I say, 'Well, fuck you and fuck your fatwa.' Meanwhile these filet mignons are starting to set me back like sixty, seventy bucks a week. So I start moonlighting at this very exclusive, very posh beauty salon uptown. Very high-profile clientele—Lainie Kazan, Kaye Ballard, Eydie Gormé, Eddie Arnold—y'know, you reach a point where you don't even notice anymore, it's like, 'There's Piper Laurie, pass the rugelach.' Anyway, one day this woman comes in, she's got a 4:45 P.M. appointment, her name is Meredith, and she's missing the top half of her cranium, and her entire brain is exposed. Y'know the line from that Eurythmics song that goes *I'm speaking de profundis. / This ain't no joke. / A medium-boiled egg with the upper portion of its shell and albumen removed reveals a glaucous convexity of coagulated yolk. / Oh yeah...It hurts...Oooo, c'mon...A glaucous convexity of coagulated yolk!* Well, that's the image. It's as if someone had taken this woman's cranium and meticulously—"

"That's Duran Duran," the operations officer interjects.

"What?" says Dad, turning to the voice that comes from behind a one-way mirror separating the control module room from the execution chamber.

"I'm pretty sure that line's from a Duran Duran song, because I remember that in the video, the guy who sucks out the yolk is Simon Le Bon."

My father furrows his brow for a moment and then nods.

"You're right," he says, "you're absolutely right. Simon Le Bon sucks out the yolk, starts choking, and then Nick Rhodes Heimlich-maneuvers Le Bon, who expels the yolk which arcs through the air and settles in a corner of the sky where it begins to throb and radiate, and the video which had heretofore been sepia-toned takes on this incredibly garish, heavily impastoed van Gogh-at-Arles coloration as they sing the refrain, *Spit the sun into the sky / I'm so hard, I think I'll die!* over and over again. It's Duran Duran. You're absolutely right."

He turns back toward me.

"Anyway...it's as if someone had meticulously sawed around the circumference of this woman's cranium at about eyebrow-and-ear level and just lifted the top right off. But the *really* amazing thing is that she has a full head of long brown hair growing directly out of her brain. So apparently her condition was not the result of a freak workplace accident or a sadistic experiment—which is what I'd initially assumed—but the result of a congenital defect. She was either born without enclosing cranial bones or had suffered some sort of massive fontanel drift. And, remarkably, her hair follicles are distributed in a perfectly normal pattern directly on the pia mater of her cerebral cortex. The other beauticians are too squeamish to work on her and, in fact, fled to the pedicure and waxing rooms the minute she walked through the door, so I volunteer. As soon as she's in the chair, it's obvious to me that she's feeling a bit uncomfortable, so the first thing I say is, 'Meredith, take your eyeglasses off.'

"She's like, 'Excuse me?'

"'Take off your glasses.'

"She doffs the thick-lensed violet frames.

"'Did anyone ever tell you how much you resemble Reba McEntire? It's uncanny.'

"She giggles, blushing. The ice is broken. I intuit immediately that Meredith is a warm, friendly person with a wonderful, understated sexiness. We start talking about what kind of a cut she wants.

"'First of all,' she says, 'I'm sick of always having to brush these bangs off my prefrontal lobes.'

"'The bangs have to go,' I say.

"Meredith explains that she'd like a hairstyle that doesn't look 'done.' She wants to be able to just wash her hair and finger-style it, without needing a brush, because the bristles can apparently nick cerebral arteries and cause slight hemorrhaging and mild dementia. She also wants to be able to let it dry naturally—hair dryers can overheat and sometimes even boil her cerebrospinal fluid. And electric rollers and curling irons are absolutely contraindicated—they tend to induce convulsions.

"I start by trimming off all the extra hair that had been hanging down over Meredith's shoulders and bring the length up to a point where the hair can curve gently against the sides of her neck. I want a fuller, more luxurious look to her hair, and since she's got plenty of it, I control the volume with a graduated cut. Meredith's hair had parted naturally between the cerebral hemispheres, along the superior sagittal sinus. I think a slight asymmetry will create a more sophisticated shape and line, so I sweep her hair over from a side part at the left temporal lobe. This is a very versatile style. It can be tied back for aerobics, worn full and smooth at the office—Meredith is a commercial real estate broker—and then swept up for evening. In other words, there are no limitations to what Meredith can do with this cut, which is exactly right considering her sports activities, her business, her charity benefits—she's co-chairperson of the Rockland County chapter of the American Acrania and Craniectomy Society—and her busy social life. Meredith's hair is a very dark, nondescript brown, so I suggest to her that we lighten it. She enthusiastically agrees. I start by coloring in a soft, cool blond to maximize the impact of the wet, pinkish gray tissue of her brain. Then I add a few extra highlights to play off the deep ridges and fissures that corrugate her cortex.

"Meredith is ecstatic about the makeover, but she has one lingering concern.

"'I won't need barrettes, will I? When I wear them, they put too much pressure here,' she says, indicating the posterior perisylvian sector of her left hemisphere, 'and it disrupts my ability to assemble phonemes into words. That can really be a problem when I'm showing property.'

"'No barrettes, clips, combs, hairpins, headbands—that's the beauty of this style. You wash it, let it dry, run your fingers through it—done. No fuss, no aphasia, no memory loss, no motor impairment. You're ready to rock.'

"'It's just perfect!' she says, turning her head this way and that, as she admires herself in the mirror.

"Before she leaves, we discuss which shampoos and conditioners won't permeate the blood-brain barrier. She gives me a big kiss, a huge tip, and nearly skips out of the shop, at which point the other beauticians filter back to their stations.

"About two weeks later, I receive a note at the salon from

Meredith. It says: 'The office manager was very, *very* impressed—if you know what I mean! Some people took a while to notice how different I looked, but all of them *love* it! You're *THE BEST*!'

"And so, son, the point is—any asshole with a Master of Social Work degree can put on a turban and start issuing fatwas about whom you can and whom you can't mail meat to, but it takes real balls to turn a brunette without a cranium into a blonde."

I've whipped out a pad and pen, and I'm trying to scribble this down as quickly as I can: *Any asshole with a Master of Social Work degree... can put on a turban and start issuing fatwas...about whom you can and whom you can't mail meat to—*

And my pen runs out of ink.

"Fuck!" I squawk. "Excuse me, anybody have a pen or a pencil?"

"Here," says the prison superintendent, reaching into his jacket pocket and handing me a syringe-shaped pen, the bottom half of which is emblazoned with the words *New Jersey State Penitentiary at Princeton—Capital Punishment Administrative Segregation Unit,* its upper half a transparent, calibrated barrel filled with a viscous glittery blue liquid that undulates back and forth as you tilt it.

"Cool pen!" I exclaim.

"Thanks," he says. "I get them from the potassium chloride sales rep. It's one of those 'put your logo here' freebies."

I finish transcribing the maxim: *—but it takes real balls to turn a brunette without a cranium into a blonde.*

And as the superintendent and warden usher me into the witness room, I experience two serendipitous visual thrills.

First, as the warden extends a guiding hand, there's a slight billowing of fabric at the top of her dress that gives me a sudden glimpse of the etiolated curvature of a breast and then (I catch my breath!) a sliver of a crescent whose slight variance in coloration might indicate—I suspect, I hope!—just maybe (gulp!) the very top of an areola!

(Or perhaps not. My seventh-grader brain could be creating an areola where there is none, my adolescent libido "filling in the blanks," investing ambiguous retinal input with its own meaning. I may be processing visual stimuli with the little head instead of the big one. In fact, this could be a perfect example of an idiomatic expression that Ms. Frey, my Spanish teacher, taught us: *Mirando con el bastón en ves de los bastoncillos y los conos.* Seeing with the rod instead of the rods and cones. In other words, this phantom areola might simply be a cathected version of the Kanizsa triangle—a famous optical illusion in which the observer perceives a triangle even though the interconnecting lines forming a triangle are missing—that we just learned about in Mr. Edelman's biology class. Weird...)

And then, moments later, as the warden lowers herself into one of the witness room's orange extruded-plastic chairs: Visual Thrill #2. A taut, faintly stubbly swath (yum!) of pale and dewy armpit flesh!

I desperately need to preempt an erection. First of all, a hard-on here would be terribly inappropriate (just because I'm only in the seventh grade doesn't mean I lack a modicum of decency), and second, it would be impossible to conceal—remember, I'm shirtless and these Versace leather pants are tight and ride really low on the hips. It might also suggest the perverse possibility that I find the imminent execution of my father sexually arousing, which would be a gross misreading. And at the very least, it might imply that I'm callous and self-absorbed. (Totally wrong. I'm empathetic and I'm sensitive, but I belong to a peer group that's temperamentally and philosophically averse to verbalizing real feelings. [For a comprehensive discussion of this psychological paradigm, see Renata Mazur's *Fetuses with Body Hair: The Loathsome World of Pubescent Boys.*] We choose to speak a language that conveys as little information as possible. Like mites signaling each other across great distances with minuscule puffs of pheromone, we identify ourselves to each other with monosyllabic, opaque shibboleths of diffidence—"huh," "cool," "fucked," "weird," etc. This is our special language and we're proud of it—in this way, we're no different from the Basques or the Kurds or any other linguacentric separatist group. But don't think that simply because we're affectless and inarticulate, and harbor a deep distrust of romantic bromides, that we don't have intensely passionate and turbulent inner lives.)

At any rate, obviously this is neither the time nor the place for what Walter Pater called "burning with the hard, gem-like flame" (my English teacher, Mr. Minter, interprets this as a kind of *aesthetic rapture,* but my friends and I believe that Pater was referring to a *hot bone*). So in an effort to quell arousal, I try conjuring unpleasant thoughts. But I can't think of anything at the moment. I guess, on balance, I'm a pretty upbeat, sanguine guy. I'm basically a morning person. And I consider this a bona fide psychological category, because when you wake up in the morning, the first thing that really hits you is that you're not dead, and if you tend to greet that basic fact with any degree of enthusiasm if not outright alacrity, then I think that's a fairly strong indicator of an optimistic disposition. And man, I'm out of the chute each morning with out-and-out zipadeedoodah alacrity! I set the clock-radio alarm to 95.7 FM, which until recently was a classical station and is now all-Pathoco. Pathoco—which was originally called "Texas 12-Step"—is a musical subgenre that originated in some of the country's most parochial, inbred, and anomic white suburbs. It features a bouncy sort of Tijuana Brass sound that completely belies its dark and often disturbing lyrics. For instance, the #1 Pathoco single right now is a song called "The Beasts of Yeast." Against a very festive, up-tempo mariachi background, a man sings of his wife's recent confession that every night she dreams of beating him with a baseball bat, covering his bloodied head with a plastic bag, sitting on his chest, punching his face, and screaming, "Die, David, Die!" and then once he dies, relaxing and smoking crack. In the next verse he sings about his five-year-old daughter, who euthanizes all of her stuffed animals and dolls. The father returns home from work each day to find his daughter's dolls and teddy bears on the floor of her bedroom with plastic bags over their heads secured with thick rubber bands. When he asks her why she's assisted her little friends in committing suicide, she says simply that they were "stressed out." Then in the ensuing verse—in the phlegmatic, acquiescent falsetto of one whose ability to register indignation has corroded from years of living in New Jersey—he reveals that the underlying cause of all his family's problems is severe food allergies. And in the chorus, husband, wife, and daughter, in shimmering three-part harmony, enumerate the offending substances: "Wheat gluten. Lactose. Yeast. Shellfish. Eggs. Tropical oils. Etc." The malevolence of the banal—Legionnaire's disease from a motel hot tub, toxic shock from a tampon, lung cancer from radon, leukemia from the electromagnetic radiation of high-voltage power transmission lines, MSG-induced spontaneous abortions from take-out lo mein—is a central Pathoco motif. But the music's irrepressibly ebullient beat and the shrill, deliriously mirthful horn arrangements rouse me like reveille each morning. Bathroom ablutions consist of ground azuki-bean scrub for the blackheads, followed by a quick yogic deep-gargle (you swallow about a foot of what's called "esophageal floss" and then pull it back out—I learned it from Mr. Vithaldas, he's my Ayurvedic Health teacher, that's my 7th-period elective), and then I descend on the kitchen and, if it's a school-day morning, I have an espresso laced with a shot of calvados and some thinly sliced bichon frisé on a plain bagel, and then I'm out the back door and I'm at the tetherball pole. It's difficult to adequately describe how important the sport of tetherball is to me. Yes, I love playing tetherball more than doing anything else in the world. Yes, I adore the way that the dew flies off the ball when I hammer that first serve each morning and the cord wraps in a tight spiral around the top of the pole and the ball caroms with such force that the cord uncoils with almost equal torque, and I crouch in a low, ballasted stance and let the ball sail over my back and then, my bodyweight cantilevered like a discus thrower's, wield a lethal and quasi-legal cupped palm to sling it in an opposite orbit, and back and forth, in clockwise and then counterclockwise centrifugal arcs that whine as they split the air. Yes, the spiritual sludge of late-second-millennium life literally evaporates in the thermal vectors of my frenzied footwork, my bobbing and weaving, my parries and pirouettes, and it becomes like this atavistic dance, and I feel as if I'm dancing in the center of the sky. And yes, I feel as if everything most precious within myself is awakened and I experience an ineffable kinesthetic beatitude. But the *coolest* thing is that after I've been hitting for a while, there's something about the way my pants smell when they get sweaty—I don't know if it's the kind of leather Versace uses or it's just the way any leather smells when it gets wet—but it makes me completely euphoric, and I enter a highly evolved, massively parallel quantum fugue state during which I achieve tachyphrenic processing speeds of ten trillion floating-point operations per second, and I have cosmological revelations (e.g., instead of subatomic particles being composed of strings—which are tiny vibrating bits of hyperdimensional space—perhaps the *ball-like* leptons and quarks are attached to hyperdimensional *tethers* and they coil and uncoil around *poles,* which are the dimensionless interfaces between matter and antimatter) and then I get this incredible sensation throughout my body as if I've been given an ice-cold mint-jelly enema and bubbles of the frigid jelly are percolating up through my spinal column and bursting exquisitely in the back of my head.

So what I'm trying to say here is that, given the fact that I'm the kind of person who starts each day exulting in the aroma of his own sweaty pants, coming up with an unpleasant memory to preempt an erection is not easy. But finally, after racking my brain for almost a minute, I manage to dredge something up from last Thursday.

Something from television, actually.

What turns a person *off* is as inscrutably subjective as what turns a person *on*. There are four major *turn-offs* in the following synopsis of a story that aired last Thursday night on ABC's *20/20*. See if you can deduce what they are. Put yourself in my Di Fabrizio boots as you read. Give yourself a time constraint—say fifteen seconds—and as you analyze the text for anaphrodisiacal elements, imagine the pressure I'm under as I frantically scan my own memory bank, scrotum tingling, the execution of my father only moments away.

To further enhance the interactive realism of the text, begin to masturbate as you read the following passage. For each *turn-off* you're able to find before coming, award yourself 1,000 points. If your point total equals or exceeds 3,000, proceed to the section beginning *All of this—the warden escorting me into the witness room, the momentary glimpse of the slope of her breast, possibly her areola...*If your total is under 3,000, return to the words *Felipe, his older sister Gretel, and I are watching TV Thursday night,* and begin masturbating again.

> Felipe, his older sister Gretel, and I are watching TV Thursday night. *20/20* is running a profile of Silvio Barnes, the painter who was blinded after being hit on the head with a frying pan while surfing the 35-foot breakers at Waimea Bay in Hawaii and then, less than a week later, suffered a massive stroke during a full-body wax at an after-hours depilation bar in Manhattan. Thanks to the Dove unauthorized biography, we all know the story by now of how, when Silvio was only fourteen, his father—the inventor of the Miracle Collar, the push-up collar for men's dress shirts that gives the appearance of a larger, more protuberant Adam's apple—offered Silvio a yearly stipend and a studio of his own. But Silvio, perceiving his father's patronage as an instrument of control, refused, and catching the next plane and hydrofoil to Chiang Mai, a resort city in northern Thailand, took a job as a busboy at the Gesellschaft für Schwerionenforschung (Society

for Heavy Ion Research), a gay dance club. Snatching a minute here and a minute there during breaks, he'd sneak off to the club's sulfurous boiler room cum atelier, where he'd eventually complete his two astonishing masterpieces:

Teenage Neofascist Skinheads Suffering From Progeria (That Rare Premature Aging Disease) Play Mah-Jongg at a Swim Club in Lake Hayden, Idaho is a 94-by-66-inch, acrylic-on-canvas work that, notwithstanding a title that leads one to expect several freakishly wizened nazi youths wanly shuffling mah-jongg tiles outside a lakefront cabana, actually depicts, in delicate flecks of color, several peonies in a vase.

Anna Nicole Smith Before and After Fire-Ant Attack is a 90-by-120-inch acrylic-on-canvas diptych. In this case, the title does literally describe the painting's content. In the left-hand panel, the former Texas checkout girl turned Guess? jeans model is splayed lasciviously on a dirt road. The right-hand panel features the identical pose except that the lasciviously splayed Smith is stippled with hundreds of Seurat-like inflamed pustules.

Barbara Walters conducts a brief interview with Silvio, whose garbled responses are subtitled. In the closing minutes, wiping drool from his chin, she says, "Silvio, you completed only two paintings in your entire career, both of which you sold for a fraction of their current value [the paintings now hang in opium warlord Khun Sa's splendid new museum in northern Myanmar] and then squandered the money on an endless succession of skanky male prostitutes. As a result of a frying pan and a body wax, you'll never paint again. And your desperate attempt to reinvent your career as a movie director was an unmitigated critical and financial disaster."

Barnes wrote and directed a film entitled *¡Hola Mami!*

about an eccentric middle-aged optometrist who marries a sullen, zit-spangled 16-year-old who loiters around his office every day after school, chain-smoking in a fuchsia PVC bustier, a huge gaudy crucifix bobbing on her bosom. The "plot" revolves around the optometrist's use of a varietal rice chart instead of the traditional lettered eye chart. Long, uninterrupted stretches of the movie consist of the following sort of dialogue:

OPTOMETRIST: Let's start with the top row, moving from left to right.
PATIENT: All right. Arborio. Valencia. Lundberg's Christmas Rice. Black Japonica. And Wehani.
OPTOMETRIST: Perfect. Second row.
PATIENT: Red. Sri Lankan Red. Wild Pecan. Jasmine. White Basmati.
OPTOMETRIST: Perfect. Let's skip down a few rows. How about row five?
PATIENT: American White Basmati. American...Umm... American Brown Basmati, I think. Maratelli. And that next one's either Black Sticky or Thai Sticky. And I'm not sure about the last one.
OPTOMETRIST: OK. How about the next row down, row six?
PATIENT: That's really tough. Converted? Sambal? Gobind Bhog? They're really fuzzy.
OPTOMETRIST: OK. Back up to the fourth row—
PATIENT: Japanese Sticky. Sticky Brown. Short-Grain Brown. Long-Grain White. And Wild Rice.
OPTOMETRIST: Is row six sharper now or...now?
PATIENT: The first way.

Following the clip from *¡Hola Mami!* they cut to Hugh Downs and Barbara Walters back in the studio.

And Walters says with her patented withering aplomb, "Hugh, in all our years together on the show, we've profiled so many wonderful people whose lives have been shattered by tragedy, but I've never before come away with the feeling that—hey, this guy is such an over-weening, self-absorbed asshole, he deserves his misfortune, and, in fact, there's something so divinely *just* about it, that it's actually funny. It's so rare that we can derive some cathartic enjoyment from another person's suffering. But every so often our fervent prayers are answered and an obnoxious enfant terrible's meteoric success is abruptly and irrevocably snuffed. Silvio Barnes—now blind, incapacitated, and anathema in New York *and* Hollywood—is an individual whose precipitous ruin all Americans can celebrate with big, hearty, guilt-free gales of laughter."

And Hugh looks at Barbara and says, "Fascinating."

As they break for a commercial, Felipe, Gretel, and I do an instant postmortem.

"I'm into Barbara's rancid schadenfreude," says Felipe.

"I hear you, dude," I say. "It had wings. But Downs killed it with that perfunctory 'Fascinating.'"

"Hugh's hot!" objects Gretel.

"Yuuuk!" Felipe and I make the international sign for hemorrhagic vomiting.

"You'll appreciate Hugh Downs when you're more mature," she says, haughtily readjusting her brassiere.

"I don't think I'll ever be *that* mature," I say, huffing glue from a brown paper bag and passing it back to Felipe.

All of this—the warden escorting me into the witness room, the momentary glimpse of the slope of her breast, possibly her areola, and the flesh of her armpit as she sits down, and then the frenzied search through my memory for just the right *20/20* segment to temporarily neuter myself so that a healthy, perfectly normal, and involuntary heterosexual reflex won't be misinterpreted in such a way that I'm seen as an execrable son—all of this takes place in a span of no more than ten seconds. I wonder if, like, Bill Gates when *he* was 13, had the ability that I have at the age of 13 to anatomize minute fluctuations of consciousness that are occurring literally in femtoseconds. Anyway...

It's 5:25 P.M. Appeals exhausted, reprieves forsaken, last words ardently orated, the execution of Joel Leyner C.P. #39 6E-18 commences.

Inside the control module room, the executioner activates the delivery sequence by pushing a button on the control panel. A series of lights on the panel indicates the three stages of each injection: Armed (red), Start (yellow), and Complete (green).

As the lights for the initial injection sequence switch on and a piston is loosed from its cradle and falls onto the plunger of the first syringe, the delivery module introduces 15 cc of 2-percent sodium thiopental over ten seconds, which should cause unconsciousness.

I nudge the superintendent with my elbow.

"Thanks," I whisper, returning his pen.

"Keep it," he says.

"Are you kidding?"

"No. It's yours."

"Cool!" I gush.

After a minute, the red light pulses again, then the yellow, and the machine injects 15 cc of pancuronium bromide, a synthetic curare that should produce muscle paralysis and stop his breathing.

Following another one-minute interval, the lights flash and the final syringe, containing 15 cc of potassium chloride, is injected, which should induce cardiac arrest, with death following within two minutes.

Thirty seconds pass.

A minute.

In the dark witness room, we are mute and absolutely still. And in this riveted silence, the physiologic obbligato of human bodies—the sibilant nostrils, the tense clicking of temporomandibular joints, the bruits of carotid arteries, and the peristaltic rumblings of nervous bowels—becomes almost a din.

Ninety seconds elapse.

Two minutes.

The muscles in my father's neck appear to become rigid, actually lifting his head slightly off the gurney.

His eyes open wide.

"I feel shitty," he says.

The doctor, who's been monitoring the EKG, frowns at the operations officer, who turns to the warden and shakes his head grimly. Scrutinizing an EKG printout incredulously, he emerges from behind the screen and approaches my dad. He checks his pupillary reflexes with a penlight and then listens to his respiration and heart with a stethoscope.

"Physically, he appears to be absolutely fine," he says, grimacing with bewilderment.

The operations officer in turn gives a thumbs-down to the warden, who's now risen from her seat in the witness room.

"Mr. Leyner," says the doctor to my father, "I'm going to give you several statements and I want you to respond as best you can, all right?"

My father nods.

"Bacillus subtilis grown on dry, nutrient-poor agar plates tends to fan out into patterns that strongly resemble this fractal pattern seen in nonliving systems."

"What is a diffusion-limited aggregation?" responds my father.

"Music played by this Vietnamese ensemble consisting of flute, moon-lute, zither, cylindrical and coconut-shell fiddles, and wooden clackers is the most romantic and, to Western ears, melodic of all Southeast Asian theater music."

"What is cai luong?"

"This Hollywood legend kept a secret cache of Dynel-haired toy trolls."

"Who was Greta Garbo?"

"According to the American Mortuary Society, these are currently the two most widely requested gravestone epitaphs."

"*Wake Me Up When We Get There* and *If You Lived Here, You'd Be Home Now.*"

The doctor brightens momentarily.

"I'm sorry," amends my father. "What are *Wake Me Up When We Get There* and *If You Lived Here, You'd Be Home Now?*"

The doctor sags.

"Neurologically, he's perfectly normal," he announces, punctuating his diagnosis with a dejected, frustrated fling of his *NJ State Capital Punishment Division of Medicine* loose-leaf binder, which skitters across the floor.

"Cool binder!" I marvel sotto voce, helplessly susceptible to logo merchandising.

My father is returned to his cell. The operations officer confers with the warden, who informs me that the doctor would like to see me in his office.

I slip two hastily scrawled notes into her left hand.

The lights have come back on in the witness room and programmed music resumes over the ambient audio system—Kathleen Battle and Courtney Love's haunting performance of Mozart's aria "Mia speranza adorata" from the *Ebola Benefit—Live from Branson, Missouri* CD (Deutsche Grammophon), which segues into "Sarin Sayonara" from the Aum Supreme Truth Monks' *Les Chants d'Apocalypse* CD (Interscope), which is followed—as I enter the elevator—by the Montana Militia Choir (accompanied by Yanni and the Ray Coniff singers) singing—I swear to god!—"The Beasts of Yeast."

Read along with me, as I peruse this *People* magazine article in the waiting room of the prison doctor:

When Viktor N. Mikhailov, Russia's Minister of Atomic Energy, invited Hazel R. O'Leary, the U.S. Secretary of Energy, to a dinner party arranged to facilitate a discussion of Russia's plutonium stocks, he probably expected Mrs. O'Leary and her retinue to arrive with the first editions and bottles of rare vintage champagne that are the traditional accoutrements of diplomatic courtesy.

What he certainly didn't expect was for Mrs. O'Leary to arrive, Fender Stratocaster slung across her back, along with bassist Ivan Selin, Chairman of the Nuclear Regulatory Commission, guitarist John Holum, Director of the U.S. Arms Control and Disarmament Agency, and drummer J. Brian Atwood, Administrator of the U.S. Agency for International Development. Instead of propounding her views over cocktails or across the dinner table—as would be the norm at such a gathering—Mrs. O'Leary and her bandmates delivered a blistering set of original songs, thematically linked, each exploring a different facet of her overarching position that Russia must render its surplus weapons plutonium unusable.

Mrs. O'Leary, soignée and austere in a black Jil Sander dress, opened with a smoldering rocker about the global security risks of stolen fissile material that seemed to gradually implode with intensity as it slowed to the tempo of a New Orleans funeral march, achieving the exaggerated slow-motion sexual swagger of the Grim Reaper bumping and grinding down Bourbon Street. Next, Mrs. O'Leary almost shattered the huge Czarist-era crystal chandelier with an opening riff that tore from her amp like shrapnel from an anti-personnel bomb. She repeated the riff—an irresistible and diabolically intricate seven-note figure—over and over again, plying each shard with the obsessive scrutiny of a monkey grooming its mate, it becoming more squalid, more lewd, more intoxicating with each iteration, until finally the band launched into the song, a hammering sermon about how Russia must mix its plutonium in molten glass and bury it deep underground.

In the midst of the song, which, like an asylum inmate gouging at his own scabs, exacerbated itself into a raging cacophony, Mikhailov; Viktor M. Murogov, director of the Institute of Physics and Power Engineering at Obninsk; Yuri Vishnevsky, the head of Gosatomnadzor or GAN, the Russian equivalent of the Nuclear Regulatory Commission; and Aleksei V. Yablokov, an adviser to President Boris Yeltsin, and their spouses formed a throbbing mosh pit in the center of the living room.

Following the set, when asked what had made her appear with the band, Mrs. O'Leary, drenched in sweat, paused to catch her breath and then replied, "I'd asked Viktor [Mikhailov] if I could bring my guitar...and he said sure. And one thing led to another...and, well..." She gestured toward the throng of guests still pumping their fists in the air.

After dinner, a bizarre incident occurred that has had the diplomatic community and entertainment industry abuzz with wild rumor and rampant speculation.

Sergei Smernyakov, a well-known nightclub hypnotist invited to the soirée by Mikhailov to provide post-prandial entertainment, hypnotized guests Dorothy Bodin, Deputy Secretary of the Department of Energy; Cynthia Bowers-Lipken, a weapons expert at the Natural Resources

Defense Council; and LaShaquilla Nuland, wife of Adm. C. F. Bud Nuland, Vice Chairman of the Joint Chiefs of Staff. Each woman was given the posthypnotic suggestion that at the tone of a spoon striking a wineglass she would become a frenzied Dionysian orgiast with an uncontrollable compulsion to instantly gratify her every carnal desire.

Brought out of their trances, the women, each one a paragon of professional accomplishment, dignity, and decorum, blushed at the suggestion, and laughingly assured their companions that—with all due respect to Mr. Smernyakov's mesmeric prowess—they could certainly never be induced to behave in such an outrageously uncharacteristic manner.

But sure enough, when Yeltsin aide Yablokov tapped a tiny silver jam spoon against his wine goblet, Ms. Bodin, Ms. Bowers-Lipken, and Mrs. Nuland immediately disrobed, rending the garments from their bodies as if they were aflame, and then, like deranged children, spreading caviar and blintz filling over each other's naked flesh. Then, after a brief huddle, they overpowered a chosen male guest, shackled his legs, cuffed his hands behind his back, and took turns sitting on his face as they swigged caraway and jimsonweed-infused vodka from cut-crystal decanters.

Having finally sated themselves and tired, the women released the man, who staggered back to his hotel covered in their juices, followed by a howling cavalcade of rutting dogs, cats, raccoons, and possums whose demented caterwauling awakened sleeping Muscovites throughout the city.

Although invited guests refuse to comment on the identity of the male victim, *People* has learned that it was none other than celebrated television personality and Tony Award–winning actor

continued on p. 115

"Mark Leyner?"

"Huh?" I say distractedly, my attention monopolized by the fore-going magazine article.

"Mark, the doctor will see you now."

"Right now?" I whine, my fingers riffling furiously through a multipage Lincoln Town Car insert in a frustrated effort to reach the jump on page 115 and learn the name of the celebrity "victim."

"Right now," answers the nurse with a peremptory lilt.

"Fuck," I mutter, and toss the magazine atop a pile.

Have you ever read an article in *People* that was so perfectly suited to your interests that it seemed as if the writer had intended it exclusively for you, so that you could—in the way that mentally disturbed individuals glean divine messages from advertising jingles or laundering instruction labels—perhaps derive some subliminal or encrypted communication or some secret gnostic insight? That's how I feel about this particular article.

I can't tell you how many afternoons I've frittered away contemplating what it would be like to be held captive and abused by various groups of fanatical and/or unbalanced and/or unwashed women. For a while, it's *all* I talked about, which I realize became rather tedious for my parents. I remember one night at the dinner table, I was going on and on about what it might be like to get kidnapped and tormented by a group of rogue policewomen, when my dad interrupted me and said, "I didn't think I'd ever hear myself saying this, but—could we talk about Napoleonic War muskets [my previous fixation] for a while?"

Actually my parents were pretty cool about it, though. In fact, they got me a subscription to one of these young-adult book series called *Around the World with Rusty Hoover*. In each book, this kid Rusty Hoover—who's about my age—invariably finds himself mistaken for someone else and then gets abducted by gorgeous women who torture him. Like in *Rusty Hoover Goes to Peru*, Rusty's on vacation with his parents, and he's misidentified as a Peruvian Treasury officer, captured and brutally interrogated for weeks in a sweltering Lima apartment by giggling cadres at a Shining Path pajama party. In *Rusty Hoover Goes to Portugal,* Rusty's on vacation in the Algarve with his parents, where he's erroneously targeted as an unethical ship-building magnate by an underground cell of shrouded fishermen's widows who turn out to be particularly sadistic and horny. There's *Rusty Hoover Goes to Law School,* where Rusty accompanies his par-ents to visit his older sister Tara at law school, and he's confused for some pervert who's been sending pornographic e-mail to fellow students in his Patents class, and he's forced to sign a confession in his own prostatic fluid, subjected to pseudoscientific experimenta-tion, and flogged by Professor De Brunhoff—a loose composite of Catharine MacKinnon and Lisa Sliwa—and her frothing aco-lytes. And then—one of my favorites—*Rusty Hoover Goes to Indi-ana,* in which, en route to Yellowstone Park, the family car's cruise control malfunctions on Route 70 near Terre Haute, where Rusty's mistaken for a locker-room Peeping Tom by a women's fast-pitch softball team that has just completed a double-header in 100-degree heat and that—in the words of the jacket copy—"teaches Rusty a lesson in pine tar and voyeurism he'll never forget."

But until I read the article in *People* magazine, this sort of thing had only existed for me in fiction and in my own febrile fantasies. And now I see that it's actually happened to some guy who was lucky enough to be in Moscow at just the right dinner party. But who is he?

Isn't it one of life's—well, maybe *tragedies* is too strong a word—one of life's most vexing conundrums, that just at the exact moment that you really get into a magazine article in a doctor's wait-ing room, the nurse calls your name?

The doctor's office features standard-issue M.D. furnishings and bric-a-brac with three notable exceptions: on his desk, a photo-graph of a dismayed woman (whom I presume is his wife) in a gauzy lavender negligee drowning a four-inch Madagascar "hissing" cockroach with spray from a White Diamonds cologne atomizer; on the wall alongside an array of diplomas and certificates, a huge LeRoy Neiman painting of Socrates drinking his cup of hemlock; and above the credenza, a framed needlepoint of Cleopatra's valediction from Shakespeare's *Antony and Cleopatra:* "The stroke of death is as a lover's pinch, / Which hurts, and is desired"—the cursive embroidery bordered by intertwined asps.

"I'm very sorry about your father, Mark."

The doctor, downcast and shaken, rises from his chair and walks out from behind his desk. "I'm terribly, terribly sorry," he says, embracing me.

Perhaps I have deferred or suppressed my emotions—numbed myself. Also—and I realize that I may have been naive or unrealistically optimistic—it simply hadn't ever occurred to me that my dad wouldn't respond to the lethal drugs. But now the emotions come surging forth. My eyes begin to fill. I sob, I heave, I weep unrestrainedly.

"Why did this have to happen?" I wail, clutching him.

"Mark, I wish there was a simple answer," he says, with a reciprocal squeeze.

I unclasp his arms and step away from him.

"But everyone said it would work," I contend with aggrieved composure.

"For the overwhelming majority of inmates, sodium thiopental, pancuronium bromide, and potassium chloride is the terminal regimen of choice and proves to be completely efficacious. Unfortunately, it was not as deleterious to your father as we would have hoped."

"Doctor, isn't there anything more you can do?"

"I'm afraid not."

"What about trying other lethal drugs?"

"The *only* drug protocol that the Food and Drug Administration has approved for executions is sodium thiopental, pancuronium bromide, and potassium chloride." He bristles. "There are literally scores of promising new lethal drugs in development, but each one is hopelessly mired in FDA bureaucracy. Glaxo Wellcome has a compound called Mortilax, which combines the industrial solvent carbon disulfide and a neurotoxic insecticide, pyrethrum, with death-cap fungus, but it's bogged down in phase-one animal studies. Johnson & Johnson's Panicidin—whose active ingredients include several nitrated derivatives of phenol, zinc phosphide (a hepatotoxic rat poison), dioxin, and tetrodotoxin (a poison extracted from the livers of Japanese blowfish)—was sailing through phase-two human efficacy trials when the FDA declared a moratorium on further testing because the drug was apparently causing moderate new hair growth in men with male-pattern baldness. And Pfizer has a very exciting new product in the pipeline called Necrotropin, which is a year into a four-year phase-three clinical trial. Necrotropin is composed of tetraethylpyrophosphate (an insecticide that blocks the enzyme cholinesterase, resulting in a fatal buildup of acetylcholine), caustic potash (for corrosive destruction of internal organs), santonin (an alkaloid from wormseed that causes cardiovascular collapse), strychnine (for tetanic spasms leading to asphyxia), methyl isocyanate (the chemical that killed 3,000 people in Bhopal), and a concentrate of Gaboon viper venom (which is both hemotoxic and neurotoxic, causing diffused hemorrhages *and* respiratory paralysis). Pfizer is planning to offer it as an injectable, a transdermal patch, and a pleasant-tasting chewable tablet.

"So, potentially—and in spite of the appalling ineptitude of the FDA—the future is very bright. I emphasize the word *potentially*—one of the things that causes me so much anguish about the destruction of the rain forest is the possibility that we're irrevocably losing indigenous plant toxins and venoms that could be used in the development of new and more powerful lethal drugs. But look, even if the FDA approved one of these experimental agents, there's no guarantee that it would prove any more effective on your father than the drugs we administered today. I suspect that your father's habitual abuse of angel dust and his hypersensitivity to gamma radiation have somehow conferred an immunity to toxins. Although I have no idea what the precise biochemical mechanisms are here, my hypothesis is that chronic anaphylactic reactions to gamma rays occurring concomitantly with sustained exposure to phencyclidine has actually altered the genetic matrix in each of your father's cells, rendering him resistant to the lethal drugs presently available to us."

"Well, why can't any of these companies develop a drug that will kill gamma-ray-sensitive angel-dust users?" I ask.

"It's more an issue of economics than scientific or technological capability. How many people in the United States with severe gamma ray sensitivity who habitually abuse phencyclidine do you think commit capital crimes each year?"

"Probably not that many...I don't know...maybe 50,000 a year?"

"Try 1,500. Compare that to the 600,000 new cases of congenital generalized hypertrichosis each year. [Individuals with this disorder, thought to be transmitted on the X chromosome, have an upper body and face covered with hair and often end up in sideshows as human werewolves.] Or the 1.2 million annual cases of Lipid-Induced Inuit Hyperthermia. [Sufferers of this malady, which primarily affects the Eskimo people of Arctic Canada, maintain exceptionally high body temperatures — about 107°F or above — as a result of heavy consumption of blubber and tallow. Geologists have long been concerned that an LIH epidemic could raise ambient temperatures sufficiently to weaken and finally destroy the ice underpinnings of the West Arctic Ice Sheet. The entire sheet would then slide rapidly into the sea, causing an abrupt and catastrophic rise in global sea levels, and flooding low-lying countries like the Netherlands and Bangladesh.] But even these are considered third-tier markets. In terms of the bottom-line mindset of the pharmaceutical industry, 1,500 cases is a negligible patient base. It's just not economically feasible for a company to expend the necessary R&D resources on a drug that's designed to kill only 1,500 people a year. So we'd be talking about an orphan lethal drug. And who do you think awards orphan-drug status? The FDA."

"It sounds hopeless," I say.

"It's not hopeless if we set a national agenda. If we as a country commit ourselves and our resources to developing a drug that can kill gamma-ray-sensitive angel-dust abusers, we can do it—and we can do it by the year 2000. But it has to be a national priority with the full support of the American people. Do you know much about North Korea?"

"Not really. I'd like to, though. In fact, I was going to take *Pariah States* as my 7th-period elective for next semester, but I decided to take *English Punk 1975–1978* instead."

"Well, you want to talk about setting agendas and making national commitments, these guys could teach us all a thing or two. Their leader, Kim Jong Il, is apparently always developing these little growths on his face and he's an extremely vain guy, so the government spends about $1.8 billion constructing this fabulous thermonuclear dermatological facility the likes of which have never been seen anywhere. The device works by firing a dazzling light from 192 lasers down a labyrinth of mirrors, focusing a titanic bolt of energy—a thousand times the output of all the power stations in the United States—onto a single tiny pellet of supercold hydrogen fuel placed on Kim Jong Il's mole, wart, or wen and creating a miniature thermonuclear blast lasting one-billionth of a second, which completely vaporizes the lesion. That's what a country can do if it puts its mind to it...."

Frustration with the failed execution, the inaccessibility of more-potent lethal drugs, and the vagaries of the federal bureaucracy; envy for the ruthless fecundity of totalitarian technocrats; and utter physical and emotional fatigue seem to cumulatively crest, as the doctor's voice trails off and, with a sort of spent serenity, he gazes out the window.

The window affords a view of an emerald-green lawn upon which sits a filigreed wrought-iron gazebo completely swathed in concertina wire. In 1996, singer Michael Jackson presented then-governor Christine Todd Whitman with the original gazebo used in *The Sound of Music* as a gift to the State of New Jersey—the only proviso being that the gazebo be used for the delectation of the state's penal population. Rotated every two years among New Jersey's several maximum security institutions, the gazebo—in which Liesl and Rolfe serenaded each other with "I Am Sixteen Going on Seventeen"—is used both for conjugal visits and punitive solitary confinement.

During this lull, I become aware of a softly pulsing obbligato— the *ch-ch-ch* of innumerable inmates engaging in unlubricated sodomy, which, like the *ch-ch-ch* of stridulating male cicadas, can be heard on summer evenings in villages and towns miles from the prison.

Emerging from his reverie, the doctor turns back to me.

"Do you play any sports? You look like you're in pretty good shape," he says.

"Tetherball," I reply, miming an overhead smash.

"Y'know, when I was your age, the jocks wore pearls...that was *the big thing* back then...freshwater pearls. You'd be in the locker room after football practice, and there'd be these big hairy naked guys wearing single strands of pearls, snapping towels at each other..."

"No way!" I snort, not bothering to hide my contempt for the fleeting fads of bygone generations.

"It's funny when you look back...the things you thought were so cool, so tough...Freshwater pearls..." he trails off, returning his gaze out toward the gazebo.

Our conversation continues desultorily, the doctor intermittently blurting a question or offering some random reminiscence, and then fading off again into mute introspection, the gaps filled with the ubiquitous *ch-ch-ch*.

Despite the fact that, beyond a gustatory preference for brains and marrow, we have almost nothing in common, I find myself bonding somewhat with the doctor. Having long accepted the stereotype of the physician as the stolid professional who views the fates of his patients with cold, clinical detachment, I was all the more moved by this doctor's genuine empathy. He responded with such grief, and with such a sense of personal responsibility, that it was almost as if it were his own father he'd failed to kill.

Perhaps also contributing to my feelings of affinity for the doctor is the fact that a V-shaped area from the waist to the crotch of my leather pants had become sodden with tears, causing a distinctive odor to waft upward. And whereas the pungent aroma of sweaty leather makes me feel omniscient, the bittersweet fragrance of tear-soaked leather engenders in me a sense of interconnectedness with all sentient beings.

"Has lethal medicine always been your specialty?" I ask, infused with *agape*.

"I was a third-year medical student when I made up my mind," he replies. "I was assigned to the pediatric-execution wing of a large state prison up in Connecticut—it was the first of my clinical rotations in what was then called Malevolent Medicine. From that point on, I was hooked. For me, the field of pediatric executions has always been the most gratifying. There's absolutely nothing in the world that compares to the look on the faces of a mother and a father after they've been told that the execution of their sociopathic, incorrigibly homicidal child has been a success. There's an instant realization—you can see it in their eyes—that the courtroom vigils, the legal bills, the civil suits, the endless hours of family therapy are all over, that they and the deceased demon seed's siblings can now go on and live a normal, happy life. It's an expression that never ceases to touch you deeply, no matter how many times you see it."

The telephone rings.

The doctor reoccupies the high-backed chair behind his desk, picks up the receiver, and swivels around so that his back is to me and his conversation—save for an initial "I think that would be wise under the circumstances"—is inaudible.

I pluck a lollipop from the fishbowl on his desk, wander over to the window, and gaze bemusedly at the gazebo.

Ch-ch-ch. Ch-ch-ch. Ch-ch-ch.

Shortly the doctor swivels back into view and hangs up the phone.

"The warden's going to make an announcement in her office in a few minutes," he says.

He stands, circumambulates his desk, and embraces me again.

"If it provides any solace, I want you to know that, medically, I've done everything at my disposal to kill your father."

"I understand," I quaver, nodding solemnly. "And thank you."

I pivot and race out of his office, heading straight for the pile of magazines in the waiting room. I retrieve the *People* I'd been reading and flip frantically to page 115 so I can finally learn the identity of the television personality and Tony Award–winning actor who was ravaged by the three hypnotized wives at a Moscow dinner party. But when I reach 115, I find—to my absolute horror—that someone has cut a rectangular section out of the page including the all-important final paragraphs of the story that had so captured my imagination. And it's all the more frustrating to discover that the excision of my article was inadvert. The culprit had cut out a coupon on the reverse page—116—for two Bradford Exchange limited-edition collector's plates commemorating, respectively, the 1977 professional debut of transsexual tennis player Renée Richards and the 1992 beating of Reginald Denny during the Los Angeles riots.

"Inmates aren't allowed to have scissors, are they?" I ask the nurse.

"No," she says.

"Well, how did someone cut a coupon out of this magazine?" I ask, wiggling my fingers through the hole in the page.

"They use shanks—y'know, homemade knives."

I shudder.

The image of hardened convicts daintily clipping coupons with their shanks gives me goose bumps.

The warden's office is a serried, murmuring Who's Who of penal officialdom: the warden, of course, seated at her desk, signing papers proffered assembly-line fashion by a feline male secretary with close-cropped orange hair; and milling about and filling the room with gossip and banter are the superintendent; the operations officer; the executioner; the doctor; two of the prosecuting attorneys from the ice-cream scooper murder case; my dad's lawyer; my dad, who, despite a slightly bilious tinge to his complexion, is chewing his gum mirthfully and talking golf with the rabbi; and a state-appointed stenographer, her fingers a kinetic blur as she endeavors to somehow transcribe the babble of simultaneous small talk.

Given the self-importance and solipsism endemic to seventh graders, I'm assuming that the warden's impending announcement is about me. After the execution attempt and just before I met with the doctor, I'd scribbled and surreptitiously conveyed to the warden two notes that read, respectively, "You wanna get high?" and "Be my sweaty bosomy lover?"

Why she would choose to make such a public response to my homey blandishments, though, I have no idea.

The lithe arm swings over her desk with one final form. The warden signs with a culminating flourish and rises. A dainty throat-clearing and a tentative, collegial "Folks..." goes unheeded. And then a great gurgling hawking up of phlegm and a stentorian imperious "Gentlemen!" effects an instant decrescendo of chitchat, the rabbi's punch line "So Moses flings the Pharaoh's ball into the Sinai and says, 'Here, use my sand wedge...'" trailing off in the corner of the room, the stenographer's fingers momentarily still.

"Gentlemen," the warden says, "I have an announcement to make concerning Joel Leyner C.P. #39 6E-18, and pursuant to Volume 2C, Part Five, Article 11-3 of the *New Jersey Department of Corrections Digest of Procedural Regulations and Guidelines,* a state-appointed stenographer will herewith transcribe all remarks germane to the disposition of Mr. Leyner's sentence.

"The State Legislature has vested in the Governor, the Attorney General, and the warden of this institution the following authority, as specified in Section 42J of the Penal Code: 'In the event of an abortive execution by lethal injection in which the condemned inmate survives, any and all further attempts to execute that inmate by lethal injection within that institution and under the medical supervision of said institution's physician(s) are prohibited. Subject to unanimous consent of the Governor, the Attorney General, and the institution's warden, said inmate shall be, with all due speed and by public decree, resentenced to State Discretionary Execution, and thereupon immediately released. Although the State is not hereby required to enforce the death sentence, it may, at its discretion, execute said inmate immediately upon his or her release into the community or at any time thereafter. Said inmate (hereafter referred to as "the releasee") is subject to discretionary execution immediately upon vacating said institution's premises and at any time thereafter. In the event of an abortive Discretionary Execution in which the releasee survives, the State may, but is not required to, make an additional attempt or unlimited attempts on the life of the releasee. The Discretionary Execution of the releasee shall be carried out — if at all — whenever, wherever, and however the State of New Jersey deems appropriate, subject only to the inalienable caprices of the State of New Jersey.'

"It is so ordered and adjudged that Joel Leyner be sentenced to State Discretionary Execution and promptly discharged from this institution, this sentence to remain in force until Mr. Leyner's decease."

"En inglés, por favor," I chafe, gnawing my lollipop stick.

"Basically, Mark, your dad's free to go, but the State reserves the right to kill him the minute he walks out the front gate," says the warden. "Plus, the State has complete latitude in terms of execution protocols and rules of engagement. In the next ten minutes your dad could be pithed with an English pub dart in the car on the way home from here. On the other hand, he might never be killed—he could live out his life unperturbed and die of natural causes in his slobbering dotage. Or the State could wait until he's 99 years, 11 months, and 30 days old and then, on his 100th birthday, replace his dentures with molded plastique so that morning, as Willard Scott is telling America what a good-looking man he is, god bless him—BA-BOOM! Now, if you'll excuse me for just a moment, there's some material I'd like you to have before you leave, Mr. Leyner," she says, exiting her office.

"And this is called what, again?" my father asks the superintendent.

"NJSDE—New Jersey State Discretionary Execution."

"I think I read about this in *Elle*," Dad says. "It's sort of like an optional fatwa."

"The feature we like to stress to releasees is the indeterminacy," continues the superintendent. "You're living your life, rowing merrily along, and suddenly one morning you wake up and there's a dwarf ninja crouched on your chest who deftly severs your carotid arteries with two honed throwing stars. Or you're on a flight to Orlando, Florida, giggling to yourself as you read the *Confessions* of Saint Augustine, and meanwhile, 35,000 feet below, a New Jersey state trooper steps out of his car, kneels alongside the shoulder of I-95, aims a shoulder-held antiaircraft missile launcher, and blows your 727 into friggin' curds and whey."

"They'd do that?" I ask excitedly. "They'd sacrifice all those people just to kill my dad?"

"NJSDE gives us a lot of leeway. We're no longer encumbered by the federal government, by the FDA, the FAA, the Justice

Department...it really unties the hands of the state. I think it's an extremely innovative piece of statutory legislation. And you have to give the Governor the bulk of the credit. She takes a lot of flak for the narcolepsy and the lathery horse posters, but she was committed to this and very savvy about the politics."

"How do you feel about it?" my father asks, turning to the rabbi.

"It's a very postmodern sentencing structure—random and capricious, the free-floating dread, each ensuing day a gaping abyss, the signifier hovering over the signified like the sword of Damocles. To have appropriated a pop-noir aesthetic and recontextualized it within the realm of jurisprudence is breathtakingly audacious. I think you're going to find it a very disturbing, but a very fascinating and transformative way to live, Joel."

Personally, I don't find it all *that* innovative, audacious, disturbing, fascinating, or transformative. It just seems like normal life to me—not knowing from day to day if you'll be pithed with a pub dart or sliced into sushi by some hypopituitary freak in black pajamas, or if your false teeth will blow up in your head. That's just late-second-millennium life. I mean, isn't everyone basically sentenced to New Jersey State Discretionary Execution from, like, the moment he's born?

Although, OK—I have to admit—a statutory algorithm designed to amplify the anarchic cruelties of human existence and arbitrarily inflict its violence upon innocent bystanders, exponentially expanding the nexus of fatal contingencies, is pretty intense. And also, I assume that any ninja who works for NJSDE is involved in the state civil service bureaucracy—and there's something really appealing to me about the image of ninjas waiting in lines for hours at state offices for application forms and photo IDs. And I absolutely adore the notion of elite units of New Jersey State Troopers, magnificently loathsome in their Stetsons and jackboots, sworn by blood oath to enforce the stringent dicta of NJSDE, wending the corniches of the French Riviera or the Spanish Costa del Sol in their emblazoned cruisers, in inexorable pursuit of some targeted releasee, some hapless New Jersey expatriate shambling along the boardwalk, camera and wine sack slung across his belly, oblivious to the cataclysmic, surreal violence in which he'll be momentarily engulfed.

But do I say any of this when the rabbi, in turn, asks me what *I* think of NJSDE? No, of course not. Instead I mutter some facile, meaningless catchphrase.

Why do I nullify my own intelligence with this willful, stereotypical inarticulateness? Why do I immure my thoughts in this crypt of sullen diffidence?

Do I perhaps derive some sadomasochistic pleasure in the mortification of my own intellect, akin to those who cut and burn their own bodies? After all, isn't the act of making oneself mute a mute-ilation?

Am I ultimately knowable?

Is it ludicrous and stilted for a 13-year-old to describe himself, even facetiously, as "an individual of daunting complexity"?

Why is it, then, that when the rabbi, in turn, asks me what *I* think of NJSDE, I glibly reply: "It's cool, like a video"?

The warden returns.

"This should help answer any questions you might have, Mr. Leyner," she says, handing my father a booklet, which I peruse over his shoulder.

The glossy brochure is entitled *You and Your Discretionary Execution.*

Q. *What is New Jersey State Discretionary Execution?*

A. NJSDE was developed by Alejandro Roberto Montés Calderón, a cashiered Guatemalan Army colonel who fled Guatemala after his counterinsurgency unit was accused of "crimes against humanity" by Americas Watch and Amnesty International. Mr. Calderón resettled in the United States, where he became a gym teacher at

Emerson High School in Union City, New Jersey. The Governor, who had Mr. Calderón for gym in both her junior and senior years, appointed him to chair the Select Committee on Capital Punishment and Tort Reform.

NJSDE is a pioneering sentencing program designed to give the State of New Jersey maximum—one might even say *giddy*—latitude in dealing with condemned inmates, like yourself, who have survived unsuccessful institutional executions.

Q. *Am I responsible for the cost of my unsuccessful institutional execution?*

A. You are responsible only for the cost of the lethal drugs. Most health insurance plans and HMOs cover lethal prescription drugs, paying for them directly or through reimbursements to the insured individual. Check your policy and consult with your broker or benefits administrator.

Q. *How does the State determine whether I will live or die?*

A. Your status is reevaluated on a daily basis. At precisely 9:00 P.M. each night, at the New Jersey State Discretionary Execution Control Center in Trenton, data processors insert every NJSDE releasee's social security number into an intricate equation whose variables include the current pollen count at Newark International Airport and the total daily receipts collected at tollbooths along the Garden State Parkway as of 7:45 P.M. If, factored through this algebraic operation, your SS number yields a prime number, any five-digit sequence from pi, or the Governor's PIN code for her MAC card, you are subject to Discretionary Execution over that ensuing 24-hour period.

Q. *Is NJSDE painful?*

A. Yes! The State avails itself of a potpourri of execution methods including bare hands and teeth, sharpened stick, flint ax, bisection by lumberyard circular saw, car bomb, drive-by shooting, rocket-propelled grenade, Tomahawk cruise missile, etc., any of which can cause significant discomfort. The *degree* of pain you experience may vary in accordance with the efficacy of the execution attempt and with your body's ability to produce natural opiates, called endorphins, at moments of extreme stress. If you choose to augment your endorphins by prophylactically self-anesthetizing through heavy alcohol consumption and you develop cirrhosis, bear in mind that some hospitals in New Jersey will not perform liver transplants on patients who face possible execution within 48 hours of surgery.

Q. *How does the State make certain it's executing the right person?*

A. Prior to any execution attempt, your identity will be surreptitiously confirmed using sophisticated DNA-fingerprinting autoradiograph techniques developed by the LAPD Forensic Crime Laboratory.

Q. *What will happen to me after I'm killed?*

A. You will experience a sense of well-being. You (i.e., your soul) will separate from your body. You will travel through a dark tunnel. Emerging from this darkness, you will encounter a field of white radiant light. And you will enter this light. You will conduct a review of your life. You may encounter a "presence." You will probably meet deceased loved ones. At some juncture, you may hear what you think is your body calling out, beseeching you. *Do not return to your body!* This bark or whooping sound is made by a spasm in the muscles of the voice box caused by increased acidity in the blood of the corpse. Your body will undergo rigor mortis (rigidity), livor mortis (discoloration due to settling of blood), and algor mortis (cooling). Tissue will break down through enzymatic action, and putrefaction will ensue through the decomposition of proteins by bacteria. Your body will be colonized by necrophage insects, including blowfly larvae and saprophagous beetles, and within three to six months, caseic fermentation should occur.

Q. *This is a change of subject, but—Why, after he'd been so successful as a starting pitcher and in fact had recently thrown a no-hitter against the Boston Red Sox, was Dave Righetti pulled from the starting rotation and put in the Yankee bullpen? Was this just the result of one of Steinbrenner's autocratic tantrums, or was there some sound baseball reasoning behind the decision?*

A. The months following Righetti's July Fourth no-hitter against the Boston Red Sox were among the most tumultuous in Yankee history. Players had the locker room repainted, replacing the traditional Yankee pinstripe motif with gyrating chained dancers and huge flying griffins bearing futuristic bare-breasted Valkyries with laser guns. Each game was preceded by a ritual team circle jerk. Postgame revels raged into the early morning. It was not unusual to find Meg Tilly, Teri Hatcher, Amanda Plummer, Vanessa Williams, Jaye Davidson, Kate Capshaw, Janet Reno, Daphne Zuniga, Helena Bonham Carter, and the like sprawled languidly across the locker-room floor as players sipped sweat from their navels with teeny coke spoons. Sports fans will not soon forget the image of a simpering Don Mattingly injecting Ritalin into his neck for the benefit of press photographers. Steinbrenner's capricious mean streak was exacerbated by the cheese-free diet he'd been put on by his cardiologist. One minute, he seemed too spaced out to recognize anyone; the next, he was clubbing or pistol-whipping whoever was handy. Predictably, players and coaches oscillated between rhapsody and despair, their heady self-confidence undermined by an involuntary nihilism. Righetti, the crotch of his uniform distended by the heavy cock rings he now insisted on wearing when he pitched, circumambulated the mound between pitches muttering what a *New York Post* headline described as "Hermetic Incantations and Insane

Glossolalia!" Righetti was ultimately placed on the disabled list and committed by Steinbrenner to the psychiatric hospital in Rodez, France, where the visionary dramatic theorist and poet Antonin Artaud had undergone sixty convulsive shock treatments. Pledging that his star pitcher would receive "the finest care money can buy," Steinbrenner stipulated that Righetti be given *sixty-one* convulsive shock treatments — one for each of the home runs Roger Maris hit in 1961. Three weeks later, Righetti rejoined the team in Kansas City. That night, in the eleventh inning, Yankee utility infielder Hector Peña hit a mammoth 600-foot shot to dead center field. Following a protest by Royals manager Dick Howser that Peña was using an illegally doctored bat, umpires confiscated his Louisville Slugger, sawed it open, and discovered two pounds of stolen Russian plutonium. The Yankees were forced to forfeit the game and effectively dropped out of pennant contention. That off-season, in an effort to restore morale, Steinbrenner took the team on a tour of Japan, Southeast Asia, and the Indian subcontinent. Although several Yankees tore anterior cruciate ligaments slipping on the raspberry-colored snail-egg pods that litter ballparks in the Mekong lowlands of southwest Laos, and during a game in the Mujahedeen Dome in Kabul, Afghanistan, rookie prospect Andre Knoblauch lost his legs when he stepped on a land mine chasing a line-drive hit into the gap in left-center, the trip was a great success. Steinbrenner was particularly impressed with the custom practiced by Japanese players of wearing glass vials of potassium cyanide on cords around their necks. And in an exhibition game against the Yomiuri Giants, a Yomiuri player, caught in a run-down between second and third base, did indeed swallow his suicide capsule rather than suffer the ignominy of being tagged out. The Yankees returned to the United States, proceeding directly to Fort Lauderdale, and throughout spring training they evinced a renewed esprit de corps and seriousness of purpose. The new season began with extremely high expectations. But on opening day, several hours before game time, as starting pitcher Dave Righetti napped on a training table, his fingers interlocked behind his head, Knoblauch—in a stupid rookie prank—put a caramel apple in Righetti's left armpit. When Righetti awoke and discovered the caramel apple stuck fast to the armpit of his pitching arm, he panicked and, seizing the wooden stick, wildly pried the agglutinated candy-coated winesap from his body, taking several layers of torn flesh with it. Righetti was rushed to a nearby hospital where surgeons performed an emergency graft using 53 infant foreskins donated by a Bronx *mohel* who was a rabid Yankee fan and had heard what happened on his car radio. Righetti returned to the stadium in time to pitch two innings of hitless relief, and remained in the bullpen for the rest of his tenure with the New York Yankees.

Q. *Could innocent people who happen to be near me at the time of my New Jersey State Discretionary Execution also be killed or injured?*

A. Yes! It's quite possible that bystanders unfortunate enough to be in your proximity during your execution attempt will be inadvertently killed or maimed. "Collateral damage" is an integral component of the NJSDE program, effectively increasing the degree and rapidity with which NJSDE releasees are stigmatized by, and ostracized from, their communities. The fact that being anywhere near you puts someone at risk of being killed or paralyzed by a stray 9-mm round, gruesomely disfigured by an errant machete, or blinded by a wayward crossbow arrow makes it unlikely that—in the gym, for instance—that person will choose the StairMaster next to yours, never mind join you in tucking away some sea leg fra diavolo and Chianti at the local trattoria, and less likely still that he or she will have sex with you later that evening. As an NJSDE releasee, you'll be amazed not only at the corrosive anxiety of living with an indeterminate death sentence, but at how quickly you'll be shunned as a pariah wherever you go. That's why *The American Spectator* awarded NJSDE five bastinados—its highest rating—in a recent evaluation of state-funded internal security apparatus, calling it "A breath of fresh air…The most whimsical deterrent program in years!"

Q. *Given the potential for "collateral damage," can I be killed while praying in a crowded church, synagogue, or mosque?*

A. Yes, you can!

Q. *Can I be killed while visiting a friend's premature infant in a neonatal intensive care unit?*

A. Sure!

Q. *Can I be Discretionarily Executed while giving someone CPR?*

A. I don't see why not!

6

THE SUGAR FROSTED NUTSACK (2012)

THE STORY SO FAR

1999 MTV pilot for *Iggy Vile M.D.* is produced. MTV executive Brian Graden calls it "the most disgusting thing I've ever seen." It never airs

2000 Writes two episodes of *Wonderland* for Imagine/ABC. After reading the first script, Imagine executive Tony Krantz asks creator/executive producer Peter Berg to fire Leyner, but Berg refuses. Krantz will later graciously concede that he was wrong and extol Leyner's work for the series

2001 Writes (with John Cusack) screenplay for *Et Tu, Babe*

2002 Writes *B Major* for Universal/Imagine

2004–2005 Writes *The World's Fair* and *Hurricane Jerry* for Robbins Entertainment

2005 Publication of *Why Do Men Have Nipples?* (with Billy Goldberg), which goes on to become a number one *New York Times* bestseller

2005 Writes (with Jeremy Pikser and John Cusack) the screenplay for *War, Inc.*

2007 In Bulgaria for shooting of *War, Inc.* (starring Cusack, Ben Kingsley, Marisa Tomei, Hilary Duff, etc.)

2007 Hit by a car in Culver City, California, resulting in serious injury to left knee; will never play basketball again

2008   Premiere of *War, Inc.* at the Tribeca Film Festival

2012   Undergoes prostate cancer surgery (Dr. David Samadi)

2012   Publication of *The Sugar Frosted Nutsack*

THE TENDER DILEMMAS OF LATER LIFE

Adam Sternbergh

FOR ACOLYTES OF Mark Leyner, the 1990s were a time of abundance. No matter when new readers had joined the cult of Leyner—maybe it was after encountering *My Cousin, My Gastroenterologist* in 1990 or *Et Tu, Babe* in '92 or *Tooth Imprints on a Corn Dog* in '95—the discovery of his fiction reliably sent such readers ecstatically scrambling both forward and backward in time: scouring his back catalog for earlier works while simultaneously scanning the horizon for the arrival of future installments.

For a time, those installments appeared with satisfying regularity, every two or three years or so. With each new book, up to *The Tetherballs of Bougainville*, in 1997, Leyner expanded our understanding of that neologistic descriptor that had increasingly become the only satisfying way to describe his work: *Leyneresque*.

And then: nothing. Nada. Silence.

Leyner, in a sense, disappeared.

This disappearance was not as deliberate and calculated as, say, the disappearances of Salinger and Pynchon. It's just that the novels...stopped.

Leyner himself would occasionally poke his head up, as he did with the publication of his bestselling collections of medical curiosities, such as *Why Do Men Have Nipples?*, written in collaboration with Dr. Billy Goldberg. (And it must be said here that the phrase "as he did with the publication of his bestselling collections of medical curiosities, such as *Why Do Men Have Nipples?*, written in collaboration with Dr. Billy Goldberg" sounds itself like a line from a Leyner novel.)

This gap between new novels, which would eventually stretch to fifteen years, is a time Leyner later called "the interregnum." As mysteries go, his long absence from fiction writing was not, it turns out, that mysterious. Leyner had gone Hollywood.

Which is to say: he'd sufficiently attracted the attention of powerful Hollywood types with overstuffed Hollywood wallets, in the grand tradition of great American novelists who are temporarily distracted and detoured from novels by the opportunities Hollywood affords.

For Leyner, this meant a long fallow period of fiction non-writing. When he did finally write a new novel — *The Sugar Frosted Nutsack*, in 2012 — it was both recognizably Leyneresque and something new.

Was it funny? Yes. Strange? Of course. Was it...Leyner? Good question. As the experimental novelist Ben Marcus wrote in a *New York Times* review of *Nutsack*, "Mark Leyner writes in a genre that could be called Mark Leyner," going on to describe this genre as "gun-to-the-head comedy delivered with a stratospheric I.Q .," resulting in novels "created by a literary mind that seems to have no precedent."

In other words: *Leyneresque.*

And yet.

"It is very important to me, maybe excessively important to me, that what I do is unlike anything else," Leyner said to me on the eve of the publication of *Nutsack* — and what's notable about that novel, as well as the two that followed, *Gone with the Mind* in 2016 and *Last Orgy of the Divine Hermit* in 2021, is not how different they are from anyone else's work (Leyner's novels have always been different) but how different they are from the fiction that made him so famous in the 1990s.

These new novels—one is tempted to call them Late Period Leyner, or at least Later Period Leyner, for who knows how many periods Leyner will eventually have—are, of course, Leyneresque. But they also signal how the definition of that term has grown, evolved, expanded, necessarily burst its seams. If Leyner's earlier novels were breakneck comic paeans sung to a supersize celebrity-engorged culture, these new novels felt...more fragile. More human. More aware of mortality. More—dare I say—poignant. With his earlier work, Leyner had been accused of many excesses, but poignancy was never one of them. He made you laugh, made you gasp, made you spit take, made you think, made you put down the book in gape-mouthed wonder—but had he ever made you cry?

Reader, these new books could make you cry.

In *Nutsack,* an unemployed butcher named Ike Karton contemplates a panoply of ersatz gods (albeit from his stoop in Hoboken, New Jersey). In *Gone with the Mind,* a son listens, rapt, as his elderly mother recounts the story of her life (albeit outside a Panda Express in a shopping mall food court). In *Last Orgy,* a father, nearing death, imparts what wisdom he's collected to his beloved adult daughter (albeit in a spoken-word karaoke bar in the fictional country of Chalazia).

Pre–the interregnum, Leyner's fiction had dazzled and careened and hummed with electric possibility. Post–the interregnum, Leyner's fiction still snapped with the familiar currents, but it had also become both more recursive and more expansive, less concerned with pop-cultural hijinks and more intrigued by the application of that familiar Leyner toolkit—gun-to-the-head comedy, stratospheric IQ, a literary mind that seems to have no precedent—to the tender dilemmas of later life, such as aging, parenting, and death.

"He demonstrates how much is still possible for the novel when tradition is left behind," wrote Bruce Sterling in an admiring consideration of *Last Orgy of the Divine Hermit,* "proving that fiction can be robust, provocative, and staggeringly inventive, without for a moment forfeiting entertainment."

Having laid his tools aside for a time, Leyner returned to reveal something surprising. Not that he could still do what no other novelist was attempting—for hadn't that been the challenge and the achievement all along?—but that he could use those tools to accomplish something he hadn't yet done himself. Novels that could break your heart. This reveal was well worth the wait.

Adam Sternbergh is an Edgar-nominated novelist and an editor at the *New York Times.* His writing has appeared in *New York* magazine, the *New York Times, GQ,* the *Independent on Sunday, The Walrus,* and elsewhere and has been collected in *The Best American Political Writing, The Best Technology Writing, Never Can Say Goodbye: Writers on Their Unshakable Love for New York,* and *New York Stories: Landmark Writing from Four Decades of New York Magazine.* His latest novel is *The Eden Test.*

EXCERPTS FROM
THE SUGAR FROSTED NUTSACK

THERE WAS NEVER *nothing*. But before the debut of the Gods, about fourteen billion years ago, things happened without any discernible context. There were no recognizable patterns. It was all incoherent. Isolated, disjointed events would take place, only to be engulfed by an opaque black void, their relative meaning, their *significance*, annulled by the eons of entropic silence that estranged one from the next. A terrarium containing three tiny teenage girls mouthing a lot of high-pitched gibberish (like Mothra's fairies, except for their wasted pallors, acne, big tits, and T-shirts that read "I Don't Do White Guys") would inexplicably materialize, and then, just as inexplicably, disappear. And then millions and millions of years would pass, until, seemingly out of nowhere, there'd be, fleetingly...the smell of fresh rolls. Then several more billion years of inert monotony...and then...a houndstooth pattern EVERY-WHERE for approximately 10^{-37} seconds...followed by, again, the fade to immutable blackness and another eternal interstice... and then, suddenly, what might be cicadas or the chafing sound of some obese jogger's nylon track pants...and then the sepia-tinged photograph from a 1933 *Encyclopedia Britannica* of a man with ele-phantiasis of the testicles...robots roasting freshly gutted fish at a river's edge...the strobe-like fulgurations of ultraviolet emission nebulae...the unmistakable sound of a koto being plucked...and then a toilet flushing. And this last enigmatic event—the flushing of a toilet—was followed by the most inconceivably long hiatus of them all, a sepulchral interregnum of several trillion years. And, as time went on, it began to seem less and less likely that another event would ever occur. Finally, nothing was taking place but the place. There was a definite room tone—that hum, that hymn to pure ontology—but that was all. And in this interminable void, in this black hyperborean stillness, deep in the farthest-flung recesses of empty space, at that vanishing point in the infinite distance where parallel lines ultimately converge...two headlights appeared. And there was the sound, barely audible, of something akin to the *Mister Softee* jingle. Now, of course, it wasn't the *Mister Softee* truck whose headlights, like stars light-years in the distance, were barely visible. And it wasn't the *Mister Softee* jingle per se. It was the beginning of something—a few recursive, foretokening measures of music that were curiously familiar, though unidentifiable, and addictively catchy—something akin to the beginning of "Surrey with the Fringe on Top" or "Under My Thumb" or "Tears of a Clown" or "White Wedding." And it repeated ad infinitum as those tiny twinkling headlights became imperceptibly larger and drew incrementally closer over the course of the million trillion years that it took for the Gods to finally arrive.

These drunken Gods had been driven by bus to a place they did not recognize. (It's almost as if they'd been on some sort of "Spring Break," as if they'd "gone wild.") At first, they were like frozen aphids. They were so out of it, as if in a state of suspended animation. It took them several more million years just to come to, to sort of "thaw out." The first God to emerge, momentarily, from the bus was called *El Brazo* ("The Arm"). Also known as *Das Unheimlichste des Unheimlichen* ("The Strangest of the Strange"), he was bare-chested and wore white/Columbia-blue polyester dazzle basketball shorts.

He would soon be worshipped as the God of Virility, the God of Urology, the God of Pornography, etc. El Brazo leaned out of the bus and struck a contrapposto pose, his head turned away from the torso, an image endlessly reproduced in paintings, sculptures, temple carvings, coins, maritime flags, postage stamps, movie studio logos, souvenir snow globes, take-out coffee cups, playing cards, cigarette packs, condom wrappers, etc. His pomaded hair swept back into a frothy nape of curls like the wake of a speedboat, he reconnoitered the void with an impassive, take-it-or-leave-it gaze, then scowled dyspeptically, immediately turned around, and returned to the bus, where he sullenly ensconced himself, along with the rest of the Gods, for another 1.6 million years. It's extraordinary that, among these sulking, hungover deities who chose to forever doze and fidget in a bus, there were several with enough joie de vivre to continue beatboxing that hypnotic riff for an eternity—that music that's been so persistently likened to a dance mix of the *Mister Softee* jingle. Perhaps it was a fragment of their alma mater's fight song. They did act, after all, like classmates, as if they'd grown up together in the same small town.

One of the first things the Gods did, once they sobered up and finally vacated that bus, was basically put things in order, make them comprehensible, provide context, institute recognizable patterns. (The Gods imposed coherence and meaning, one suspects, as an act of postbender penance.) And that spot in space where they'd fatefully decamped became consecrated forevermore as the celestial *downtown*, the capital of a very hip, but unforgiving, meritocracy. It was very much the Manhattan Project meets Warhol's Factory. And there was that chilly vibe of militant exclusivity, that cordon sanitaire, that velvet rope which segregated the Gods from everyone and everything else. From the outset, it was clear that these Gods had very rigid opinions about who *could* and who *couldn't* be part of their exclusive little clique. No socialites. No dilettantes. No one who was merely "famous for being famous." Just Gods. But their affect was so labile that, depending on your angle, they'd appear completely different from one instant to the next. It was like those lenticular greeting cards. There they'd be, ostensibly a group of elegantly accoutered eighteenth-century aristocrats, straight out of Watteau's rococo *Fête Galante* paintings, amorously cavorting in some sylvan glade with the lutes and the translucent parasols and the flying cupids…but if you shifted your vantage point ever so slightly, they'd look exactly like the members of some Japanese noise band smoking cigarettes backstage at All Tomorrow's Parties at Kutsher's Hotel in Monticello. One minute they'd have assumed the guise of a bunch of tan, well-heeled, ostentatiously casual CEOs chitchatting at the annual Allen & Company Sun Valley media conference…but then you'd tilt your head a bit, and they'd have metamorphosed into a little army of street urchins with matted hair and yellow eyes scavenging for food in garbage dumps, sucking on bags of glue. And because they were omniscient and so tight-knit, they could be very adolescent and pretentious in the way they flaunted their superiority. It wouldn't be unusual for a God to use Ningdu Chinese, Etruscan, Ket (a moribund language spoken by just five hundred people in central Siberia), Mexican Mafia prison code, Klingon, dolphin echolocation clicks, ant pheromones, and honeybee dance steps—all in one sentence. It's the kind of thing where you'd be like, was that *really* necessary?

Everything we are and know comes from the Gods. From their most phantasmagoric dreams and lurid hallucinations, we derive our mathematics and physics. Even their most offhanded mannerisms and nonchalant, lackadaisical gestures could determine the fundamental physical and temporal structures of our world. There was once a birthday party for the God of Money, *Doc Hickory,* who was also known as *El Más Gordo* ("The Fattest One"). Exhausted from feasting, El Más Gordo fell asleep on his stomach across his bed. *Lady Rukia* (the Goddess of Scrabble, Jellied Candies, and Harness Racing), who'd been lusting after El Más Gordo the entire night, crept stealthily into his bedroom, rubbed a squeaking balloon across the bosom of her cashmere sweater, and then waved it back and forth over his hairy back. The way the static electricity reconfigured the hair on his back would become the template for the drift of continental landmasses on Earth. Another great example would be, of course, the God *Rikidozen,* also known as *Santo Malandro* ("Holy Thug"). Rikidozen was once absently tapping a Sharpie on the lip of a coffee mug, and the unvarying cadence of that tap-tap-tap became the basis for the standard 124 beats-per-minute in house music. The Gods were the original (and ultimate) bricoleurs. They created almost everything from their own bodies. From their intestinal gas — their flatus — we get nitrous oxide, which we use today as a dental anesthetic and in our whipped cream aerosol cans (our "whippits"). From the silver-white secretions that crystallize in the corners of their eyes after a night's sleep, we obtain lithium, which we use to make rechargeable batteries for our cellphones and laptops. Once the God named *Koji Mizokami* had a small teratoma — a tumor with hair and teeth — removed from one of his testicles. He took it home and fashioned it into the composer Béla Bartók. He went outside in order to fling him into the future. But he wasn't sure into whose uterus (and into what epoch and milieu) he wanted to jettison the musical genius. Several Gods happened to be strolling by at that moment. They were the ones known as *The Pince-Nez 44s* or *Los Vatos Locos* ("The Crazy Guys"). Frequently, they had completely off-the-wall suggestions, but sometimes these actually turned out to be pretty decent ideas. "Why don't you have him born to a family of racist Mormons?" one of them suggested. Mizokami looked down at the wriggling larval Bartók in the palm of his hand. "I'm not at all sure about that," he said, in his languid drawl. And then someone else said, "Maybe it would be funnier if he were Joel Madden and Nicole Richie's son? Or make him a Taliban baby." (Eventually, of course, Mizokami-san decided to hurl Béla Bartók into the womb of a woman in Nagyszentmiklós, Austria-Hungary, in the 1880s.)

Generally, the proprietary realms of the Gods were organized and assigned in a very conscientious, collegial manner. There'd usually be some taxonomic category that would ensure a high degree of structural and/or functional relatedness among the various domains that fell under a particular God's purview. But, occasionally, the link between jurisdictions was so tenuous and slapdash that it smacked of reckless endangerment or criminal negligence. For instance, the giantess *C46*, the Goddess of Clear Thinking (i.e., *lucidity*) was, for a brief period, also the Goddess of Clear Skin! It's said that at the end of a long, grueling day, *Shanice* (the very cute, unfailingly effervescent Goddess who functioned as a sort of traffic manager at meetings) noticed that no one had claimed Clear Skin, and she was like, "C46, since you already do Clear Thinking, how about taking this one?" And everyone was so fried at that point that they all just shrugged and acquiesced. On the first Wednesday of the next month, though, everyone realized that Clear Skin should have obviously gone to the God of Dermatology, *José Fleischman* (who was sometimes called *The Jew from Peru*). And, without objection, C46 courteously relinquished the realm to The Jew from Peru (who was also known as *The Valiant One* and *He Who Never Shrinks from Anything Pus-Filled*). The point here is that even these kinds of remedial decisions were almost always made by consensus. But sometimes there were disagreements over turf which would escalate into savage internecine conflicts among the Gods, intractable conflicts with ever-widening ramifications.

El Burbuja, the God of Bubbles—a stubby, pockmarked, severely astigmatic deity—originally just ruled over the realm of inflated globules. At first, everyone assumed he'd be satisfied as a kind of geeky "party God" whose dominion would be limited to basically balloons and champagne. And no one paid much attention when he published an almost impenetrably technical paper in some obscure peer-reviewed journal in which he claimed sovereignty over Anything Enveloping Something Else. He then named himself, in rapid succession, God of Ravioli, God of Kishkes, God of Piñatas, God of Enema Bags, God of Chanel Diamond Forever Bags, God of Balloon Angioplasty, and then God of Balloon Swallowers (the drug smugglers who swallow condoms full of drugs). This then enabled him to proclaim himself God of the Movie *Maria Full of Grace*, which gave him entrée not only into the movie industry but—by simply parsing words in that title—into the music business. He immediately became God of the Song "How Do You Solve a Problem Like Maria" and then claimed the entire Rodgers and Hammerstein music catalogue as his own. This all happened, of course, millions of years before these songs were even written. A shrewd, uncannily prescient, and relentlessly enterprising businessman, El Burbuja quietly parlayed a series of discreet lateral "acquisitions"—kielbasa, snow globes, inflatable bounce houses, boba balls (the tapioca balls used in bubble tea), and soft gel encapsulation— into a vast empire of interlocking realms that included Asian magnesium smelting, automated slot machines, first-person shooter games, social networking websites, and iTunes—again, eons before any of these things existed. If ever there were a God destined to appear on the cover of *Cigar Aficionado* magazine, it would be El Burbuja. Probably the most stunning example of how El Burbuja tirelessly maneuvered under the radar to expand his empire is when he proclaimed himself God of Those Blue *New York Times* Bags People Use to Pick Up Their Dogs' Shit. The other Gods' initial reaction to this was, predictably, one of complete befuddlement. Who'd want *that*? But El Burbuja was playing many moves ahead of the others. He quickly assumed the mantle of God of Dogs, God of New York, and God of Shit. Again, this is before there was ever such a thing as "New York" or "dogs" or even "shit." (The Gods' excrement is called "loot drops." It's a slurry of coltan—the metallic ore used today in many cellphones and laptop computers.) No one seemed to even notice or particularly care when he took the next logical step and made himself God of Times, because all that really entailed was track and field records and multiplex showtimes (e.g., 11:50 am, 2:15 pm, 4:45 pm, 7:20 pm, 9:45 pm, 12:15 am). But then El Burbuja, on a late Friday afternoon before a long holiday weekend—and as he'd been planning to do all along—lopped the "s" off "Times" and became the God of Time. It was a characteristically ingenious, some might say cynical, even unscrupulous, ploy, but once everyone realized that what had appeared to be a proofreading correction was actually a coup of epic proportions, it was too late—they were presented with a fait accompli and had no other choice than to acquiesce. And that is how this unprepossessing, chubby God with the bad skin and the weak eyes parlayed jurisdiction over bags of warm crap into irrefutable control over one of the fundamental dimensions in the universe, thereby making himself one of the most formidable Gods in the whole fucking pantheon! But even though El Burbuja had clearly finagled for himself the vast Realm of Time, the other Gods continued to indulge the astigmatic "Mogul Magoo" (as he came to be called) basically because he was *so* homely and *such* an obsessive workaholic, and they just found his insatiable acquisitiveness sort of...*cute.* They'd say, "Oh, that's just how little Mogul Magoo rolls" or "Oh, that's just Mogul Magoo being Mogul Magoo." (And they knew, of course, that he was destined to become the tutelary divinity of plutocrats and rich, pampered celebrities.) Granted, sometimes the other Gods were like, "Magoo, what the fuck? Relax." But no one ever really felt like begrudging him the fruits of his monomaniacal labor. It was something relatively mundane that caused Magoo to run afoul of the irascible El Brazo, who sometimes referred to Magoo as *Fräulein Luftblase* ("Miss Bubble")— a taunting homophobic slur. Without any fanfare, one day, Magoo had asserted himself as the God of the Breast Implant and God of the Nutsack. He dutifully submitted his boilerplate rationale: Anything Enveloping Something Else. Just as a bubble is a globule of water that contains air, the scrotum is a pouch of skin and muscle that contains the testicles, and the breast implant is an elastomer-coated sac containing a thick silicone gel. Ergo, it's perfectly logical and reasonable to conclude that both spheres fall within my purview. This completely infuriated El Brazo, who, as the God of Urology and the God of Pornography, considered the nutsack and the breast implant his inviolable domains. The antipathy that developed between these two Gods (and, subsequently, between Magoo and the Goddess *La Felina*) would have significant consequences throughout the ages. El Brazo began to routinely, and very publicly, threaten Magoo and his cohorts with liquidation in a sort of Night of the Long Knives. And Magoo began traveling around with a posse of "Pistoleras"—half a dozen divine, ax-wielding mercenary vixens who were total fitness freaks with rock-hard bodies. Each of them had a venomous black mamba snake growing out of the back of her head, which she'd pull through the size-adjustment cutout on the back of her baseball cap. And this is the origin of today's fashion in which women gather their hair into a ponytail or a braid and allow it to hang through the hole in the backs of their caps.

The Gods used a drug called "Gravy," also known as *Pozole* ("stew"). Their drug use was heavy and appeared to be both ritualistic and recreational. At one time, it was considered to be what actually made the Gods deities, and there was speculation that consumption by human beings might bestow certain divine qualities on them. Gravy was originally thought to be a smokable version of the Vedic drug Soma and assumed to be hallucinogenic and derived from psilocybin mushrooms or *Amanita muscaria* (psychoactive basidiomycete fungus). Some have speculated that Gravy is a form of hallucinogenic borscht—a theory endorsed by such scholars as Mircea Eliade, Georges Dumezil, and University of Chicago professor of the history of religions Wendy Doniger. Today, though, many experts believe that Gravy is a solvent similar to what's found in glue, paint thinner, and felt-tip markers. This theory has gained considerable support among a wide range of prominent people, including TMZ's Harvey Levin, forensic pathologist

Cyril Wecht, criminal defense attorney Mark Geragos, and professional beach volleyball player Misty May-Treanor. Before the imbibing of Gravy, ritual protocol required the recitation of a sacred oath, and then the guest would clink his golden chalice against that of his divine host and solemnly ask, "You gonna shoot that or sip it?" There are about fourteen Weight Watchers Points in a half-cup serving of the rich hallucinogenic beverage. Smokable Gravy — made by heating liquid Gravy and baking soda until small pinkish-white precipitates ("rocks") form — is more quickly absorbed into the bloodstream, reaching the brain in about eight seconds. (Side effects can include: Progeria, Necrotizing Fasciitis, Bovine Spongiform Encephalopathy, Craniopagus Twins, Elephantiasis of the Testicles, Projectile Anal Hemorrhaging, and Gangrene of the Eyeballs.)

Yagyu — a God who was also known as *Dark Cuervo* ("Dark Raven") and *Fast-Cooking Ali* — created "Woman's Ass," which was considered his masterpiece. Nothing he'd done before prepared the other Gods for the stunning, unprecedented triumph that was "Woman's Ass." His previous accomplishments had been deliberately banal. He'd created the Platitude, for instance. When the Gods first *came to* — once they'd finally recovered from whatever dissipated spree they'd been on — they came to with a jolt, pulsing with intensity and ambition. They worked nonstop, didn't sleep, their pupils were dilated, they were jittery, quivering with nervous tics, and they talked incessantly — they had this self-indulgent, hyperintellectual diarrhea of the mouth. Like, instead of just muttering "Fuck," a God who cut himself shaving would launch into an anguished soliloquy in the iambic tetrameter of John Milton's *Il Penseroso*. And the simplest, most perfunctory questions, like "Hey, how's it going?" would elicit long, recondite Spinozan disquisitions on "attributes" and "modes" and discursive, inferential perception. Fast-Cooking Ali was a very shy, introspective, solitary individual. So he created a series of stock phrases that more reticent, self-effacing Gods like himself could use in response to the query "Hey, how's it going?" These included "It's going," "Hangin' in there," "Same shit, different day," and "If you want to live, don't come any closer." Fast-Cooking Ali's bromides quickly became part of the standard repertoire, but he pretty much disappeared from the scene and became a recluse and no one after that knew what he was working on or if he was even working on anything. It was said that he was spending his days holed up in a room somewhere, by himself, smoking Gravy, muttering to himself, lost in masturbatory fantasies about loop quantum gravity and supersymmetric particles. And then one day he emerged with "Woman's Ass." El Brazo was the first to see it. "That's so fucking hot! It's genius," he exclaimed, immediately summoning the other Gods. There was considerable discussion about hair—how much, how little (final decision: none on the cheeks, some along the perineum, downy fuzz above the crack)—and the pigmentation of the skin around the anus (final decision: slightly darker for white women). Despite the great acclaim he received for "Woman's Ass," Fast-Cooking Ali dropped out of sight again. Although it would not become public knowledge for millions of years, he had begun a very secret, very intense affair with La Felina, the Goddess of Humility. La Felina would, over the course of time, have many relationships with mortal men. She has a heavy sexual thing for Hasidic and Amish guys, as well as anarcho-primitivists, including Theodore Kaczynski (the Unabomber). Sometimes she wears a Japanese schoolgirl sailor outfit. La Felina hates the rich and she hates celebrities. (She has recently tried to induce a deranged person to stalk and kill the designer Marc Jacobs.) El Brazo is the God who fills our bodies with desires that can never be satisfied. But La Felina is the Goddess responsible for making ugly women more erotic than beautiful women.

The God of Head Trauma (who was also, of course, the God of Concussions, the God of Dementia, the God of Alcoholic

Blackouts, the God of Brainwashing, Implanted Thoughts, and Cultural Amnesia) was called *El Cucho* ("The Old Man"). This was a facetious epithet because El Cucho had a lustrously youthful appearance — a million-watt smile and a streaming surfer-boy mane of blond hair. He wore a tiger-skin loincloth. In the eternal schism between El Brazo and La Felina on one side versus Mogul Magoo and his snake-headed Pistoleras on the other, El Cucho (who was also known as "Kid Coma" and "XOXO") was firmly in the El Brazo / La Felina camp. XOXO liked sitting around with circus performers and hockey players and boxers and plying them with drugged sherbet. He liked to mess with people's minds — to make them forget things or put alien ideas in their heads. (Year after year, he was consistently voted both "Most Sadistic" *and* "Friendliest" God by his peers!) Once, he gave Pittsburgh Penguin center Evgeni Malkin a concussion during a game at Mellon Arena, and although Malkin's body (his "mortal husk") lay unconscious on the ice for about ten human-minutes, XOXO actually "kidnapped" Malkin's soul and took it to his garish hyperborean hermitage miles beneath the earth's surface in what is now Antarctica, where he kept it captive for two and a half God-years. There was a suffocatingly sweet smell at the hermitage, as if Eggnog Febreze was being continuously pumped in through the ventilation system. XOXO served Malkin's soul drugged sherbet, which made Malkin's soul woozy and disinhibited enough that it agreed to be dressed up in a U.S. Marines tank top and PVC diaper briefs. Then the two of them played a card game called snarples, and every so often XOXO would chastely kiss Malkin's soul on the mouth. Then XOXO shampooed and cornrowed Malkin's soul's hair, and, using a sharp periodontal curette, he carved short secret phrases into the furrows on his scalp (like "Puppy Love" and "Book Club" and "New You"). It was creepy. Each time XOXO would kiss him, he'd exhale fervently into his mouth. It was really more like CPR than making out. XOXO's breath was like mentholated Freon. And when Malkin finally came to on the ice at Mellon Arena, he pawed violently at his throat saying over and over again in Russian, "My uvula is frozen!" All Malkin could remember was being given a ticker tape parade. But then he realized with a shudder that it wasn't ticker tape at all but the gossamer scales of his own molting mind that were falling all over the streets of Pittsburgh! XOXO also delighted in abducting legal proofreaders from midtown office buildings in the middle of the night and taking their souls to his remote, sweet-scented hermitage, where he'd keep them captive and toy with them for years. They'd wake up back in their office cubicles thinking they'd lost consciousness from anaphylactic allergic reactions to ingesting peanuts in candy bars they'd gotten out of the vending machines. XOXO had once shown a poem he'd written to Shanice, the irrepressibly chipper Goddess of Management—the adorable one with the awesome organizational skill set—and her reaction was uncharacteristically negative. XOXO had literally asked for it, though. He had explicitly requested that Shanice not give him one of those glib "Oh, it's really great!" responses, but to take her time, read it over carefully, and provide him with a very honest critique. And he told her, furthermore, that the more unsparing the critique was, the more meaningful it would be to him, and that he was only showing the poem to her because he considered her the most trustworthy of all the Gods and he could depend on her, and only her, to be completely candid with him. What Shanice didn't realize at the time—although she would eventually—was that the offering of the poem was a gesture of seduction. Not that the content of the poem was seductive per se—it was not a "love poem" in any sense. The poem depicts a group of businessmen who are returning home from work one evening. On a lark, they diverge from their customary route and end up deep in the woods. They gang up on the "new guy" (someone who'd only recently been transferred to their division), and, in what appears to be a sort of hazing ritual, they tie him to a tree and whip him with his own belt. His pants fall to his ankles, and it's obvious that he's aroused. *But*—as the poem goes on to suggest—he's aroused not by the robust flagellation but because he sees an ineffably beautiful butterfly flit by. Everyone had always considered XOXO to be kind of frivolous. He actively pursued his hobby of snatching hockey players' souls and messing with their minds and whatnot, but he didn't seem to apply himself diligently to much of anything else. He came across as something of a dilettante and an underachiever. XOXO thought that the poem would show Shanice a more serious side and a more delicately registered sensibility than he was usually given credit for. Shanice had always assumed that XOXO was unequivocally gay—something confirmed, in her mind, by the homoerotic tenor of the poem. One could certainly discern an element of shame in the poem or at least a desire on the part of the poem's protagonist to displace or mitigate the cause of his arousal. And Shanice did, in fact, discern this strain of discomfort in the poem. She wasn't at all what she seemed either. And, in this way, she had a great deal in common with XOXO. They both felt underestimated by the other Gods. (It was Shanice's sense that the other Gods considered her to be affable and competent, but basically pedestrian.) Anyway, if Shanice had realized at the time that XOXO was offering her the poem to read and critique as a gesture of seduction, she probably would have finessed her evaluation a bit. But she didn't. And it was quite a blow. The incident made things tense between Shanice and XOXO, left them somewhat estranged, and undoubtedly influenced Shanice—whether she was conscious of it or not—to align herself with Mogul Magoo (on whom she soon developed an insane crush). It also left XOXO embittered and implacably hostile to anyone who ever tried to put his or her thoughts and feelings into words. And so XOXO, this resentful poet manqué, became the God who delights in spitefully snatching brilliant thoughts from people's minds and casting them into oblivion. When you're lying in bed, in that hypnagogic state, neither awake nor asleep, and you have a lovely idea that seems to evanesce almost as soon as you're conscious of it—that's XOXO snatching it away. And when you're high and you have an extraordinarily inspired and unprecedented idea and then you wake up the next day and have to glumly acknowledge how banal and derivative it actually was—that's also XOXO's doing. During the night he came down and sabotaged the idea, gutted it—leaving only the banal and derivative. He keeps a vast cache of stolen ideas in his hyperborean hermitage.

WHY DO GODS LIKE HAVING SEX WITH HUMANS SO MUCH?

For them it's a kind of slumming, rough trade, a *nostalgie de la boue* ("nostalgia for the mud"). And many of the Gods—including several of the *major* deities—feel that human beings' finite life expectancies and their comparatively limited intelligence simply make them SUPER-SEXY! These Gods find human existential angst—being aware that death is inevitable, but not knowing, at any given moment, exactly when or how it might occur—to be a total TURN-ON! They paradoxically find those very characteristics that so definitively subordinate human beings to the Gods—mortality, benightedness, and impotence—to be HOT, HOT! HOT!! And the very thought of abjectly defiling themselves—of *wallowing*—in all the pungent excretions and effluvia of the human body maddens them with desire. This is the good news. The bad news is that, for a human, having a sexual/romantic relationship with a God can be a daunting, traumatic, and even tragic experience. You have to be very careful! Gods are self-important. They tend to have ADD. They love to fuck with your head. Because they're immortal, they tend to be late all the time. And because they're omnipotent, they usually exhibit a complete lack of empathy. They are narcissistic and furiously self-absorbed. If they want to have sex with you, it doesn't really matter to them how you're feeling or what you're going through. So don't expect understanding or patience from a God just because you're getting your period or you have to study for your SATs or you're leaving the next day for a tour of duty in Afghanistan. And if a God does seem to evince some concern or betray any vulnerability, you have to be very skeptical because their behavior is frequently insincere and manipulative. And they're supermercurial and you have to always put up with their cryptic moods and petulant fatwas. And they can come and go (i.e., materialize and disappear) so that no one else can see them — which can make you feel very isolated from other people. Mi-Hyun, age twenty-nine, worked at a florist shop. She was *very* pretty. She had a pageboy with cute blunt-cut bangs. One day, *Bosco Hifikepunye,* the God of Miscellany (including Fibromyalgia, Chicken Tenders, Sports Memorabilia, SteamVac Carpet Cleaners, etc., etc.) espied Mi-Hyun as she smoked a Parliament Light outside the florist shop. He couldn't believe how HOT she was! And soon the God and his "Little Flower Girl" were having completely insane sex-a-thons. But, of course, Hifikepunye would arrive and depart invisibly, unbeknownst to anyone but Mi-Hyun. Mi-Hyun's neighbors — the old Dominican ladies — would always tease her: "You're a pretty girl, Mi-Hyun. When are you going to get a boyfriend?" And Mi-Hyun would be like, "I have boyfriend. He visit me every night." "But we never see him," the old ladies would reply. "We never see *anyone* visit you." And soon they started to think that Mi-Hyun was crazy. At first, it didn't really bother Mi-Hyun. She was too happy. The God, Hifikepunye, was GREAT in bed! He'd anoint her clitoris with Witches' Flying Ointment (aka *Lamiarum Unguenta* or "Witches' Unguent"), a mixture of Gravy, belladonna, chimney soot, clove oil, and the fat of an unbaptized child. Once he made her fifty feet tall and put the mummified body of King Tutankhamen into her ass as she came. She liked that so much that he turned Lenin's corpse and Ted Williams's cryonically preserved head into anal sex toys too! These are things that, of course, Mi-Hyun would excitedly tell her coworkers at the florist shop the next morning, but they would just shake their heads and say, "Mi-Hyun, you need to see a psychiatrist." Soon Mi-Hyun was let go from the florist shop. And she became alienated from her neighbors. And, worst of all, the Goddess Lady Rukia (Scrabble, Jellied Candies, Harness Racing), who coveted Hifikepunye and was jealous of his mortal paramour, gave Mi-Hyun periodontal disease so she'd have bad breath and bleeding gums and be less alluring to the God. Sure enough, Hifikepunye lost interest in her and stopped coming around. (One Christmas, he felt guilty and put a winning Pick 6 Lotto number into one of her dreams. But XOXO made her forget it as soon as she woke up.) Heartbroken, lonely, penniless, and now dying from the high levels of bacterial endotoxins that her infected gums had released into her bloodstream, Mi-Hyun lay across the tracks at the West Side Rail Yards one freezing night and waited for a freight train to end her misery....She was picked up by the police and brought to the Emergency Room at Bellevue Hospital where she was admitted with a fever of 104 degrees, refractory hypotension, tachypnea, and a white blood cell count of 14,000 cells/mm^3. She was immediately administered oxygen, fluids, and antibiotics and transferred to the ICU where she was given an APACHE II score of 25 and diagnosed with severe sepsis. She was put on norepinephrine and a continuous infusion of piperacillin-tazobactam with aminoglycoside. Three weeks later, it was determined that she was healthy enough to be transferred to the psychiatric unit. After telling psychiatrists and nurses about her sexual liaisons with the God Bosco Hifikepunye and about how he made her fifty feet tall and used Ted Williams's cryonically preserved head as an anal sex toy and about how XOXO, the God of Dementia and Implanted Thoughts, had made her forget the winning Pick 6 Lotto number that Hifikepunye had hidden in her dreams and about how Lady

Rukia, the Goddess of Scrabble and Jellied Candies, in a jealous rage, had given her periodontal disease that eventually developed into endotoxemia and sepsis...she was diagnosed with paranoid schizophrenia and put on 15 mg per day of the antipsychotic drug Zyprexa. When she failed to respond to the medication (i.e., when she continued to insist upon the veracity of her stories about the Gods), she was given electro-convulsive therapy four times a week for the following several months. And although this resulted in severe retrograde amnesia (she no longer has *any* memories of her parents or her childhood), her memory of being fifty feet tall and fucking a God remains vividly intact. And this memory, like a single calligraphic stroke on the white page of her erased mind, caused a dreamy smile to permanently settle across the catatonic impassivity of her face. XOXO had ineradicably inscribed the memory in Mi-Hyun's mind at the behest of La Felina (who detests the vain, the rich, the celebrated and champions the humble, the indigent, the anonymous, the unknown and inaccessible, the marginalized, the deranged, the antimodernists, the anarcho-primitivists, the fanatical Luddites, the bedraggled, plump, sweaty working-class women with hairy pussies, etc.). The Gods glorify chosen mortals ("the elect") by having XOXO ineradicably inscribe in their minds the story of the Gods. Now this particular story brings up a very interesting point about the Gods and their complex and often opaque relationships. Why would XOXO ineradicably inscribe into the mind of a mortal woman an amorous memory about Bosco Hifikepunye (who was also sometimes known as *Cara de Papa* ["Potato Face"])? After all, wasn't XOXO aligned with the El Brazo / La Felina / Fast-Cooking Ali axis, which generally contended against the Mogul Magoo / Shanice / Lady Rukia / Hifikepunye camp? Yes, but although the Gods' roiling antipathies and interpersonal feuds were genuine and their larger schisms intractable and polarizing, they constituted, in the grand scheme of things, a kind of "play." The Gods disported themselves by endlessly acting out their essential natures, the affirmation of their own wills and the fulfillment of their own desires—this "sport" perpetually reproducing (as if inadvertently) the harsh patterns and eternal recurrences of human life. The settlement of divine differences inevitably results in human collateral damage for which the Gods feel absolutely no responsibility or remorse. But the bonds of kinship among them are indestructible. And their protocol—their lordly code of precedence and etiquette vis-à-vis one another—as inscrutable as it will forever remain to us, is scrupulously observed, without dissent, by them. When, by some unspoken consensus, the Gods determine to glorify a chosen mortal by having XOXO ineradicably inscribe in his or her mind the story of the Gods, it's done, regardless of whomever's proxy or fuck-buddy that mortal might have been. Just as when, by some unspoken consensus, the Gods determined one day that their Belle Époque was over and that it was time to disperse for a while, for each God and Goddess to go his or her own way.

During the Belle Époque—that period of time, about fourteen billion years ago, after the Gods were delivered by bus from some sort of "Spring Break" during which they are said to have "gone wild"—the Gods put things in order, made them comprehensible, provided context, imposed coherence and meaning, i.e., they created the world as we know it today. But although, as it's been said, they abide by a stern, hieratic protocol, these Gods—Rikidozen, Los Vatos Locos, José Fleischman, The Pistoleras, etc.—when viewed from a certain perspective, can seem like harebrained cartoon characters lurching haphazardly from one debacle to another, motivated as much by mischievousness and perversity as anything resembling intent or design. For instance, most of the butt-calls that people make today are the result of bored Gods just fucking around. And a lot of the weird, unexplained things that happen to people in Florida are the work of the Gods. In a Gravy-fueled tantrum one night in a Pensacola Motel 6, the Dwarf Goddess *La Muñeca*

("The Doll") turned her mortal girlfriend Francesca DiPasquale, a Chief Warrant Officer in the U.S. Navy, into a macadamia nut, then a jai alai ball, and then into 100,000 shares of Schering-Plough stock. How credible did Pensacola chief of police Ellis Moynihan consider speculation that a lesbian Dwarf Goddess high on a smokable form of hallucinogenic borscht called "Gravy" might have turned the missing DiPasquale into Schering-Plough stock? In other words—was Moynihan one of the *elect*, one of the *illuminati*? Unfortunately, we'll never know. Two weeks after DiPasquale disappeared, Moynihan died of anaphylactic shock from a severe allergic reaction to peanuts in a vending machine candy bar. Strange, isn't it? Moynihan had never previously shown *any* symptoms of even a mild sensitivity to peanuts. In fact, he *loved* peanuts and consumed them in such quantities that his coworkers in the squad room had begun referring to him as *El Hombre Elefante* ("The Elephant Man"). (Although, perhaps, as Desk Sergeant Nate Seabrook confided with a nudge and a wink, that nickname actually derived from the massive plexiform neurofibroma that obscured half of Moynihan's face.) Stranger still—when officers looked frantically for the epinephrine auto-injector in the emergency first-aid kit, they found that someone had replaced it with a whippet, a small cartridge of nitrous oxide (aka "Laughing Gas"). A taunting cosmic joke? Yeah, maybe. But what does this wild oscillation between the sublime (e.g., the creation of musical harmony, the electromagnetic spectrum, prime numbers and the Riemann Zeta Function, etc.) and the gratuitously sadistic (e.g., giving someone a grotesquely disfiguring facial tumor) reveal to us about the Gods? La Muñeca was the Goddess of Architecture—she designed some of the most spectacular of the Gods' hyperborean hermitages, in addition to the huge biomorphic resin and silicone dining table for the Hall of the Slain that's considered as radical today as it was eleven billion years ago when she first impulsively sketched the design on a napkin at a club! Doesn't sabotaging a first-aid kit in a Pensacola, Florida, police station so that someone suffocates to death, someone whose only offense seems to have been suspecting that you turned your girlfriend into a jai alai ball when you were high—doesn't this, in addition to being mind-bogglingly petty and vindictive, seem like a colossal waste of time for the Goddess of Architecture? Well, first of all, a God would contend, you can't waste something of which you have an inexhaustible supply. And secondly, since anything a God does is an expression of that God's essential nature and thus imparts meaning and transfigures the manifold totality of the real, gradations of significance don't exist—everything is equally important.

Think of the sweetest, most wonderful things you've ever experienced in your life...just randomly, off the top of your head... things as ineffably sublime as the beautiful butterfly which aroused the businessman in XOXO's poem....Now, make a list. For instance:

- It's 1960 in Jersey City and you're falling asleep in your mom's lap on a Hudson Boulevard bus to the metronomic cadence of the windshield wipers and the sound of the tires on the rainy street, and sitting all around you are nuns and stooped gray men in fedoras.
- Egg-drop soup and egg rolls at the Jade Restaurant in Journal Square, Jersey City.
- The gurgle of water coolers and the pungent aroma of legal accordion folders in the supply room at 26 Journal Square.
- Mid-1960s, late afternoon, drinking Yoo-hoo with your dad at the driving range, and then, later that night, sitting in front of the TV with him and the intro for *Combat!* comes on ("*Combat!* Starring Vic Morrow and Rick Jason"), and your dad offers you a stick of Black Jack gum.
- Eating tea sandwiches with your mom at the Bird Cage in Lord & Taylor, in Millburn, New Jersey.

- The first movie scenes that gave you a hard-on: when seaman John Mills (played by Richard Harris) gets flogged with a cat-o'-nine-tails in *Mutiny on the Bounty* (also Harris's O-Kee-Pa suspension initiation ritual in *A Man Called Horse*); and when Candace Hilligoss gets out of the bathtub in *Carnival of Souls* (to creepy organ music), also the scene where Candace Hilligoss tries different stations on the car radio (but can only get creepy organ music), and the scene where Candace Hilligoss takes her clothes off in the dressing room at the department store (to creepy organ music); and also when Martine Carol emerges from her bathtub in *Lucrèce Borgia* (aka *Sins of the Borgias*), and also, in the same movie, when she's whipped by her brother, Cesare (played by Pedro Armendáriz).
- That moment in the early '90s when there were three made-for-TV movies about Amy Fisher: *The Amy Fisher Story* (Drew Barrymore), *Amy Fisher: My Story* (Noelle Parker), and *Casualties of Love: The Long Island Lolita Story* (Alyssa Milano); and then, soon, Tonya Harding and Jeff Gillooly's "Wedding Video" sex tape came out.
- That total goose bump moment in the Pet Shop Boys song "What Have I Done to Deserve This?" when Dusty Springfield starts to sing ("Since you went away, I've been hanging around / I've been wondering why I'm feeling down").
- In 2004, the long-awaited pedestrian bridge over Kennedy Boulevard (formerly Hudson Boulevard) links the East Campus and the West Campus of St. Peter's College in Jersey City.
- Nice and drunk on Chivas Regal, eating ravioli, first heavy snow falling outside, fat girl at the bar (nice and drunk too) smiles at you.

Each of these numinous moments, these epiphanies, is *of the Gods, a manifestation,* a *Godding* (*Götterung*), and in each we are able to unmistakably discern the hand of a specific God. Mogul Magoo's fingerprints are all over those egg rolls at the Jade in Journal Square. And, surely, we can identify, in the pedestrian bridge that spans Kennedy Boulevard, linking the two campuses of St. Peter's College, the animating spirit of La Muñeca. And who else could have been behind the unprecedented phenomenon of Amy Fisher and Tonya Harding but La Felina, the fanatical champion of unsublimated passion and base motives, who glories in authentic intensities like lust, jealousy, and vengeance? The Fisher/Harding upheaval seemed to augur an astonishing revolution in the sociology of glamour—the erotic exaltation of the homely, unscrupulous, working-class girl. But it was so short-lived as to actually be a last gasp, because reality entertainment almost immediately reverted to a depressingly predictable perversion of all that, exalting instead the Hilton/Richie/Kardashian axis of "beautiful" celebutantes. This development so infuriated La Felina that, at one point, she was about to unleash a hybrid of Charles Manson and Pol Pot on America to completely purge it of every single "beautiful" celebutante when Fast-Cooking Ali dissuaded her at the very last minute, not because he was against the idea but because they were incredibly late to something, and La Felina—who exalts the physically deformed and the mentally unbalanced and the sans-culottes and the scum of the earth, and who wet her pants during the September Massacres of 1792—decided to shelve the plan for another time.

By some unspoken consensus, the Gods determined one day that their Belle Époque was over and that it was time to disperse for a while, for each God and Goddess to go his or her own way. This was the Diaspora of the Gods. Several stayed in the vicinity of the Gods' original "bus stop," which experts have speculatively situated in the Abell 1835 Galaxy, some 13 billion light-years from Earth, while others place it in the Markarian 421 Galaxy, which is located in the constellation Ursa Major, a mere 360 million light-years away. Some Gods (e.g., El Brazo), of course, moved into Versailles-like coral and onyx palaces and sumptuous frangipani-scented hermitages miles underground in what is now Antarctica. Los Vatos Locos submerged themselves in a peat bog in Denmark for several million years. While some pursued esoteric, purely theoretical existences in strange, impalpable, zero-dimensional realms, others chose drab, quotidian lives (à la Jenny from the block) in small cities in the Midwest. Mogul Magoo, Shanice, and the Pistoleras inhabited the lush mountains of the Gondwana supercontinent. Lady Rukia and Doc Hickory lived on a cul-de-sac in Chula Vista, California. The lovers La Felina and Fast-Cooking Ali—both avatars of humility and self-denial—shrunk themselves down to about three micrometers tall (the size of a typical yeast cell) and lived in the anal scent-gland of a capybara named *Dawson* in the remote Caura forest in southern Venezuela. And then, one day in 1973, by some unspoken consensus, the Gods determined that their Diaspora was over and that they would all reconvene and, from here on in, occupy the top floors of the world's tallest and most opulent skyscraper. Thus began a nomadic period during which the Gods constantly moved, en masse, from what had become the former tallest-building-in-the-world to the latest tallest-building-in-the-world. So, in the summer of 1973, the Gods and Goddesses all moved into the top floors of the Sears Tower (now known as the Willis Tower) in Chicago, Illinois. They then relocated, in 1998, to the Petronas Twin Towers in Kuala Lumpur, Malaysia; the Taipei 101 in Taiwan, in 2004; the Shanghai World Financial Center in China, in 2008; and finally, in 2009, the Burj Khalifa in the Business Bay district of Dubai, United Arab Emirates. The Burj Khalifa is 2,717 feet tall. And this is where the Gods currently reside.

* * *

The Sugar Frosted Nutsack is the story of a man, a mortal, an unemployed butcher, in fact, who lives in Jersey City, New Jersey, in a two-story brick house that is approximately twenty feet tall. This man is the hero IKE KARTON. The epic ends with Ike's violent death. If only Ike had used for his defense "silence, exile, and cunning." But that isn't Ike. Ike is the Warlord of his Stoop. Ike is a man who is "singled out." A man marked by fate. A man of Gods, attuned to the Gods. A man anathematized by his neighbors. A man beloved by La Felina and Fast-Cooking Ali, and a man whose mind is ineradicably inscribed by XOXO. Ike's brain is riddled with the tiny, meticulous longhand of the mind-fucking God XOXO, whose very name bespeaks life's irreconcilable contradictions, symbolizing both *love* (hugs and kisses) and *war* (the diagramming of football plays).

What will give us goose bumps and make us teary-eyed when, in the end, Ike dies? It's the same thing that gave us goose bumps and made us teary-eyed when we heard Dusty Springfield sing "Since you went away, I've been hanging around / I've been wondering why I'm feeling down" in the song "What Have I Done to Deserve This?" It's the same thing that makes all pop music so heartbreaking. Even when Miley Cyrus sings "So I put my hands up, they're playin' my song / The butterflies fly away / I'm noddin' my head like 'Yeah!' / Movin' my hips like 'Yeah!'" in her song "Party in the U.S.A." It's that chirping mirth against a backdrop of despair, that juxtaposition of blithe optimism against all the crushing brutalities and inadequacies of life. The image of an ineffably beautiful butterfly flitting by the shattered windows of a dilapidated, abandoned factory is not so poignant because it highlights the indomitable life force. To the contrary, the butterfly (and the pop song) is like a PowerPoint cursor; it's there to whet our perception of and strengthen our affinity for what's moribund, for what's always dying before our eyes. Loving the moribund is our way of signaling the dead from this shore: "We are your kinsmen…"

When Ike dies, at the hands of the ATF snipers or Mossad assassins or Interpol agents, or is beset by a swarm of nanodrones (depending on which story you choose to believe), he dies with a metaphysical coquettishness that befits a true hero, greeting his violent demise with silly, sweet, uninhibited laughter. All the Gods are suddenly talking at once; it's this Babel, this incomprehensible cacophony, that just degenerates into white noise. And then it's as if he's stepped into an empty elevator shaft on the top floor of the world's tallest building, and as he plummets down, he whistles the *Mister Softee* jingle—"those recursive, foretokening measures of music; that hypnotic riff"—over and over and over and over again to himself...

A hero.

1.

*What subculture is evinced by **Ike**'s clothes and his shtick, by the non-semitic contours of his nose and his dick, by the feral fatalism of all his loony tics — like the petit-mal fluttering of his long-lashed lids and the **Mussolini** torticollis of his Schick-nicked neck, and the staring and the glaring and the daring and the hectoring, and the tapping on the table with his aluminum wedding ring, as he hums those tunes from his childhood albums and, after a spasm of **Keith Moon** air-drums, returns to his lewd mandala of Italian breadcrumbs?*

So begins the story of **Ike Karton,** a story variously called throughout history **Ike's** *Agony, T.G.I.F. (Ten Gods I'd Fuck),* and *The Sugar Frosted Nutsack.* This is a story that's been told, how many times?— over and over and over again, essentially verbatim, with the same insistent, mesmerizing cadences, and the same voodoo tapping of a big clunky ring against some table.

Every new improvisational flourish, every editorial interpolation and aside, every ex post facto declaration, exegetical commentary and meta-commentary, every cough, sniffle, and hiccough on the part of the rhapsode is officially subsumed into the story, and is then required in each subsequent performance. So, for instance, the next time *The Sugar Frosted Nutsack* is recited, the audience will expect that the sentence "Every new improvisational flourish, every editorial interpolation and aside, every ex post facto declaration, exegetical commentary and meta-commentary, every cough, sniffle, and hiccough on the part of the rhapsode is officially subsumed into the story, and is then required in each subsequent performance" be included in the recitation, and if it's not, they'll feel — and justifiably so — that something vital and integral has been left out.

The audience will, in fact, demand that the sentence "So, for instance, the next time *The Sugar Frosted Nutsack* is recited, the audience will expect that the sentence 'Every new improvisational flourish, every editorial interpolation and aside, every ex post facto declaration, exegetical commentary and meta-commentary, every cough, sniffle, and hiccough on the part of the rhapsode is officially subsumed into the story, and is then required in each subsequent performance' be included in the recitation, and if it's not, they'll feel — and justifiably so — that something vital and integral has been left out" *also* be included in the recitation. And also the sentence that begins "The audience will, in fact, demand that the sentence 'So, for instance, the next time *The Sugar Frosted Nutsack* is recited, the audience will expect that the sentence "Every new improvisational flourish...,"'" etc. And also the sentence that begins "And also the sentence that begins..." And also the sentence that begins "And also the sentence that begins 'And also the sentence that begins...'" Et cetera, et cetera.

To a critical degree, this infinite recursion of bracketed redundancies is what gives *The Sugar Frosted Nutsack* its peculiarly numinous and incantatory quality. Everything *about* it becomes *it*.

Keep in mind that the original story (what we've gleaned from cave walls, cuneiform on clay tablets, and papyrus fragments) was only one paragraph long, consisting in its entirety of: *What subculture is evinced by **Ike**'s clothes and his shtick, by the non-semitic contours of his nose and his dick, by the feral fatalism of all his loony tics—like the petit-mal fluttering of his long-lashed lids and the **Mussolini** torticollis of his Schick-nicked neck, and the staring and the glaring and the daring and the hectoring, and the tapping on the table with his aluminum wedding ring, as he hums those tunes from his childhood albums and, after a spasm of **Keith Moon** air-drums, returns to his lewd mandala of Italian breadcrumbs?*

For hundreds, even thousands, of years, this was all there was to the "epic" story of **Ike**, the 5'7" unemployed butcher, incorrigible heretic, and feral dandy who slicked his jet-black hair back with perfumed pomade and dyed his armpit hair a light chestnut color and who was dear to the Gods (themselves ageless, deathless).

Then, sometime circa 700 B.C., the subhead <u>**Ike** Always Keeps It Simple and Sexy</u> was added. And over the ensuing centuries, as this was told and retold, and with the accretion of new material with each successive iteration, the complete story that we all know today as *The Sugar Frosted Nutsack* came into being.

Don't expect soaring "epic" rhetoric from the 5'7" forty-eight-year-old **Ike Karton. Ike**'s first extended speech wholly concerns itself with the mundanity of breakfast. ("I can't decide what to have for breakfast today. I don't want something *breakfasty*—that's the problem. You know what I'd really like? A shawarma and a malt. But you can't find good shawarma in this fuckin' town now that it's full of Jews and Freemasons….I'm *serious!* So I'm either gonna have a pastrami and sliced beef tongue with cole slaw and Russian dressing on rye and a Sunkist orange soda, or maybe just a big bowl of Beefaroni and some chocolate milk or something.") He's an unassuming, plainspoken (albeit delusional and antisemitic) man. He speaks with the air of a hero accustomed to—even weary of—fame (even though he's completely unknown outside the small Jersey City neighborhood of attached and identical two-story brick homes where he's considered an unstable and occasionally menacing presence—although it must be added that women overwhelmingly find him extremely charming and sexy, and many suspect that **Ike** playacts his indefensible antisemitism only to make himself a more loathsome pariah on his block, i.e., to make himself even *more* charming and sexy).

As you hear this or read it, the God **XOXO** is indelibly inscribing it into your brain. But **XOXO** is a puzzling figure. It's not possible to characterize him as "good" or "bad"—these terms are meaningless when applied to the Gods. He's mischievous—a trickster. Though frequently innocuous or merely "naughty," his meddling can cause enormous inconvenience and suffering, i.e., it can be wicked in its consequences. And it certainly seems as if he often acts under the compulsion of his own ancient grievances—primarily the humiliation he suffered when the Goddess **Shanice** criticized his poem about the businessman who became so terribly aroused when he was flogged in the woods by some of his colleagues. Like some disturbed stenographer, interjecting his own thoughts into the court record, **XOXO** will constantly try to insinuate his own lurid "poetry" into this story. For instance, you will soon come upon the unfortunate passage "Pumping her shiksa ass full of hot Jew jizz." Now that may be an appropriate phrase for some **Philip Roth** novel, but it has no place in *The Sugar Frosted Nutsack*. This is a perfect example of a gratuitous interpolation on the part of **XOXO**. This is **XOXO**—the embittered poet manqué—trying to ruin the book, trying to give the book Tourette's, trying to kidnap the soul of the book and ply it with drugged sherbet. And make no mistake about it—he *will* try to kidnap the soul of the book and ply it with drugged sherbet.

You can actually help preserve the integrity of *The Sugar Frosted Nutsack*. You can help wrest control of the story back from **XOXO**. When you come upon a patently adventitious phrase, one that can, with a reasonable degree of certainty, be attributed to **XOXO**, like

"Pumping her shiksa ass full of hot Jew jizz," you can ward off the meddlesome mind-fucking God with the rapid staccato chant of **"Ike, Ike, Ike, Ike, Ike!"** It should sound like **Popeye** laughing, or like **Billy Joel** in "Movin' Out (Anthony's Song)"—"But working too hard can give you / A heart attack, ack, ack, ack, ack, ack." It's similar to that moment when, after **Captain Hook** has poisoned **Tinkerbell, Peter Pan** asks the audience to clap their hands if they believe in fairies, or when, in *The Tempest,* **Prospero** beseeches the audience, in the play's epilogue, to "Release me from my bands / With the help of your good hands….As you from crimes would pardoned be, / Let your indulgence set me free." But remember, when you chant **"Ike, Ike, Ike, Ike, Ike!"** to fend off the spiteful interpolations of **XOXO**, it absolutely has to sound like **Popeye** laughing or like **Billy Joel** in "Movin' Out (Anthony's Song)," or it won't work.

2.

EACH SECTION OF *The Sugar Frosted Nutsack* is called a "session." The sessions were produced—over the course of hundreds, even thousands, of years—by nameless, typically blind men high on ecstasy or ketamine, sipping orange soda from a large hollowed-out gourd or a communal bucket or a jerrycan. The brand of orange soda traditionally associated with *The Sugar Frosted Nutsack* is Sunkist.

The first session, the ninety-six-word paragraph beginning with the phrase *"What subculture is evinced by **Ike**'s clothes and his shtick, by the non-semitic contours of his nose and his dick"* is considered the only original session. Everything else is considered a later addition to, or a corruption of, that original session. But if one were to recite or perform only the original session without all the later additions and corruptions, the audience would feel—and justifiably so—cheated. And they would probably feel completely justified in killing and ritualistically dismembering and cannibalizing the blind, drug-addled bard. At the very least, they'd demand their money back.

Some experts have gone so far as to propose the hypothesis that that "original" ninety-six-word paragraph is itself an addition and a corruption, and that the only true, historically valid version of *The Sugar Frosted Nutsack* (the urtext) is the four-word phrase "The Sugar Frosted Nutsack." They surmise that blind men high on ecstasy, seated in a circle, and sipping orange soda from a jerrycan would chant the words "The Sugar Frosted Nutsack" over and over and over again, for hours upon hours, usually until dawn. As time went on, a stray word or phrase would be appended, resulting, eventually, in the ninety-six-word paragraph now generally accepted as part of the first session, under the subtitle: **Ike Always Keeps It Simple and Sexy**.

The Sugar Frosted Nutsack was never actually "written." A recursive aggregate of excerpts, interpolations, and commentaries, it's been "produced" through layering and augmentation, repetition and redundancy. Composition has tended to more closely resemble the loop-based step sequencing we associate with Detroit techno music than with traditional "writing."

5.

POOR, POLYTHEISTICALLY DEVOUT, sex-obsessed **Ike**, cosseted and buffeted by his Gods, their marionette. With the exception of his own family, and possibly his daughter's louche, drug-peddling boyfriend, **Vance** (who finds **Ike** endlessly entertaining and secretly reveres him), no one else in **Ike**'s neighborhood of modest two-story brick homes or perhaps the world (though, for **Ike**, his neighborhood *is* The World) seems to believe in the Gods. So, from a certain psychiatric perspective, one could say that the **Karton** family is clearly and deliberately portrayed as suffering from a form of *folie à famille*—a clinical syndrome in which a psychotic disorder is shared by an entire family, its essential feature being the transmission of delusions from the "inducer" to other family members ("the induced"). Typical characteristics of families with *folie à famille* include social isolation, codependent and ambivalent family relationships, repetitive crises (especially due to economic causes), and the presence of violent behaviors. The "inducer," the original source and agent of the delusions, is usually the dominant family member (almost invariably the father and the symbol of authority, and almost always a Taurus). The other family members, who constitute the "induced," frequently display passive, suggestible, and histrionic personality traits. The suggestion that the **Kartons** suffer from a *folie à famille* raises an interesting question about *The Sugar Frosted Nutsack*. Are the Gods real or is **Ike Karton** just crazy? And the answer is: Yes. There are four explanations for the ambiguous portrayal of the Gods' empirical existence especially as it relates to **Ike**'s (and his family's) mental health. First, obviously the Gods themselves have determined that **Ike**—their mortal champion, their chosen one, their "elect of the elect"—should be anathematized as "a nutbag" by his neighbors, perhaps as a test of **Ike**'s devotion and fortitude, or perhaps to give him the most masochistic bang for his buck, because it doesn't take a psych major to glean from *The Sugar Frosted Nutsack* that **Ike** is a hard-core masochist who has a very florid martyr's complex and chronic, almost continuous fantasies of being flogged by unkempt, overweight, world-weary women. Secondly, perhaps **Ike** (whose cellphone ringtone is **2 Live Crew**'s "Me So Horny") encourages people in his neighborhood to think of him as "crazy" because he is planning to commit "suicide-by-cop" and the determination of an individual's mental capacity, or "soundness of mind," to form an intent to commit suicide may be of consequence in claims for recovery of death benefits under life insurance policies—in other words, if **Ike** seems crazy, his family will get the insurance money after he provokes the ATF or Mossad into killing him (as is his fate). The third explanation is that this is the God **XOXO** fucking with the book, trying to ruin it by making it too confusing, by creating insoluble contradictions and conundrums, by essentially tying the shoelaces of the book together. It's obvious, after all, that **XOXO** has hacked into *The Sugar Frosted Nutsack,* that **XOXO** has contaminated *The Sugar Frosted Nutsack* with a malicious software program or a botnet that's able to compromise the integrity of the book's operating system and/or **Ike Karton**'s mind and/or the entirety of **Ike Karton**'s genome, including, most significantly, his expiration date (i.e., the date upon which, driven by his daemon, his destiny will be fulfilled). Or—and this is the fourth possible explanation— perhaps, in a kind of "false flag operation," it's the Goddess **Shanice** who, upon becoming so indignant at not being named by **Ike** as one of the "Ten Gods I'd Fuck (T.G.I.F.)" in the Second Season, infects **XOXO**'s sharp periodontal curette (the one he uses to ineradicably engrave *The Sugar Frosted Nutsack* into **Ike**'s brain) with a botnet. Most experts now agree that there's overwhelming validity to all four explanations. Though at times it may seem as if the Gods are portrayed as only existing in **Ike**'s mind, *The Sugar Frosted Nutsack* unequivocally represents the Gods as having, in fact, created the world ("During the Belle Époque—that period of time, about fourteen billion years ago, after the Gods were delivered by bus from some sort of 'Spring Break' during which they are said to have 'gone wild'—the Gods put things in order, made them comprehensible, provided context, imposed coherence and meaning, i.e., they created the world as we know it today"). Also, there are frequent instances in which one or several Gods clearly intervene on behalf of or in opposition to **Ike**. For instance, in the Third Season (sometime around 1100 A.D., "sessions" became known as "seasons"), **Doc Hickory**, the God of Money, who was also known as *El Más Gordo* ("The Fattest One")—the God whose static-charged back hair became the template for the drift of continental landmasses on Earth—tries to finagle **Ike** a free rice pudding at the Miss America Diner on West Side Avenue in Jersey City. In the Fourth Season, the Gods **Los Vatos Locos** (also known as **The Pince-Nez 44s**) prevent someone from coming to the aid of **Ike**'s daughter's math teacher when **Ike** threatens to sodomize him. (They're watching this all take place from their perch at the 160-story Burj Khalifa in Dubai, and they're totally cracking up.) In the Fifth Season, **Koji Mizokami**, the God who fashioned the composer **Béla Bartók** out of his own testicular teratoma, helps **Ike** shoplift an Akai MPC drum machine from a Sam Ash on Route 4 in Paramus, New Jersey. And, in the Sixth Season, **Bosco Hifikepunye**, the God of Miscellany (including Fibromyalgia, Chicken Tenders, Sports Memorabilia, SteamVac Carpet Cleaners, etc.) begins supplying **Vance** with the hallucinogenic drug Gravy to sell on the street and also impregnates **Ike**'s daughter. And, as **Colter Dale** (the offspring of that union) postulates—in a postscript that would become the Final Season— "That the Gods only occur in **Ike**'s mind is not a refutation of their actuality. It is, on the contrary, irrefutable proof of their empirical existence. The Gods choose to only exist in **Ike**'s mind. They are real by virtue of this, their prerogative."

6.

PUTTING ASIDE WHAT might be construed as a cynical attempt to pathologize an authentic oracular hero in order to sell him drugs (e.g., Clozaril, Zyprexa, Risperdal, etc.), in other words, for the financial benefit of the pharmaceutical industry (once we assume an organic basis for *deviant theologies,* we legitimize a market for diagnostic assays and treatment modalities), and putting aside the even more fundamental issue of the pharmacological colonization of the Western psyche, is there any validity to the diagnosis of *folie à famille* for the **Kartons** (the family, not the band)? **Ike Karton** doesn't seem to fit the textbook profile of "the inducer." He can't really be described as domineering, for instance. Of course, in his unassuming way, he casually offers up incidental remarks and observations about the world—that people like **Anna Wintour, Gisele Bündchen, Ronald Perelman,** and **Jon Bon Jovi** should be dragged from their offices or homes and guillotined on the street, or how it would be much more entertaining in the Winter Olympics biathlon if, instead of shooting at targets, the biathletes shot ski jumpers at the apex of their flights like human skeet, or his admiration for the ferocious Renaissance politician **Cesare Borgia** and Chechen strongman **Ramzan Kadyrov** and the ruthless one-eyed prime minister of Cambodia, **Hun Sen**. But he has never tried to "proselytize" or "indoctrinate" his family. He has never sat his wife and daughter down and formally told them the entire saga (i.e., the entirety of *The Sugar Frosted Nutsack*) in the classic style—that is, high on ecstasy, swigging orange soda from a gourd, tapping his aluminum wedding ring on the tabletop to maintain that mesmerizing cadence—from beginning to end. In fact, he won't formally tell the whole saga in the classic style from beginning to end until—in the Penultimate Season, and shortly before being gunned down by ATF or Mossad sharpshooters—he sits down with his half-divine infant grandson, **Colter Dale**, pours out a sacred libation of Sunkist, and, tapping his ring on the tabletop, begins chanting to the rapt, wide-eyed infant from the very beginning: "There was never *nothing*. But before the debut of the Gods, about fourteen billion years ago, things happened without any discernible context. There were no recognizable patterns. It was all incoherent. Isolated, disjointed events would take place, only to be engulfed by an opaque black void, their relative meaning, their *significance*, annulled by the eons of entropic silence that estranged one from the next. A terrarium containing three tiny teenage girls mouthing a lot of high-pitched gibberish (like **Mothra**'s fairies, except for their wasted pallors, acne, big tits, and T-shirts that read 'I Don't Do White Guys') would inexplicably materialize, and then, just as inexplicably, disappear…" And with that unprecedented gesture, **Ike** incorporates (and consecrates) what had heretofore been simply an academic prologue into the very body, the very heart of *The Sugar Frosted Nutsack* (and it has been considered its First Season ever since). But prior to the Penultimate Season, over the years, **Ike** has, every now and then, sat down with his wife and his daughter and his daughter's disreputable boyfriend, **Vance**, and, in his soft, confidential, hoarse whisper, informally shared with them several vivid but isolated and disjointed little fragments. And despite the fact (or maybe due to the fact) that these disjointed little frag-ments seem to lack any discernible context, **Ike**'s wife, his daughter, and **Vance** are sufficiently enthralled so that they appear (to some experts) to suffer from a form of *folie à famille*. Such is **Ike**'s galvanic (albeit diffident) charisma, his *magnificence*. Such is the inky dye of his faith that, over time, drop by drop by drop, it slowly seeps into and stains the porous minds of his loyal, loving family. (There are some experts, although they constitute a persecuted minority within the expert community, who believe that there has actually been only one bard—that one being **Ike Karton**. And within this group, there is a dissident faction who also believes that there has actually been only one expert, that one also being **Ike Karton**. Although this is an extremely controversial and virtually indefensible position, it does have one vehement and disproportionately influential proponent: **Ike Karton**.)

Ike's "10 Things That I Know for Sure About Women" List

Soon after **Ike** and **Ruthie** first met (at the A&P where, at that time, **Ike** was employed as a butcher in the meat department), they had a conversation one spring day in the park about each other's past relationships and about love and about what one could realistically hope for in a marriage, etc. **Ruthie** asked **Ike** if he thought he understood women well. **Ike** got very quiet and thought about this for a while, as he tossed handful after handful of croutons to the swans and mice that had gathered at their feet. Finally, he told **Ruthie** that he was going to make a list. "Not a list of which celebrities you think should be guillotined," she said, coyly averting her eyes and smiling flirtatiously at him. "No," he said, "a list of ten things that I know for sure about women." About a week later—to show **Ruthie** a more delicately registered sensibility than he, a gym-rat and butcher, suspected **Ruthie** gave him credit for—**Ike** presented the list (entitled "10 Things That I Know for Sure About Women" but including an 11th) to **Ruthie** as they sat on the very same bench in Lincoln Park:

1. Even little girls, in all their blithe, unharrowed innocence, have a presentiment of sorrow, hardship, and adversity… of loss. Women, throughout their lives, have an intrinsic and profound understanding of **Keats**'s sentiments about "Joy, whose hand is ever at his lips / Bidding adieu."

2. This sage knowledge of, and ability to abide, the inherently fugitive nature of happiness somehow accounts for the extraordinary beauty of women as they age.

3. Women have an astonishing capacity to maintain their equilibrium in the face of life's mutability, its unceasing and unforeseeable vicissitudes. And this agility is always in stark and frequently comical contradistinction to men's naively bullish and brittle delusions that things can forever remain exactly the same.

4. Women are forgiving, but implacably cognizant.

5. Women are almost never gullible, but sometimes relax their vigilance out of loneliness. (And I believe most women abhor loneliness.)

6. In their most casual, offhand, sisterly moments, women are capable of discussing sex in such uninhibited detail that it would cause a horde of carousing Cossacks to cringe.

7. Women are, for all intents and purposes, indomitable. It really requires an almost unimaginable confluence of crushing, cataclysmic forces to vanquish a woman.

8. Women's instincts for self-preservation and survival can seem to men to be inscrutably unsentimental and sometimes cruel.

9. Women have a very specific kind of courage that enables them to fling themselves into the open sea, into some uncharted terra incognita—whether it's a new life for themselves, another person's life, or even what might appear to be a kind of madness.

10. Women never—no matter how old they are—completely relinquish their aristocratic assumption of seductiveness.

11. And here is one last thing I know—and I know this with a certitude that exceeds anything I've said before: that men's final thoughts in their waking days and in

their lives are of women...ardent, wistful thoughts of wives and lovers and daughters and mothers.

Ruthie found this so beautiful and so moving that she wept as she read it. In the coming weeks, though, she'd discover that **Ike** had plagiarized it, from beginning to end, word for word, from something that had appeared in the November 2008 issue of *O, The Oprah Magazine.* But by then she'd already fallen deeply in love with him, and not at all *in spite of* what he'd done, but, in large part, *because* of it—here was a man willing to steal for her, a man with a big enough nutsack that he was willing to brazenly steal another man's *words,* another man's *ideas* (his most precious intellectual property)...for *her.*

Ninety-seven percent of people think that it was SUPER-SEXY of **Ike** to totally plagiarize that from *O, The Oprah Magazine*!!

7

GONE WITH THE MIND (2016)

THE STORY SO FAR

February 3, 2014   In a miraculous case of pareidolia, Leyner discovers the face of the Imaginary Intern in the craquelure of a bathroom tile while seated on the toilet

2015   Awarded the Terry Southern Prize by the *Paris Review*

2016   Publication of *Gone with the Mind*

DISAPPEARING ACT

Mark Leyner's Self-Consuming Fictions

Jonathan Dee

Gone with the Mind, Mark Leyner's seventh book of fiction, might seem like a high-spirited satiric romp if you haven't read the other six. It is the transcript of a fictitious reading delivered by a fictitious writer named Mark Leyner as part of the Nonfiction at the Food Court Reading Series at the Woodcreek Plaza Mall. Mark, who has come to the mall to read excerpts from his new memoir, also entitled *Gone with the Mind,* is introduced by his mother. Her introduction is forty pages long; it commences with her description of the crippling morning sickness she suffered when Mark was in utero. The number of people in attendance at the reading, it is important to note, is zero; two workers, from Sbarro and Panda Express, are technically seated in the food court, but they are on break, and they resist all attempts by Leyner *mère* and *fils* to get them to look up from their phones and pretend to be a legit audience.

Mark means to preface his reading with a few remarks about the genesis of *Gone with the Mind*; it becomes clear after a while that the reading proper is probably never going to begin—that Mark, standing atop a plastic table in order to be better seen and heard (at least in theory), will do pretty much anything to keep the meta-narcissistic experience of talking about writing about himself from coming to an end. (His mother, the only one listening, reassures him periodically that he's doing great and that she could listen to him indefinitely.)

"Just a little background before I get started," he says:

Gone with the Mind *was originally going to be an autobiography in the form of a first-person shooter/flight-simulator game....The, uh... the goal of the game is to successfully reach my mother's womb, in which I attempt to unravel or unzip my father's and mother's DNA in the zygote, which will free me of having to eternally repeat this life.*

Though the novel we're reading does, in a very loose fashion, describe how the *Gone with the Mind* project morphed from this idea—with the collaboration, Mark insists, of a key hallucinatory figure known as the Imaginary Intern—into the memoir from which he is nominally about to read, it has little resemblance, and even less aspiration, to what might conventionally be called a story. Mark makes plenty clear his revulsion toward any "rigid chronology of pivotal incidents," at one point advocating the replacement of "incumbent imperial narratives" with a new artistic medium based entirely on smell. What we get in lieu of such a chronology is a long, associative series of memories, digressions, and musings, some about Mark's own life (mostly identical to that of his author, from the Jersey City childhood to the actual name of the Manhattan doctor who performed his robotic prostatectomy) and others on subjects ranging from Mussolini to a proposed reality TV show about self-endoscopy to a recent article in a scientific journal: "South Korean Microbiologist Discovers That Even Amoebae Fall into the Five Basic Archetypal Categories: Nerd, Bully, Hot, Dumpy, and New Kid."

The word *riff* sometimes seems pejorative in a literary context, but it's hard to avoid here—not for reasons having to do with jazzlike improvisational skill but simply because Leyner is very funny. While anecdotal experience in getting people to agree with me on this point suggests a certain gender divide, I will assert nevertheless that he's as funny as any writer I could name. His frame of reference, within the space of a paragraph, or even a sentence, is dizzying. (He was once called "the poet laureate of information overload.") He gets a great deal of mileage out of the names of things. Sometimes it's a familiar high-low move, as when he refers in passing to "a group of experts" consisting of Alan Greenspan, Dog the Bounty Hunter, and "controversial Beverly Hills plastic surgeon Dr. Giancarlo Capella." More often, though, it's his specificity with obscure common nouns and his establishment of a Buster Keaton–style deadpan through his fastidious verbal exactitude. Most writers would have stopped this sentence eleven words sooner:

And I tend to believe that this inclination to look back on one's life and superimpose a teleological narrative of cause and effect is probably itself a symptom of incipient dementia, caused by some prion disease or the clumping of beta-amyloid plaques.

Or spot the Leyneresque word near the end of this sentence about the Imaginary Intern:

Life's a harrowing fucking slog—we're driven by irrational, atavistic impulses into an unfathomable void of quantum indeterminacy—but, still…it's nice to have a friend, a comrade, a paracosm, whatever, to share things with.

He is, to pick the kind of arcane cultural referent he might enjoy, the Alexander Popov of comic fiction: not renowned for endurance but unbeatable in a sprint. "If it weren't for Internet porn," he says in apology to his "audience" at one point, "I'm sure we would have finished *Gone with the Mind* a lot sooner. If it weren't for Internet porn, there'd be a cure for cancer, there'd be human photosynthesis, levitation, time travel, everything."

In the aggregate, *Gone with the Mind*'s uninterrupted associative riffing resembles narration, or even stand-up comedy, much less than it does psychotherapy. Mark has been prompted—it scarcely matters how—to start talking about how he came to be the fifty-eight-year-old son, husband, father, and writer he is today; as with any venture into talk therapy, maybe something comes of it, maybe not. The mountainous exercise in narcissism that is this "reading" is of course dramatically undercut by the fact that no one is listening, that no one (with the exception of Mark's mother) cares, and that it requires a heroic effort of magical thinking on Mark's part to keep this awareness of his own insignificance at bay. It also requires that he not stop talking. *Gone with the Mind* is a triumph of the will: it's as funny as Lucky's monologue in *Waiting for Godot* and as horrifying. Mark has to work really, really hard—tragically hard—to maintain the fiction not simply that he is a public figure but also that he exists at all. You get the sense that if his mother weren't there, he would disappear.

It's not easy to think of another contemporary literary career with which Leyner's might be fairly compared. He was and is considered a prophetic satirist of various unflattering aspects of our age: the obsession with fame, the focus on self-aggrandizement, the lightning-fast yet meaningless connectivity of the search engine, the memoir and reality TV boom, even autofiction. (The "poetic I" constructed so subtly in the work of Ben Lerner and Rachel Cusk is, in Leyner's hands, blown up to the proportions of a Macy's Thanksgiving Day Parade balloon.) By the time he published *Et Tu, Babe,* his third book (and first novel), in 1992, he had begun to build his fictions around a magnificently exaggerated, grotesquely famous, and powerful version of himself. Other novelists (Martin Amis, Philip Roth) had played similar identity games, just as other writers (Thomas Bernhard, Gordon Lish) had explored the medium of the riff, the rant, the endless digressive introduction to a story that never gets told. Leyner's marriage of these techniques in the service of broad intellectual comedy hit the zeitgeist square in its sweet spot.

You can still find on YouTube a 1996 episode of *Charlie Rose* devoted to "the future of fiction in the information age" whose three participants are David Foster Wallace, Jonathan Franzen, and Leyner. (So high has Wallace's star risen in the intervening twenty years that one of the first facts some people now recall about Leyner is that he's the writer Wallace once called "a kind of Antichrist.") The *New York Times Magazine* ran a cover story about Leyner. He wrote monthly columns in *Esquire* and the late *George* magazine. His origins as a member of an avant-garde artistic coalition called the Fiction Collective notwithstanding, his novels and story collections became wildly popular, until, in as sure a sign of shark jumping as exists in the world of literary fiction, new editions of his work began to feature his photograph on the front cover.

Yet there seemed something paradoxically modest about his always making "Mark Leyner" the largest and crudest and most egocentric figure in his work, offering up his own persona as a kind of lamb to the satire. In *Et Tu, Babe,* that persona lives inside the heavily fortified Leyner HQ, surrounded by an army of toadies known as Team Leyner and protected against constant assassination attempts by an elite corps of cyborgs. Occasionally he takes time off to teach writing workshops, in which he singles out the most promising students and has them killed. In *Tooth Imprints on a Corn Dog* (1995), Mark Leyner shops for a $3,450 Armani backpack for his daughter's Haute Barbie and sequesters himself, Belushilike, in the Chateau Marmont in order to compose a thousand lines of free verse on deadline for a German magazine. In *The Tetherballs of Bougainville* (1997), a thirteen-year-old Mark seduces the zaftig warden bent on executing his father, offers his consulting services to a grateful foreign dictator, and creates a hit TV show called *America's Funniest Violations of Psychiatrist/Patient Confidentiality*. Thus did Leyner mock his own desire for fame even as he worked hard to maintain it. Inevitably, perhaps, his commitment to this monstrous version of himself began to seem a little like shtick; still, by the end of the millennium Leyner had as high a profile as any fiction writer in America. And then he vanished.

Well, okay, he didn't vanish; he stopped writing fiction. He went to Hollywood, where, in fifteen or so years, his only credit was as cowriter of a 2008 John Cusack movie called *War, Inc.* He also, bizarrely, cowrote with a doctor friend a bestselling series of answers to laypeople's medical questions, one volume of which was distinctively titled *Why Do Men Have Nipples?* In an interview, he said this about his long hiatus:

I was on Letterman. *I read from one of my books on* Conan. *I almost lost my place, thinking, How fucking great is this? You're reading from one of your books on television. But I would also think, Why did I ever even want this? I'd just rather be home. We wouldn't do what we do if we loved being with people. We like to be by ourselves.*

There's something a little boilerplate about that, though, something too pat to account for Leyner's own pathology. In his twentieth-century work there was always a naked eagerness to entertain; in retrospect, it seems like what he was really satirizing, or coopting, or purging from himself, in his outsize portrayals of a world wherein he was worshipped like a god, may have been his actual need to know that we liked him. As anyone who fits that sort of psychological profile might recognize, the maintenance of success is so demanding that it almost inevitably generates fantasies of failure. Maybe the tension that he was opting out of by ceasing to write stories about "Mark Leyner"—by retreating into a kind of authorship in which his identity was submerged (I don't remember a lot of *War, Inc.* posters with his face on them)—was more interior: less about the war between the heroically solitary artist and the culture that demands things from him than about the war between his own impulses.

In 2012, Leyner returned to literary fiction with a novel called *The Sugar Frosted Nutsack.* As in *Gone with the Mind,* the entirety of the novel—whose central character is not Mark Leyner but an unemployed butcher from New Jersey named Ike Karton—consists of a digressive ramp-up to a hypothetical epic that never actually begins. But the discontinuity of those digressions—the discontinuity between individual sentences, sometimes—is so aggressive as to feel almost hostile. Though the book has many champions to whom attention must be paid (Sam Lipsyte, Rick Moody, Ben Marcus), I confess I find it nearly unreadable. And while unreadability was probably not the precise effect Leyner was going for, it's not as far off as you might think.

In an interview conducted by Moody that was appended to the paperback edition of *Nutsack,* Leyner mentioned his affinity for Antonin Artaud, the founder of the Theatre of Cruelty—this just after he has said, "I have always thought of what I do as an enormous act of generosity....My impulse is just to give the reader enormous pleasure." Conceiving of one's art as a generous attempt to provide pleasure might seem at first blush a little hard to square with the confrontational views of Artaud, who professed that "no one has ever written, painted, sculpted, modeled, built, or invented except literally to get out of hell." Still, wanting to assault one's audience and needing reassurances of its love at the same time: if that's the tension *The Sugar Frosted Nutsack* fails to reconcile, it's also, in its very irreconcilability, an interesting lens through which to view both Leyner's early work and his decision to stop producing it.

"Yama nashi, ochi nashi, imi nashi," Mark reminisces at one point in *Gone with the Mind,* quoting a motto from Japanese manga: "No climax, no resolution, no meaning. Because, I have to say, even then, at eight years of age, every other kind of writing struck me as banal and outdated, and just boring beyond endurance." He says this, of course, to an empty food court, to an audience that is not there.

The conflict in Leyner's work between the desire to please and the desire to alienate has always had heavily Freudian undertones. *Gone with the Mind* plays those undertones loud and proud, not only in the absurdity of its premise (the son, now fifty-eight, standing on a table and putting on a show for his admiring mother) but also, more sadly and self-consciously, in Mark's own narration:

Like the preening narcissism of so many physically repulsive men, nothing matches the overweening, magisterial pride of the abject failure, the son manqué. Freud said: "A man who has been the indisputable favorite of his mother keeps for life the feeling of a conqueror." And I believe this remains especially true for the son who has clearly demonstrated that he's capable of accomplishing absolutely nothing.

Elsewhere Mark refers to himself as "the eternal little man, inflated with dreams of flamboyant success but forced back on his own futility," and, with an extra knife twist at the end, "Oh sad, sad, Ferbered prince...sad, sad, Ferbered, oedipally conflicted, impotent prince and poseur...ever posing autobiographically as yourself."

Even when—especially when—the real-life Mark Leyner was at his most famous, we never quite got what he was doing. We thought he was satirizing us, but maybe the thing that he was mocking was never really outside him. Though of course Mark never gets around to reading the reputedly brilliant ending of *Gone with the Mind*—an ending so ingenious as to represent "an astonishing victory over the forces of 'storytelling,' the decadent pastime of white-guard counterrevolutionaries"—we are, as in Mark's original video-game conceit, repeatedly reminded of the longing to begin:

There was a golden age for me when it was just my mother and myself, and this is still the idealized world I long for, still the mythic, primordial time, the paradisiacal status quo ante that I persistently hearken back to, whose restoration is at the core of a mystico-fascistic politics.

Gone with the Mind scarcely resembles the sort of conventional novel for which both Mark and Leyner share a principled artistic revulsion, but it's as close as they're likely to come, in that it embodies, and is driven by, a conventionally dramatic idea, that of tension between opposites. That tension—in the words of Leyner's *War, Inc.* cowriter, "the fundamental preposterousness of being a writer or even a person. That feeling that you have to be the best in the world, versus the terror that you are nothing and you are no one"— convincingly generates the emotional element one might once have voted Least Likely to Appear in a Mark Leyner Novel: pathos.

Jonathan Dee is the author of eight novels, including *The Privileges* and *Sugar Street*. He teaches in the creative writing program at Syracuse University.

EXCERPTS FROM
GONE WITH THE MIND

INTRODUCTION

MARK'S MOTHER

Hello, my name is Muriel Leyner, and I'm coordinating director of the Nonfiction at the Food Court Reading Series here at the Woodcreek Plaza Mall. This series has been made possible by the generosity of the International Council of Shopping Centers and Douthat & Associates Properties. And I'd like to single out Jenny Schoenhals, the senior general manager at Woodcreek Plaza Mall, who has worked so diligently on providing us with such a commodious venue here at the food court, and without whom none of this would be possible. I see you couldn't make it tonight, but thank you so *very* much, Jenny, wherever you are. And last, but certainly not least, I'd like to thank our indispensable sponsors: Panda Express, Master Wok, Au Bon Pain, Auntie Anne's Pretzels, California Pizza Kitchen, Cinnabon, Jamba Juice, KFC Express, McDonald's, Nathan's Famous, Sbarro, Subway, and Taco Bell.

Before I introduce our reader for tonight, I should point out that, because of the heavy rain and the flash-flood warnings that have been issued by the National Weather Service, no one—not one single person—has actually shown up for the reading...except, uh, I see that we've got some of the staff of Panda Express and Sbarro with us. I don't know if you two guys are just taking a break over there or are actually here for the reading...

PANDA EXPRESS WORKER

We're just taking a break. We're definitely not here for the reading!

MARK'S MOTHER

Well, welcome. There's nothing more dispiriting for a writer than to have traveled hundreds, sometimes thousands of miles to give a reading, and then find him- or herself facing rows of empty seats. So, I'm especially appreciative that you guys braved such inclement weather and at least showed up for work tonight. At least it provides the semblance of an audience.

"I've survived two assassination attempts: one on a highway between Sofia and Plovdiv, Bulgaria, on November 11, 2006, and one in front of a hotel in Los Angeles on February 4, 2008. On December 3, 2012, I was raped by a robot on the corner of Fifth Avenue and 101st Street in New York City. In the summer of 2014, desperate for cash and back on crack, I sold the rights to my life story to a start-up indie video-game developer called MirRaj Entertainment (named after its founders, Miriam Rubenstein and Davesh Rajaratnam)." So begins *Gone with the Mind*, my son's autobiography, excerpts from which he will be reading tonight.

Mark Leyner was born at the Margaret Hague Maternity Hospital in Jersey City, New Jersey, on January 4, 1956. I was twenty-one years old. During my pregnancy, Mark's father (my ex-husband, Joel) and I were living in a one-bedroom apartment in a small brick building at 225 Union Street in Jersey City, between Bergen Avenue and the Boulevard. We paid, as I remember, fifty dollars a month in rent. I don't know why I remember all that so exactly...perhaps because it was our very first apartment. At any rate, about five or six weeks into the pregnancy, I began experiencing terrible, terrible morning sickness. Severe morning sickness. This was at the end of April in 1955. I would throw up all day and all night. (The medical term for this is *hyperemesis gravidarum*.) And I lost a significant amount of weight. I was down to something ridiculous like eighty-five pounds. My obstetrician-gynecologist, my *ob-gyn*— although we didn't abbreviate it back then—was a man named Dr. Schneckendorf. This Dr. Schneckendorf, interestingly enough, had been my own mother's doctor when she gave birth to me in 1934. And he was a kindly old gent. But nobody really helped with the nausea. Most men, and I'd say *especially* doctors, looked on it as a form of self-indulgence. I valiantly tried to do everything humanly possible to keep it under control, but...people really thought of it as some sort of psychosomatic malady, almost like a form of malingering, as if I were simply this spoiled Jewish princess. That's the overwhelming feeling I got from most men, and certainly from most men in the medical profession at that time....I kept a bowl cradled in one arm to throw up in. I'd spend days at my mother Harriet's house or she would come over to my house. Afternoons were better, a little better, and I'd try to eat. Chinese food—fried rice—seemed to set better in my stomach. And Mark's father, after work, would stop at the Jade, which was a Chinese restaurant in Journal Square, and bring me cartons of fried rice. Whenever I felt that I could actually eat something, actually keep something down, I could be very peremptory about it. I remember that summer being down at the Jersey shore, at a beach club in Long Branch, and barking at my sister, Francis, "Get me a well-done hamburger and fries, now!" because I knew how fleeting that appetite could be, and I was absolutely determined to try to stay as healthy and as strong as I possibly could for this baby inside me. That summer we were staying at these little apartments in West Long Branch. There were lots of Jersey City people. And almost every day, the men would go out on fishing boats. And there were rough seas out there. And later in the afternoon, when these guys would get off the boats, they were green, staggering. And I'd say, "Dr. Rubenstein, Uncle Harry, what happened?" I was a fresh kid. I had a fresh mouth. "Uncle This and Uncle That, what happened out there? You don't look so good." The fact that they were so seasick, so nauseous, delighted me to no end. Because as far as they were concerned, my terrible, relentless nausea was all in my mind. "If you kept yourself busy. Maybe if you had more floors to wash." They were all such imperious chauvinists. "If you continue this, we're going to have to put you in the hospital and feed you intravenously." Believe me, if this were an ailment of men's testicles, they would have found a treatment, a cure for it a thousand years ago. But they didn't give a flying fuck. I got vitamin B shots from a doctor who was a friend of my husband, and that helped a bit. But that's about it. Other women would tell me that morning sickness was a sign of a healthy pregnancy, which was certainly a consolation. And I think that I endured it all with a genuine sense of martyrdom, determined to persevere, in the face of all the sexist, condescending bullshit, for the sake of my baby, for Mark's sake. And so, that first week in January of 1956, the third, on a Tuesday, my water broke. And Dr. Schneckendorf said come right into the hospital. I remember it was snowy and I had my little bag with me. And Schneckendorf and all the residents told me, "What you need to do is walk. Walk up and down on the hall." So I walked up and down on the hall. I had my robe—a pale blue-and-white-printed corduroy robe with white linen embroidered collar and cuffs. Buttoned down the front. Like a college girl's. Slippers. Long, fair hair in a ponytail. And I'm walking, walking, walking…and the pain is getting a bit worse, but I'm thinking, *This actually isn't* so *bad, it's like bad cramps.* And this sallow-looking young man appears and he says, "Hello." I thought, *That's strange.* "What are you doing here?" he asked, in his very thick Italian accent. I thought that was obvious. "I'm in labor! What are *you* doing here?" "I'm an anesthesiologist," he replied. He was flirting with me! I thought that was the funniest thing. Imagine—making a pass at a pregnant woman in a maternity ward! I suppose men just think they can make use of their position whenever the whim strikes them, and women should think it's wonderful that they think you're sexy. "I love it, the green-eyed blondes," he said to me in his accent. Several hours later, I was screaming at the top of my lungs, and I knew what *real* labor was, what *real* pain was. And at three o'clock in the morning, after twelve hours of labor, with no painkillers until the very end, this nice, little, perfectly round head emerged. I was ecstatic at the sight of him. I was thrilled and happy and delighted. I was as overjoyed as a human being can be. From the moment I looked at him, I knew how wonderful he was and would always be. There was just this atavistic thrill. It was physical and emotional. My mother came to see us that morning, and she held him. And then the next day, when I woke up, I brushed my hair and brushed my teeth. And I looked up. And there was that young man again—the Italian anesthesiologist. And he had a bouquet of flowers! And again, this struck me as very, very amusing. Mario. His name was Mario. He was from a titled family in Italy, and he'd only been in the U.S. for a short period of time. It was the beginning of a funny friendship. He met Mark's father. He was a typical mad Italian driver. He had these Italian sports cars and got into frequent accidents. Mark's father, who had recently graduated from law school and was clerking for a judge at the time, would help this Mario with the legal ramifications of all his numerous car accidents. It was clear that he liked the way I looked and liked the way I spoke...that he thought I was a cut above the typical people he saw... When I look back, these aren't things I'm particularly fond of—that kind of class snobbery and being such a big flirt. Anyway, it was a week's stay in the hospital in those days—that was just the protocol then. And there I was, this thin, fragile-looking girl, but I was strong. I'd walk around and stand in front of the nursery window. And I could always immediately tell which cart he was in — those skinny, naked, red legs. They'd bring the baby every four hours to be fed, bottle-fed — I didn't nurse. His circumcision was scheduled for the last day that week — the *bris* with a *mohel*. And I was extremely anxious about that on every level. I'm very concerned about cleanliness. The idea of some old geezer with his own equipment filled me with foreboding. But I was reassured by Harry Gerner, the pediatrician, and by my parents and my in-laws. I had another issue, though. I have very serious problems with clotting. I have a genetic inability to clot properly and almost died getting my tonsils out when I was ten. I had massive hemorrhaging. So I demanded that before they even think of performing Mark's circumcision, they get a clotting time done. I insisted on it. And they did. And it was normal. And they had the bris, in a special room. I don't remember if I was wearing clothes or my robe. And all the grandparents were there. And it all went perfectly well. And the next day we went home. I can regale you with all the ensuing milestones — at ten days, he raised his head and rolled over; at six weeks, he giggled; at about five months he could crawl backwards, shake his head no, and play hide-and-seek; he stood up all alone and got his first teeth at six months; at six and a half months he stood up all alone holding on to the crib; he took his first steps holding on to his playpen at seven months; he said his first word, *Da-da,* at eight months, and walked all by himself at eleven months; his favorite toys were a set of colored disks on a chain and a stuffed fuzzy cocker spaniel that his uncle Richie gave him — because I dutifully recorded all of this critical information in a white satin-bound baby diary, in which I also inscribed the following account of his first birthday: "Mark had a birthday party on Sunday the 6th of January, and we took movies of him and all the family. Both Grandmas and Grandpas, Great-Grandmas and Great-Grandpas were there, and his aunts and uncles too. He received beautiful gifts, put both fists in the cake, cried at the company, and later in the evening 'performed' for them and for the camera.".…

We didn't have any real money; his father was just about beginning his practice, and when Mark was born, Joel had been clerking for a judge, and you make virtually nothing. So when I would get lamb chops, from my mother's kosher butcher, or wherever else I got them, I would cook them for Mark, I would get them and give them to him for lunch and for his dinner. It wasn't what his father and I were having for dinner, and he would get the meat. I would cut…like if it was two or three little rib chops, I would cut up all the meat, and that was for him, and I would be salivating, and I would eat the bone when we were finished. And sometimes he would nibble on a bone, but he didn't seem to care about that as much as I did. I should have known from those days that he was the person who was going to like rare meat. But I liked the crispy well-done part, and I couldn't wait to get hold of those bones and eat them, but I was…When I was growing up, and I could see from the way that my mother behaved, that everything was for the children, I mean, that's simply the way it was, and without consciously making a decision that the *kinder* or the children were the important thing, that was certainly the case. Everything was done to make him comfortable and clean and some of that was for my own ego I'm sure. I liked the way it looked, I liked the way he looked, I liked the way it appeared to me that I was capable, you know…as I said, his crib was beautiful and his room was lovely, and everything that he had was crisp and at the same time soft, and he never ever had dirty, torn play clothes, it just wasn't like that. But it also turned out that he was a pretty clean kid and a pretty clean-lookin' kid. And he was very easy to take places. He sat there quietly, I mean, he didn't have temper tantrums and carry on like his sister, Chase. I used to have to carry Chase out of places under my arm. But Mark and I would go to the office in Journal Square, take the bus sometimes, and go up to the office and have lunch downstairs with his grandpa Ray or with his father and with his uncle Lewis. And we'd have lunch at the Bird Cage at Lord & Taylor's—that's when we moved to the suburbs and I had a car, so it was a little easier, and we would just go to the Bird Cage. And I know Mark loved it there. I was always very careful and very caring about the food he ate. When Mark was an infant, Harry Gerner wouldn't let me feed him regular food the way, for example, Phyllis Leyner did. She stuffed huge globs full of food into those kids' mouths, like they were grown-ups, and Rose couldn't bear it. And Uncle Harry said, No, one food at a time, and when we know his reaction to that, 'cause his father is very allergic and you know we've got to watch out for those things, and that's the way I do it. So the first thing he had was rice cereal, he liked it a lot, and then, like, two weeks or three weeks, whatever, he had applesauce, same thing, same thing, then after that I think it was some other fruit, I don't remember exactly...pears was one of them. But I don't remember the others. But then finally when we got to meat and vegetables and that stuff, I knew the drill, but he was eating the ground chicken and potatoes and sweet potatoes and carrots—carrots he loved and sweet potatoes he loved. I remember that the applesauce he loved, but by that time the rice cereal was okay, but it certainly wasn't a big treat. That was the first regular food, so then it seemed like a big deal, but months later he knew the other things seemed more interesting. But then it was time to start some of the more esoteric vegetables, so I bought beets and green beans or whatever, and I had the little tiny baby spoon, which is really little! And I just dipped the end of it into the beets, so I had about *that* much on a spoon that was about *that* big, and just the little edge over there was beets, and I put it in his beautiful little pink mouth and he sort of—his eyes got very round and he sort of rolled it around for a couple of seconds and then he went *spew!*...I had beets in my eyelashes. I had beets up my nose. I had beets on my clothes. You would have thought that I had given him a quart of beets! And I thought, *That does it, he'll never get*...I rolled it around, it was on him, it was on his clothing, it was on the table. And I don't think I gave him beets again until he was pretty grown up. He likes beets now. Well, it just shows you.

Ladies and gentlemen, I give you Mark Leyner.

READING

MARK

Before I start, I'd like to say: Fuck everyone who said I was too paradoxical a hybrid of arrogant narcissism and vulnerable naïveté to succeed in life (even though they were right). Also, I'd like to dedicate this to all the nematodes and hyperthermophilic bacteria who live in deep-water sulfide chimneys around the world. Good days are coming, boys.

My mom gave me a ride here tonight, and, uh…I don't really like to talk to her when she's been drinking and she's driving over ninety miles an hour, because I don't want to distract her, so I was just sitting there in the passenger seat, looking out the window, sort of *musing* to myself…I think that mothers and sons, silent in a car, sometimes exchange telepathic soliloquies, but perhaps because we sensed that this could be our last night together, that one or both of us might very well be assassinated tonight, we left each other to our respective *musing*…that whole implosion of semioticity that is *musing,* that hypercaffeinated chatter of anthropomorphic cartoon animals in one's head that is *musing,* that whole *danse macabre* of singing little piglets in one's head…At ninety miles per hour, the empirical world rushes past in an impressionistic blur. You're thinking, *There's some weird, retro-looking, brown transgendered individual jerking off in the woods.* And then you're like, *No, that's a tree.* But sitting there — the eternal little man, inflated with dreams of flamboyant success but forced back on his own futility — my memories of childhood were not impressionistic at all, they were hyperrealistic. My mind's eye — my mind's *eyeball* — had shot back, it had shot back to 1961…and I, uh…I could see myself at the age of five, I could see myself there so vividly…I was a little boy, playing on a hot concrete alley on Westminster Lane in Jersey City one day…God spoke to this little boy, as He speaks to all pure-hearted children, in his simple, binary language of blue sky and radiant sun. And suddenly, in a kind of seizure, in an explosion of unfurling clairvoyance, he saw everything that would ensue in his life. *Everything.* His entire autobiography fast-forwarded in the most extraordinary detail. The birth of his daughter, his prostate cancer, his books (every word of them!), these final moments in this food court, in this mall, tonight. *Everything.* So we have two of the mind's eyeballs, the mind's eyeball of a fifty-eight-year-old man seated in the passenger seat of his mother's car, daydreaming as he stares out the window and the mind's eyeball of a drooling five-year-old boy with blond bangs seated rigidly on a concrete alley, one speeding back in time from 2014, one speeding into the future from 1961. Assuming they are traveling at approximately the same warp speed, they would collide at around 1988, the year Pan Am Flight 103 exploded over Lockerbie, Scotland, and an earthquake in Armenia killed sixty thousand people. These are the uncanny transtemporal ballistics of the mind's eyeballs. And this is one of the things we (my mother and I) mean by *Gone with the Mind.*

* * *

Okay…just a little background before I get started: *Gone with the Mind* was originally going to be an autobiography in the form of a first-person shooter / flight-simulator game. And it was going to start at a breakfast meeting with my old editor Michael Pietsch during which I'm either assassinated or "commit suicide" in the men's room. And my ghost has to travel back in time, revisit each transformative event in my life, and execute or otherwise degrade or disable the central dramatis personae in order to get to the next (prior) event. The, uh…the *goal* of the game is to successfully reach my mother's womb, in which I attempt to unravel or unzip my father's and mother's DNA in the zygote, which will free me of having to eternally repeat this life. And I'm ferried from event to event by Benito Mussolini, who pilots a flying balcony. And along the way, he offers counsel and gaming advice kind of like Krishna in the Bhagavad Gita or like Virgil in Dante's *Inferno*. And if the player succeeds in unknitting the entirety of his (my) life, thus flinging himself into utter oblivion, into an ontological black hole (or to put a more positive spin on it, reintegrating himself into the oceanic void), he wins.

I think an autobiography in the form of a first-person shooter game that ends with unraveling the zygote in your mother's uterus *sounds* really cool, and Michael and pretty much everyone I mentioned it to also thought it *sounded* really cool, but what *is* that, actually? I mean, what would a book like that actually be, y'know? Once you start thinking about sitting down and actually writing something, it's an entirely different matter. But I remained totally committed to doing it, because that's just the kind of person I am—I'm not going to bail on something I said I was going to do. I think I'm a sort of exceedingly boring person (which certainly doesn't make me the best candidate for an autobiography!)…I mean *boring* in that I'm very dutiful, very responsible…and if I say I'm going to write an autobiography in the form of a first-person shooter game that ends with unraveling the zygote in your mother's uterus then I'm going to write an autobiography in the form of a first-person shooter game that ends with unraveling the zygote in your mother's uterus, and that's that. And I expect that of other people too, by the way. If you say you're going to be in the schoolyard waiting for me in a certain place at a certain time, then be at that place at that time. Don't send some proxy who doesn't even know where the hell to wait, y'know what I mean? If you say you're going to stay overnight with me at the hospital when I get my tonsils out, then stay overnight at the hospital, for God's sake.

I said I'm an exceedingly boring person...I don't *really* think that. I think I'm a sort of weird composite of thrill-seeking heedlessness and crippling hyperanxiety—I mean, I've taken LSD before a root canal, but I'm equally capable of calling the police and area hospitals if my wife is even five minutes late coming home from a pedicure, so...

At some point in this preliminary stage when I'm still just trying to figure out what this book could actually be, the Imaginary Intern appears...which changes *everything*. I was sitting on the toilet one morning, gazing down at the tiles on the bathroom floor, uh...just staring at the vein patterns and at the craquelure on this one particular tile, and I discerned a legible face...I discerned the lineaments of the Imaginary Intern in the craquelure of a tile on the bathroom floor. That's exactly how the Imaginary Intern was conjured up. This is a textbook *delusion of reference*, specifically a *pareidolia*, a psychological phenomenon that involves seeing meaningful patterns, frequently faces, in random information—a common example of which is, um...something like seeing the face of Jesus in a Cool Ranch Dorito or something along those lines.

The Imaginary Intern initially functioned mainly as a kind of archivist or production manager on *Gone with the Mind*, helping me collate and categorize autobiographical material, but soon he became more like a, I don't know...more like a coach or a trainer. Y'know that term in pharmacology, *mechanism of action*? It's the specific biochemical interaction that basically enables a drug to do what it does. When you're writing something, its mechanism of action is a very difficult thing to identify. It's a very subtle, very elusive thing. But it really is *the* crucial fucking thing. And when I felt that I'd lost it, that I suddenly just didn't know what it was...or when, y'know, I just felt kind of discouraged or dispirited about how it was all going, the Imaginary Intern would exhort me, he'd pump me up, y'know? He'd be, like, "Denzel Washington can land a plane upside down stinking drunk, and you can't write an autobiography? A book about your own life? Are you *fucking* kidding me?"

So, quickly on, he became a very active collaborator with me, very much a creative partner, and the fundamental principles of the project, its...what's that word?...its...its *donnée,* began to evolve quite rapidly.

I'm trying to think of a good way to describe the Imaginary Intern...um...He sort of reminded me of Billy Name, the guy who designed Andy Warhol's Silver Factory on East Forty-Seventh Street back in the early sixties, the guy who pretty much functioned as the Factory's foreman during its most fecund years...He was very earnest and forthright and affirmative in a sort of Jeff Koons / Ferris Bueller way...I'm not sure if any of this is really helping give you a sense of what the Imaginary Intern was actually like (and I'm going to talk more about him—and especially about when he left, which was a pretty big, traumatic deal for me—in a few minutes), but, for now...I mean...he was just a very friendly, very smart, upbeat, hardworking guy. Youthful, eager, open-minded, pragmatic...very much in sync with what I was thinking (obviously!) and very adept at devising practical solutions to notions that were fanciful or completely hypothetical. I was always struck by his antipathy for abstraction and how constantly he was on the alert for whatever smacks of mere theory as against the solidity and efficacy of worldly practice.

I'd wash a Klonopin down with a beer and sit on the couch and mute the TV, and I'd picture the Imaginary Intern and me just strolling down a long Brutalist concrete promenade leading to an abyss, walking and talking...

The Imaginary Intern could get very enthusiastic, very excited by our ideas, very animated, sometimes even a little strident, whereas I'd tend, as the night progressed, to become more and more recessive and sedate, and I'd sort of tilt my head and purse my lips and just listen. And I know sometimes that sort of bugged the Imaginary Intern. And one morning, after I woke up, I came downstairs and there was a note left on the couch in the Imaginary Intern's handwriting:

Yes, it was late,
and, yes, I was being very
dented-in-the-head-mutant-hillbilly,

But you...
you just sat there
like some shitty poem.

And I remember thinking, *That's such a lovely line—"you just sat there / like some shitty poem."*

Once I said to the Imaginary Intern that reading about Achilles defiling the corpse of Hector gave me a hard-on. Do you think that makes me a fascist? I asked him. And he paused for what seemed like an eternity, and finally asked me if I knew that German soldiers on the front called crystal meth *Panzerschokolade* (which means "tank chocolate"), and we talked about how the world could be divided between people with *sitzfleisch* and people with *shpilkes,* and about how movies of a certain era used the donning of a frilly apron to signify how effete or inadequate a man was (for example, Jim Backus in *Rebel Without a Cause* or James Stewart in *The Man Who Shot Liberty Valance*), and about how the government not only knows that there's life after death, they know that life after death is fantastic, and they're suppressing it, because they don't want everyone finding out and immediately committing suicide, which would ruin the economy, and about how profoundly sad the lyrics to that old song "Red Rubber Ball" are ("The roller-coaster ride we took is nearly at an end / I bought my ticket with my tears, that's all I'm gonna spend"), and we talked about the similar chemical composition of tears and seawater, of tears and great diluvial catastrophes, and about the tears of feckless, moribund men in frilly aprons, and how the brutal indifference of time was like a vast inexorable army of locusts, and how there'd been 10^{26} nanoseconds since the Big Bang...

Given all the cosmic aperçus and trippy metaphysical speculation we'd indulge in for hours on end, you'd think we were high, except we *weren't* high. Y'know? We were just sitting there.

Anyway...the Imaginary Intern thought that the whole video-game idea—this whole thing about a first-person shooter fighting his way back to his mother's uterus and unraveling the DNA in the zygote—was completely dope. *But,* he had serious, emphatic reservations about what that entailed for me. He didn't think I really wanted to get involved with this sort of rigid chronology of pivotal incidents (even one that was retrograde). He thought I would so much prefer a more associative approach to autobiography, whatever that might be.

"I know you," he said. "And whether you're going backwards or forwards, you're still obliging yourself to hew to this strict chronology, and, trust me, this is not something you're going to really want to do."

So, it was the Imaginary Intern's idea that, though *Gone with the Mind* should probably still be somehow in the form of a first-person shooter game, it should take place at a mall...with some kind of mall shooter peering through the crosshairs of a telescopic gun scope. And I don't remember the exact conversation, but I do recall him suggesting to me that even if it ultimately turned out that I retained only some vague vestige of the video-game idea, I needed to actually sit down and play a video game—something I hadn't really ever done (with the exception of arcade games like *Ms. Pac-Man* and *Donkey Kong* years ago).

So I went out, purchased an Xbox, bought myself a copy of *Call of Duty: Black Ops II*, and, uh…it didn't take me long to realize that I was astonishingly, exasperatingly terrible at it…I mean seriously, terminally inept at it…I could not, no matter how many times I tried, get beyond the most rudimentary level, and after about a week, thoroughly disgusted with myself, I just gave up and never played it or any other video game again, ever again. But I've maintained an abiding, avid interest in video games—just in theory, not in practice. I'm really in love with this whole idea—this sort of mythic and, to me, exemplary notion—of a new breed of cultural intelligentsia comprised of maladjusted, *otaku* kids holed up in their tiny bedrooms in Nagasaki or wherever, subsisting on Hot Pockets and Red Bull, inventing games, producing music, making films, whatever… this idea that our culture is now generated by disaffected, socially phobic kids who won't come out of their rooms. It obviously resonates with me because I tended to be such a bedroom recluse myself. One of my very favorite books is David Kushner's account of John Carmack and John Romero (the cocreators of *Doom*, that pioneering, classic first-person shooter series) entitled *Masters of Doom: How Two Guys Created an Empire and Transformed Pop Culture*…in fact, at one point, the Imaginary Intern and I wanted to call the autobiography *Gone with the Mind: How Two Guys, by the Inversion of a Single Letter—Simply by Turning One Letter Upside Down!—Transformed a 1939 Historical Epic Starring Clark Gable and Vivien Leigh into the Story of a Fey Little Demagogue with Blond Bangs on a Flying Balcony*. The ambivalent relationship I have with video games is actually very similar to the relationship I have with couture—it's all in theory and not at all in practice. I'm really fascinated by designers, but I have no interest in or, um…inclination to wear designer clothes myself. I just wear T-shirts and flannel pajama bottoms every day basically…some version of that. That said, I love Alicia Drake's book *The Beautiful*

Fall: Lagerfeld, Saint Laurent, and Glorious Excess in 1970s Paris. And I couldn't wait to see Bertrand Bonello's film *Saint Laurent* when it opened at the New York Film Festival. And I've always been, unsurprisingly, extremely interested in Rei Kawakubo and in the Maison Martin Margiela, especially the way that everyone who worked at that particular atelier wore identical white lab coats...that kind of anonymity, that idea of eliminating any trace of individuality, and that kind of inclusively collaborative environment was very appealing to the Imaginary Intern and me. The way the ownership of ideas was shared equally by everyone was very much the way we wanted to work together. And we were actually toying around with this movie idea once about a fashion house very much like Maison Martin Margiela, except that it was also a cult...an apocalyptic cult like Heaven's Gate, that group in San Diego whose members all committed suicide (all of them wearing identical black shirts, sweatpants, and Nike Decade sneakers) so their souls could be picked up by a UFO trailing the Hale-Bopp comet (the UFO, their version, I suppose, of the flying balcony). And I'd written a scene that takes place during a very elaborate runway show that's situated in the summer palace of an eighteenth-century Russian tsar:

INT. SUMMER PALACE

Tsar Poet weeps into tear pots. Apes trot past. Servant brings silver platter with rat pesto on pre-toast. (Pre-toast is bread put in a toaster just long enough to warm it.)

And I read the scene to the Imaginary Intern, and I remember him saying, "Do you realize that *tsar poet, tear pots, apes trot, rat pesto,* and *pre-toast* are all anagrams of *prostate*?"

And I immediately realized that, without my having been consciously aware of it, the entire movie (although we never actually got much beyond those first few lines from that opening scene) was essentially about my recent bout with prostate cancer. (The robotic prostatectomy I underwent at Mount Sinai Hospital is what we—my mother and I—are referring to when we say, "On December 3, 2012, I was raped by a robot on the corner of Fifth Avenue and 101st Street in New York City.")

The Imaginary Intern wore a T-shirt that said *Amor Fati*—"love your fate." And he'd say, "Whatever happens to you, however degrading and humiliating and fucked up, you should appreciate it, because you can put it in the autobiography. So if no one comes to your reading, incorporate it, put it in."

I guess the jury's still out on whether or not anyone's "officially" here for the reading…I mean, since you two guys are here, and I'm reading…

PANDA EXPRESS WORKER
(Looks up from scrolling Tinder on his phone.)

What?

MARK

I said—I guess the jury's still out on whether or not you're "officially" here for the reading…since you're here, and I'm reading…

Y'know, something interesting just occurred to me…the Imaginary Intern once said something to me—I don't remember his exact words—but it was something that gave me the vague impression that he might have had a sort of *nostalgie de la boue* predilection for blue-collar workers and sailors…but aside from this one fleeting, enigmatic allusion (and I wish I could remember what it was that he said…it's possible it was in relation to that merry-go-round operator who tried to seduce my mother…when I told him that story…but I'm just not sure), nothing of the sort was ever overtly broached again. But I have to say, thinking about it right now, that in all the countless hours we'd sit on the couch and watch TV together, he never once said anything like "Hey, isn't that woman gorgeous?" or "Don't you think such-and-such an actress is hot?!" Though, on the other hand, he never evinced any kind of erotic enthusiasm for men on TV either. He was really all about the work, every single thing he saw he processed as potential fodder for the project. He was one of these totally...*esemplastic* kind of guys—y'know, he had a very synthetic, very practical and resourceful kind of sensibility, always about cobbling together the most disparate, miscellaneous things. We were watching some show once or some hockey game or something, and this Twizzlers commercial came on where everything in the world is made out of red Twizzlers—the cars, the highways, the bridges, the skyline, trees, the signage, the Statue of Liberty, Mount Rushmore, the hot-air balloons, everything—and this really, really impressed the Imaginary Intern and he said, "That's exactly what *Gone with the Mind* should be like! It should all be made out of the same thing!"

And I said it's a little like that commercial for Lay's potato chips where the Mr. Potato Head husband comes home from work and he says, "Sweetie, I'm home," but he can't find her, and he's looking all around, and finally catches his Potato Head wife clandestinely eating potato chips in this closet, this pantry...and he's appalled and he's like, "But you're a potato!" Here, it's a world all made of potatoes. It's potatoes eating potatoes.

And the Imaginary Intern said, "I don't know...that seems to me to be about nonprocreative desire, about autophagy as the apotheosis of self-love. The husband catches his wife in an act of masturbatory self-consumption and he's reflexively pissed about it, but then the last shot of the commercial reveals *both* of them in the closet eating the potato chips (i.e., masturbating), so...I think that's really about overcoming heteronormative shame, whereas Twizzlers World is all about monism. To me, it's all about turning everything into, or everything being made out of, a kind of unitary material…It's about all things originating from a single source. That's what I was saying before about *Gone with the Mind*…It should be all red Twizzlers."

I'm paraphrasing the Imaginary Intern, who was extremely plainspoken…I mean, he never used any kind of academic or post-structuralist or psychoanalytic jargon…He expressed himself in a very, very simple, very childlike way, actually. In fact, he did a lot of phumphering, a lot of stammering…but in all his unguarded speech disfluencies, in all his uhs and ums, sometimes I thought I discerned some sort of encrypted content. My grandmother Rose (my dad's mom) was a blinker. She had this cute, coy way of blinking when she talked that always made me think of Betty Boop for some reason. I think that's probably why, when I was ten years old, I became so obsessed with that American POW who, during a televised press conference in North Vietnam, blinked his eyes in Morse code spelling out the word T-O-R-T-U-R-E. So I kind of suspected that the Imaginary Intern's uhs and ums constituted some kind of code too, but he left before I could determine what that code actually was, if there even was one in the first place. (My grandmother, who became very mischievous when she had even the slightest bit of alcohol, once told me that she saw a man climb into my mother's bedroom window when my father was away on a business trip about nine months before I was born. And she said that she suspected that this man was my real, biological father.

"What did this guy look like?" I asked her.

And she said, "He was a short, pudgy, mustachioed Italian man in a red shirt and blue overalls."

"Was he wearing a red cap, white gloves, and brown shoes?" I asked.

"Yeah," she said.

"And was there a red *M* in a white circle on the front of his hat and gold buttons on his overalls?"

"Yeah!"

And I was like, "Nana, that's Mario, from *Super Mario Brothers*, the video game."

And she gave me that double Betty Boop *blink-blink*.

Now that I think of it, it was a kind of feigned daffiness, a kind of playing dumb. She really was absolutely brilliant at playing dumb, a virtuoso, and she was capable of just driving people to distraction with that, particularly my dad. It never bothered me really, I just sort of went with it. In the last few years of her life, when she was living at a...what do you call those places?...not a nursing home...an assisted-living facility...on Ventura Boulevard in Studio City out in California...I used to call her every week or so, and she'd always ask me how my Mexican wife was, knowing full well that my wife, Mercedes, is Ecuadorean, not Mexican. But I'd just go with it and I'd tell her how she was doing. And once, I called her and, over the course of maybe an hour-long conversation, she insisted on speaking to me as if I were my dad's brother, my uncle Richie. And again, I just went along with it. But I knew that she knew it was me, because at one point she asked "Richie" how his Mexican wife was.)

While we were working on *Gone with the Mind*, I was extremely superstitious about anything remotely related to the book. I work out at the gym (NYSC on Fourteenth and Garden) every other day lifting weights and I run for about an hour or so along the Hudson River on my off days from the weight training, and the midpoint of my run is the train station, Hoboken Terminal, and there's a sign in stenciled letters on the window-pane of the door to the waiting room that reads:

WAITING ROOM
CLOSED BETWEEN
1:00 A.M.–5:30 A.M.
DAILY

And each and every single time I'd reach that door, panting and floridly OCD, I'd press the appropriate letters—as if I were keying in a password on an ATM touchscreen—to form the acronym for *Gone with the Mind:* The *g* in *Waiting,* the *w* in *Between,* the *t* in *Between,* and the *m* in *5:30 a.m.*

Also, if I made a decision about the book and within the next couple of hours I saw a woman's exposed armpit, I would take that to be a mystical ratification of that decision. (I'm not really talking about an armpit with encrypted content—more like a yea-saying armpit.) For example: Once, when I was in my early twenties, my father got drunk at a dinner party, and said something extremely cruel and derisive about me to a guest whom he very much admired and, I think, emulated to a significant degree—he was an advertising executive who was becoming very rich and politically influential. (He's dead now.) I was having a lot of problems at the time—feeling very unfulfilled, rootless, un-actualized, unemployable, I guess feeling sort of worthless, and having all sorts of debilitating and undiagnosable and probably psychosomatic stomach ailments...so I was particularly vulnerable, and I remember thinking an instant after the slur came out of his mouth, *Hitler, where art thou?* I was so hurt and so exquisitely humiliated, and I remember thinking at that moment that if the Gestapo had shown up (we were living in West Orange, New Jersey, at the time) looking for Jews, I would have led them straight into the dining room and said, "There's a big one right there—the drunk guy playing the clarinet." (I remember this *so* clearly. Injured—in this case, *mutilated*—pride leaves extraordinarily eidetic, graven memories.) It was a singular aberration for my father, who's an extremely principled and scrupulously considerate person—none of which, I suppose, would make him immune to a mother-besotted boy's Oedipal fantasies of patricide. (In traditional folktales, the revenge of the father for his son's Oedipal ideation is, of course, to pass along to that son a genetic predisposition for prostate cancer, which is precisely what my father, in fact, did.) I can't remember my dad being either that drunk or unthinkingly nasty ever again. I, on the other hand, have been drunk and unthinkingly nasty thousands of times—a pattern which began when I was very young, like five. I had a big, nearly life-size stuffed orangutan that my uncle Richie had given me, with fur and a rubber face and hands and feet (I think my mom might have mentioned him in her introduction), and I'd prop him up next to me on my bed, and I'd pretend that we were at a bar together, and I'd sip from a bottle of Novahistine Elixir, a decongestant/antihistamine the color of green crème de menthe, until I was pretty fucked up. There were always bottles of it in my room because (as my mom said) I was prone to colds and earaches. This was obviously before the advent of child-resistant packaging and safety caps. And I remember I'd get very loud and very irascible and aggressive with the orangutan, and say some really awful, insulting things to him…it wasn't funny. It would start off amicably enough, my arm around his shoulders (the way I'd seen guys on TV do it), joking around, telling him stories, singing (mostly Civil War songs I'd learned from an album my parents had gotten me, "The Battle Hymn of the Republic," "When Johnny Comes Marching Home," "Just Before the Battle, Mother," things like that), but after a while my mood would sour, I'd take something the wrong way, a look, a completely innocuous gesture, and my temper would flare, and I'd end up flinging him down the stairs. In my memory, the orangutan sort of *floated* through the air—I don't know, maybe he had an unusually high lift-to-drag ratio for a stuffed animal or something—but he'd hit the floor at the bottom of the stairs with an awful thud, and my mother would come frantically running from wherever she was in the house, breathless and flushed, thinking I'd fallen down the stairs. (I never named the orangutan. I think even at that age I somehow intuitively understood that *all* names are slave names, that the absolute fixity of a name constitutes a form of captivity.)

For whatever reasons (discretion, embarrassment, etc.), I had very mixed feelings about including all of this in the book, but I thought it through and finally decided to put it in, and I went for a run, and the first thing I saw once I got out along the river was a woman with her arms raised as she gathered her hair into a pony-tail with a scrunchie, exposing her armpits, which I took to be an unmistakable sign that including these anecdotes about my dad and the stuffed orangutan was absolutely the right thing to do.

I've had an armpit fetish since I was a boy, and I think its origin was this Modigliani painting of a recumbent woman with one arm lifted behind her head that was hung up on the wall in my child-hood bedroom in Jersey City. There's the visual allure...the, uh... the, uh, *iconography* of that exemplary gesture of sexual surrender, of surrender to one's own pleasure...and then there's just the whole erotics, the appreciation, the connoisseurship...I'm trying to think of a word here that doesn't make it seem overly perverse...the *fondness* for the animal smells of the human body. In Elizabethan times, lov-ers would stay in touch by exchanging peeled apples which had been soaked in their armpit sweat before they parted company. Napo-leon famously wrote Josephine from one of his military campaigns, "I will return to Paris tomorrow evening. Don't wash." And Anton Chekhov wrote, "I don't understand anything about the ballet; all I know is that during the intervals the ballerinas stink like horses." Well, I don't understand anything about Chekhov, but I can only assume he meant that approvingly. And I was watching the reality show *Couples Therapy* on VH1 the other night, and there was this whole poolside conversation between Jenna Jameson and her boy-friend, MMA-trainer John Wood, about men's fixations on women's armpits.

So, it's not just me.

There was a woman at my gym who would work out and get very sweaty, and I loved the way she smelled. It reminded me a little of Wite-Out, and also that smell when you open the flip top of a can of new tennis balls…I didn't really run into her that frequently, but this one day I walked into the gym and there she was working out…on a tricep machine, I think…and I really, really wanted to get on that machine as soon as she was done with it…while her scent was still in the air. I don't know if that sounds creepy or not, but I'm just being honest here, I'm really being, like, *totally* nonfictional. Anyhow…she finishes up, and she's about to clean the seat and the, uh…the arm pads, or whatever you call them…

"You don't have to do that," I said.

"I'm really gross," she said, an assertion which obviously only served to inflame me further.

And, in order to prevent her from wiping it down with one of those antiseptic towelettes, I threw myself across the apparatus, as one would shield a tree from a chain saw.

And one of those idiotic trainers came over, one of those little meatballs with a clipboard, and he asked her if she wanted to lodge a complaint with the manager, etc., etc.

And out the corner of my eye, I noticed this guy in his mid-sixties whom I recognized immediately as the psychiatrist I'd gone to a few times after my prostate cancer surgery. He was working out sort of perfunctorily with a set of very light kettlebells. I hadn't seen him for years, and I had no idea he even belonged to my gym. He's a gaunt, pockmarked man with a gold incisor, who, when I used to see him in his office (on Eleventh and University), always wore very beautiful, very elegant bespoke suits. So it was more than a little jarring to see him so incongruously casual in baggy red nylon shorts and a Jiffy Lube T-shirt. Seeing him again made me remember the first thing I told him in that initial visit—a story about how, when I was in the second grade, at James F. Murray No. 38 Elementary School on Stegman Parkway back in Jersey City, I swindled some color-blind classmate I was supposed to be sharing crayons with out of all the brightly colored ones, giving him basically just the browns and the blacks, because I knew he couldn't really tell the difference. And I confided to the psychiatrist that ever since then I've thought of myself as an almost pathologically selfish, sort of monstrous human being. And I remember him just sitting there and not saying anything at all in response, and then I told him that since my surgery, I've had a very disturbing recurrent nightmare in which surgical robots go wild and stalk the countryside, tearing out men's prostates. And I remember him staring down at his notes, and saying that my dream reminded him of Vincent Bugliosi's description of members of the Manson Family (specifically Susan Atkins, Patricia Krenwinkel, and Tex Watson) as "heartless, bloodthirsty robots." And then he finally looked up at me and said, "You don't really strike me as either a bloodthirsty robot or a monstrous human being."

So I turned to this trainer with the clipboard and—in the way that one sometimes distractedly blurts out something from a reverie that doesn't quite but, in a weird way, almost perfectly suits present circumstances—said, "I'm not a robot, I'm a human being," a fact which, by the way, I'm not particularly proud of. But *that* whole can of worms—cyborgs, prosthetics, DIY synthetic biology, techno-sodomy, posthumanism, whether one's aggregate self, one's "mind," can be downloaded—is something that I'm planning on dealing with ad nauseam in the excerpts I'll be reading tonight. For now, if you're wondering what fragrances a withdrawn fifty-eight-year-old man, who still confides primarily in stuffed animals, action figures, and his mother, wears: my three current scents are: for writing, Jo Malone Vetyver; for the gym, L'Eau de Jatamansi by L'Artisan Parfumeur; and for going out at night (e.g., to the mall), Bois d'Arménie by Guerlain.

I don't know if you guys can smell me from way over there...

(The PANDA EXPRESS WORKER and the SBARRO WORKER are ignoring all this completely.)

MARK

We (the Imaginary Intern and I) used to talk a lot about an olfactory art, some kind of postlinguistic, pheromonal medium that would be infinitely more nuanced than language (and without language's representational deficiencies), a purely molecular syntax freed from all the associative patterns and encoded, ideological biases of language, that could produce the revelatory sensations of art by exciting chemosensory neurons instead of the "mind," that could jettison all the incumbent imperial narratives and finally get to something *really* nonfictional. And we both tremendously admired Helen Keller's militantly pro-olfactory polemic "Smell, the Fallen Angel" in her book *The World I Live In*. And we both agreed that if all the highly anticipated virtual- and augmented-reality technologies turn out to be just based on sight and sound, they'll be complete dead ends. And we both thought that *Diners, Drive-Ins and Dives* or *Beat Bobby Flay*, which are predicated upon olfaction and gustation, are more sophisticated shows epistemologically than, say, something like *Bill Moyers Journal* or *Charlie Rose*, which are based on archaic discursive practices. And we both felt very strongly—for a completely different reason (basically because *Baylisascaris procyonis* worms and *Schistosoma mansoni* flukes are infinitely more interesting characters than advertising executives or a police commissioner)—that *Monsters Inside Me* (the Animal Planet documentary series about parasites) is a better show than probably anything else on television.

Not sure about any of this, just throwing it out there...but this all seems to represent a fairly radical revision of Descartes, whose "I think, therefore I am" becomes instead "I stink, therefore I think."

Right?

There are smells that your own body produces that can have the same effect as Proust's madeleine, producing that extraordinary, unbidden gust of remembrance, the *mémoire involontaire*. I once mentioned this in passing to the Imaginary Intern, adding that I was reluctant to talk about it because I thought people might think it's juvenile or gross, and he said, "No, no, no, dude...you should *absolutely* talk about it, it's something so many people can identify with," which is such a totally Imaginary Intern thing to say, by the way—he was so perspicacious about things like this, but without even the slightest bit of self-importance or pretension. I, on the other hand, have always been squeamish and neurotically reticent about things like this, but I do think it's particularly pertinent here: there's a certain bowel movement of mine—and it's not something I can reduplicate at will; I've yet to figure out what food or combination of foods actually produces it—whose smell immediately transports me back in time to a very specific men's room at the Deal Casino, a beach club in Deal, New Jersey, that my family frequented during summers when I was a little kid. This was a very lovely and carefree, very richly experienced, almost psychedelically vibrant time in my life (a time when I first saw zeppelins in the sky, first heard the sound of mah-jongg tiles being shuffled, first caught glimpses of naked Marlboro-smoking middle-aged women in cabanas, etc.) and that particular fecal smell, and the memories it instantly evokes, buoys me for hours and sometimes days on end, and it's something that probably got me through my almost unassuageable grief when the Imaginary Intern left, and I'd sit there on the toilet desperately hoping to re-conjure his face from the configuration of cracks in the tile floor.

I think I mentioned before all his elaborate variations on my own motifs, which seemed to me so much more brilliant than the original ideas...Well, after he suddenly left—which I'll talk about more in a minute—in my grief, in my anguished disbelief (which almost immediately exposed long-repressed memories of my dead sister and swelled into a pain of infinite yearning that's never quite abated), I ransacked the house in search of any remnants of him, and I found a trove of his "poems," which were not originally intended as poems at all, I suppose, but were simply artless collations of my own fragmentary notes, but which have the numinous, elegiac, oracular quality (in my opinion, at least) of the greatest poetry, of, say, a Friedrich Hölderlin or, uh...of a Gérard de Nerval...whose disdain for the material world matched that of the Imaginary Intern ("This life is a hovel and a place of ill-repute. I'm ashamed that God should see me here"), who famously walked his pet lobster Thibault at the end of a blue silk ribbon through the gardens of the Palais-Royal, and who hanged himself from a sewer grating in the rue de la Vieille-Lanterne with an apron string he believed to be the Queen of Sheba's garter. As the Imaginary Intern would say, you can't make this stuff up...which, come to think of it, is a sort of ironic thing for an Imaginary Intern to say.

In a very literal sense, the Imaginary Intern existed for the project—he was all about the project...all about the production of *Gone with the Mind,* that was his sole remit, as they say. So, thanks largely to him, everything we talked about, no matter how seemingly extraneous or irrelevant—Twizzlers commercials, the molecular basis of infrared detection by pit vipers, Betty Boop, Helen Keller, Jenna Jameson, parasitic worms, whatever—somehow or other wound its way back to our work. The only exception to this, the only thing we didn't treat in a utilitarian way, the only thing that was completely sacrosanct, was the epic, heroic role the Soviet Union played in the defeat of Nazi Germany in World War II, and, in particular, the defense of Stalingrad.

One afternoon, I got back home from the gym and he was gone. I found a note he'd left behind entitled "Ciao":

One just keeps saying, "No... No...No..."
Head bowed, hat in hand,
A cringing, cunning little step back,
With each dialectical evasion,
Retreating, receding, "no...no...no..."
Until one simply disappears...

* * *

I miss, so terribly, working on *Gone with the Mind* with him. And I miss the times when we'd just sit around, listening to music together in the dark (usually moody, British postpunk pop) or watching TV.

Life's a harrowing fucking slog—we're driven by irrational, atavistic impulses into an unfathomable void of quantum indeterminacy—but, still…it's nice to have a friend, a comrade, a paracosm, whatever, to share things with.

The earliest folktales tended to be about single-cell organisms which lived deep below the surface of the earth, where temperatures routinely exceeded one hundred degrees Fahrenheit. Soon, though, folktales began to feature tiny multicellular worms which had evolved to survive in the extreme, inhospitable conditions of the subsurface biosphere. These worms—belonging to "the vast and diverse phylum of nematodes"—ate bacteria and often grew no bigger than two-hundredths of an inch. Then, for a very, very long period of time after this, almost all folktales pivoted around a cobbler, his fat, conniving wife, and their gullible daughter. But the degree of refinement was extraordinarily high, each ensuing folktale an almost imperceptibly subtle modification of its predecessor. Today, these elegant algorithms have given way to *autobiography,* with the hope that it might carry the same breadth of allegorical signification.

So were I to say something like…I don't know…something like…and I'm just riffing here, I'm just freestyling…something like…"I was a delicate little boy with flaxen bangs from Jersey City, who was alternately titillated and revolted by other children my age…those, those filthy, cross-eyed children in Jughead whoopee caps who'd run around screaming at the tops of their lungs with long pink roundworms wriggling out their nostrils…and my pretty, my pretty young mother—she was *so* young then!—in her, in her, her pink Izod polo shirt and her short, khaki wraparound skirt and her penny loafers—would prepare me a lunch of cream of mushroom soup, with banana Turkish taffy for dessert, and she'd read aloud folktales about other delicate little boys *just like me* (whose pretty mothers *also* read to them as they ate), exertions which would leave her almost too exhausted to fend off the coarse advances of the stooped, hook-nosed peddlers and the, uh...the sweaty merry-go-round operators who seemed to be endlessly ringing our doorbell"... something like that...I think you could discern in even something like that, certain folkloric elements, certain of the, the, uh...the generic narratemes that the Soviet folklorist Vladimir Propp enumerated...And even though the lexicon (Jughead, Turkish taffy) and the clothes (the Izod polo shirts, the penny loafers) clearly situates it in a very specific time, in a relatively contemporaneous reality (the early sixties), there's still, to my mind at least, an *illud tempus* (to borrow Eliade's phrase) suggested here...a kind of, uh...a vaguely medieval, once-upon-a-time-ness suggested by these roving peddlers and those caterwauling, parasite-infested children...We are—all of us—so deeply, so atavistically inculcated with the structures and the tropes that inhere in the very act of storytelling, that no sooner do we begin narrating our own presumably unprecedented childhoods than we—no matter who we are—reflexively conjure up the very same brigands and woodsmen, the very same vagabonds and troubadours and ogres, the very same hermits and sly, anthropomorphic animals, or recognize their interchangeable avatars whom we have inescapably become, through the telling and the retelling...And I think you're going to find in some of the excerpts I'm planning on reading tonight...and right now I can just pick arbitrarily a couple of lines off the top of my head, lines like "I was fascinated by the nuns who seemed to float across the boulevard on rainy afternoons," for instance...or, uh..."I got my first hand job from a schizophrenic girl with webbed fingers"...or even in a passing recollection like—and I don't remember the exact words off the top of my head here—something like "I'm pacing outside the club, smoking a cigarette, it's like mid-January and I'm fucking freezing in this filthy Trix T-shirt, one of those little blue dental bibs with the metal-ball chains, red plaid flannel pajama bottoms with this giant hole in the crotch, and a pair of white clogs...and my father calls to tell me that he's surprised I hadn't been included in Philip Roth's list of 'formidable postwar writers'" or...or even in a section that appears toward the very end of the autobiography where I say something like "I'm fifty-eight years old, and I'd still rather try to support myself by mowing people's lawns and babysitting than by teaching" or, uh—and this is one of the last lines in the whole book—"Would it be so terrible for a man who perseveres under the Damoclean threat of cancer and the ever-present specter of assassination to simply try and have one last meal with his old mother in the food court of a mall?" I think even in these lines, you can find a sense of the *fantastic*...a sense of fairy-tale enchantment...But that idea of enchantment, as we move through the second decade of the twenty-first century, seems ever more adulterated, ever more degraded...and, one wonders, by what exactly? As chronologies of diagnosis and treatment replace the surrealist poetry of our symptomology, how quickly it can all begin to seem like a PowerPoint presentation at a TED talk or the strobe-effect of PTSD flashbacks in a Lifetime movie...

Of course the battle between the materialist rationalists and the anti-materialist irrationalists is long over, and the anti-materialist irrationalists lost, and we await our UFOs and our flying balconies to come and bear us away.

The chorus in Seneca's *Thyestes* asks: "Will the last days come in our time?" And I would say, Yes, absolutely. I mean, the last days might very well come during this reading tonight. I think my mom mentioned before that the floodwaters are rising, right? And assassins, *onryōs* (vengeful spirits), first-person shooters...mall shooters, whatever you want to call them...are all wandering around, floating around. And I don't think any of this should especially disturb anyone. I don't think it's anything to get all bummed out about. I think it should actually make everyone feel really good. Oprah said to Lindsay Lohan: "Vultures are waiting to pick your bones...that should *liberate* you." Someone in the video game *Total War: Shogun 2* says something to the effect of: "a samurai should not scandalize his name by holding his one and only life too dear." In other words, the true samurai enters the battle with no thought of return. And I really think that's how you have to look at it when you do a non-fiction reading, when you really commit to only presenting empirically verifiable material, when you're really *deadly* serious about that. And I bring up the Japanese writer Yukio Mishima now, not because he was a sickly, pale, pampered introvert of a child who grew up to become obsessed with bodybuilding and who, as an adult, when his mother complained that "Mommy's foot hurts," proceeded to lick the sore area in front of friends and family, but because he gave, on November 25, 1970, one of the best nonfiction readings ever given when he stepped out onto a balcony (not the flying balcony of the Palazzo Venezia, but a balcony nonetheless) and declaimed a prepared manifesto to several hundred soldiers gathered below who mocked and jeered him (and who, by the way, weren't officially "there for the reading" either), returned inside, disemboweled himself, and was then beheaded by a member of his private militia. I'm qualifying this by calling it one of the *best* nonfiction readings ever given. It could have been one of the *great* nonfiction readings ever given if Mishima's mother, Shizue Hiraoka, had been there, but she wasn't (although she did attend his funeral). I mean, you'd have to say—and I think this is *so* obvious given the fact that being mocked, jeered at, and martyred in the presence of one's mom is the key, the key ingredient here—that Christ on the Cross (in the presence, of course, of his mother, the Virgin Mary) gave one of the greatest nonfiction readings ever given.

Now, I just want to fast-forward six hours or so in the Gospel narrative to make a small point. The Virgin Mary was *not* a

Ferbering mother. And though the lifeless body of Christ did not literally cry out for her, the exigencies of Christian doctrine surely did. And unlike *my* mom on those unfortunate nights alluded to earlier, Mary did respond, and unlike *my* mom, Mary cradled *her* son in her arms...and hence the enormously popular, endlessly reproduced, and invariably eroticized image of the Pietà. Now, in all fairness, we can't underestimate the influence on young mothers—and my mom was only, what, barely twenty at that time?—we can't underestimate the...the enormous influence of pro-Ferbering authorities like Dr. Spock who, when it came to children's sleep problems—and this may surprise you guys—was more draconian than even Ferber himself.

(The PANDA EXPRESS WORKER and the SBARRO WORKER are paying absolutely no attention to anything MARK is saying.)

MARK

But the simple truth of it is that if you take a certain type of boy with an extremely delicate temperament and you turn his bedroom into a dark, terrifying sort of prison cell (even if it's only for a couple of nights), a significant amount of self-radicalization is going to occur with *that* type of child in *that* type of environment. I still suffer, to this day, from an intractable compulsion to fold things into thirds instead of halves, which I believe is directly attributable to the Ferbering.

Okay, you guys might be thinking to yourselves, *how does Christ on the Cross constitute a nonfiction reading?* The Seven Statements from the Cross ("Father, forgive them, for they do not know what they do," "Truly, I say to you, today you will be with Me in paradise," "Woman, behold your son. Son, behold your mother," etc.) were extemporaneous utterances, they were not recited from any kind of preprepared text, so how is that a reading? To which I would say, very simply, that for a divine being like Jesus Christ, all of history—from the beginning ("word one") through eternity—has already been inscribed. All of it has already been written. To a divine being, it's all already a book, or a script, whatever. So, anything a divinity says, any seemingly spontaneous utterance He or She might make, constitutes a *reading*.

As I look out tonight, there are no Roman soldiers...but there are empty chairs to mock me. And some sort of...some sort of, at least virtual martyrdom impends; I can feel that in my bones. And my mom is right here, and I appreciate that tremendously. And so, I'm very proud tonight to be here at the Nonfiction at the Food Court Reading Series. And as I look out at my mother right now, eating pork fried rice out of a Styrofoam shell from Panda Express, I can't help but be reminded of when that teacher at James F. Murray No. 38 Elementary School in Jersey City used to hold me up to the window to show me that my mom was waiting for me outside in the schoolyard, to reassure me, to demonstrate to me that she hadn't "abandoned" me again, as I apparently felt she had during her second pregnancy. I guess like a lot of kids that age, I'd occasionally fabricate the vocations of my parents, and I remember once telling that particular teacher that my father, an attorney in Jersey City, was—and I'm paraphrasing here, I don't remember my exact words—that he was actually a tropical agronomist who specialized in diseases of the banana, perhaps a sly Oedipal dig at his virility. I remember the teacher smiling at that. She was a very smiley, very accommodating woman. But I always suspected that her smile was a mask. To me, even at that tender age—I think I was six—it suggested a latent misery, hidden by a great labor of repression and dissimulation. But as I look out at my mom tonight...Y'know, Heraclitus said, "No man ever steps in the same river twice, for it's not the same river and he's not the same man." But I also think that no son sees the same mother twice, for it's not the same mother and he's not the same son. So as I look out at my mom tonight, I see not only a woman with a unique sociocultural history as a daughter, as a mother, as a grandmother, a woman with an autobiography of her own, but I also see a techno-organic aggregate body that is bacterial, fungal, mineral, metal, electrochemical, digitally informational, etc., and then, if I put on these reading glasses, which help me a lot with close-range vision, but pretty seriously degrade my ability to focus on anything in the distance, I see a sort of flat, two-dimensional, distorted female figure composed of splintered planes, and then the more I squint through the reading glasses, the more she now seems reduced to a purely geometric abstraction, a vertical element perpendicular to a horizontal element, and she's achieved an object's phenomenological status as a thing prior to any meaning…and if I look through them like this — backwards — she seems to disaggregate completely. She becomes an exploded diagram of herself. Like the instructions you get with furniture from Ikea. And here the intelligible dimensions of the mother are extended into infinite space — the macroscopic realm of celestial bodies and the vast distances between them, and the intimate realm of microscopic organisms and cells. And the image of the mother as exploded diagram is, of course, the image of the mother as suicide bomber.

On May 28, 2013, I tweeted: *Spent the weekend just wandering around outside, caramelizing things with my crème brûlée torch.*

And then on August 28, 2014, I tweeted: *Just learned this morning that my Imaginary Intern is an ethnic Chechen.* I was being facetious, of course, and I wasn't sure if the Imaginary Intern had even seen the tweet, because we were both very busy that morning, off doing our separate things. I think he was reviewing and archiving childhood crayon drawings and digitized 8-millimeter birthday-party footage that my dad had shot in the early sixties, and I was, uh…you know what?…I think this was a period of time when I'd become, like, mildly obsessed with Spaten lager beer…so I'm pretty sure that that day I was out looking for a place that sold it by the case. But it turned out that he had indeed seen the tweet, because once the two of us reconvened later that evening, he asked me, "What ethnicity do you actually think I am?" And I don't remember exactly what I said, probably something like, "Oh, you're a paracosm." Or "Oh, you're a quasi-autonomous notional entity." Or "You're an apparition from Figmentistan." Or something like that. Just kidding around with him. And I remember he said, very seriously, "I think I'm a teratoma." And it took me a minute before I realized he was alluding to an incident that had occurred, I don't know, some fifteen years ago when my mom had an ovarian cystic teratoma removed. I didn't know what a teratoma was at the time, so I did some research and I discovered that it's a kind of tumor that can contain hair and teeth and, in rare cases, eyes and feet, but much more commonly the hair and teeth, so I went out and bought a tiny comb and a tiny tooth-brush (I think they were from a set of toiletries for one of those Troll dolls that I found at a Toys "R" Us) and I gave them to my mom at the hospital. And I immediately regretted the "gift"—I'd orig-inally thought it was sort of cute and clever in a completely innoc-uous way, but then it just seemed like a creepy morbid attempt at humor at her expense, and I was really apprehensive that she'd be hurt and angry. And she so easily could have hobbled me with a glare or a pained aversion of her eyes if she'd wanted to…because I don't think it was funny to her at all…I mean, she had two huge heliotrope bruises—one from a tourniquet they'd used to start the IV drip in her arm and one from a catheter she'd had on the dorsum of her hand—that made me wince when I looked at them, she was still nauseous from the anesthesia, and she was still in a consider-able amount of pain from the surgery itself. But she just smiled at me, in that beautiful, gracious, indulgent way she has of smiling at me, the way she's always smiled at me. This is the Noh mask of her immutable benevolence.

I said a little while ago when I was talking about how my mom drove me to the mall tonight that I don't really like to talk to her when she's been drinking and she's driving over ninety miles an hour, because I don't want to distract her. And I was just being facetious. And it was a glib, thoughtless thing to say. Just for cheap laughs at her expense. And I just want to say that my mom does not drink and drive. And as soon as I said what I said, I regretted it completely. And, Mom, I looked over at you and you could have just glowered at me, which would have ruined the whole reading for me, the whole night...but you didn't. You just took it in stride. You just looked up at me, and smiled that beautiful, indulgent, luminous smile of yours, and went right back to your pork fried rice.

One stands up here, on a table in the middle of a food court, as one would upon a balcony overlooking a piazza thronged with swooning Fascists. And one becomes heedless, one becomes disinhibited, indiscreet...and one says all sorts of things one shouldn't say—

(MARK'S MOM, as if on cue, reaches furtively across the table to snare MARK'S egg roll.)

MARK

Don't eat mine, Mom.

(MARK and his MOM exchange a conspiratorial wink, as if this whole little pas de deux about the drunk driving, the ovarian tumor, and the egg roll had been predesigned to finally coax a reaction—any reaction—from the PANDA EXPRESS WORKER, who simply shrugs indifferently...whatever.)

MARK

I think one of the first things I ever wrote was a puppet play. Not a play that was intended to be performed *using* puppets, but a play intended to be performed *for* puppets — for an audience of puppets — for the stuffed animals and action figures in my bedroom. (So, given the fact that I still think that the ideal audience for my work is inanimate objects, a roomful of empty chairs actually constitutes a full house!) These plays, these productions, performances, whatever you want to call them, sort of bounced back and forth between dialogue and dance, and they were mounted in my room, as I said, and the audience would typically consist of my stuffed orangutan, maybe a G.I. Joe or two, and several dozen plastic Civil War soldiers. Many of the topics at play in these early works were those with which I'd been fixated since I was a little boy: Pietà sculptures, claustrophilia, fascism, flagellate protozoa, androgenized female Eastern European athletes, the fragility of persona, etc. And, as I said, there was dance. The choreography was spare, rudimentary. There were two basic movements that I'd perform simultaneously as I recited my monologues. I suppose in the way a sensitive child, say, in the Middle Ages, might see the threshing motions of men and women harvesting grain in the fields and make from that a formalized dance movement, a sweep of the arm could represent the eternal rhythm of the seasons, I repurposed two motions I'd seen adults perform many times in the milieu I grew up in. The first was a shifting of weight from my right foot to my left foot, back to my right, then to my left, back and forth and back and forth — this was a particular kind of swaying or *shuckling* I'd gleaned watching men preparing to hit a golf ball at the driving range or at an actual course. The other movement derives from women shuffling mah-jongg tiles. I would extend my arms out in front of my body, palms down, and make circles with my hands, flat, horizontal circles, clockwise with my left hand, counterclockwise with my right. I'd perform these movements as I recited my stammering, maudlin soliloquies and the rabid harangues to my plastic soldiers. I guess this was a kind of, of…what's the word?…a kind of…*liminal* gesturing, a gesturing that announced that we were about to cross a threshold…that we were waiting…not knowing what's next…not knowing what violence or calamity my words might bring down upon us…This was my little *Totentanz*…my little dance of death…something along those lines, I guess…And I loved putting on these plays very, very much, alone in my room, with my rapt audience of inanimate aficionados. And, honestly, I never wanted to do "more" with it…or become "known" for it…or pursue it as, y'know, any kind of vocation or career.

Which reminds me of something interesting…Soon after the Imaginary Intern left, I found a postcard from him. There was a photograph on one side…it was a close-up of a white skinhead and behind him was this Black guy (whose face and torso were out of frame) sort of standing over him, straddling him, so that his penis was lying down the center of the skinhead's shaved white skull, giving him, like, a penis Mohawk. And under the photograph was a caption that had originally read *Stay relevant.* But the Imaginary Intern had added, I guess with a Sharpie or something, the prefix *ir-* in front of the word *relevant,* so it read *Stay irrelevant,* meaning—at least this is my interpretation—don't do anything, whether it's having a friend drape his dick across your head or putting on little, sort of experimental USO performances for your plastic Civil War soldiers, or whatever—for the sake of becoming well known. Do the contrary. Cultivate your irrelevance, cultivate your gratuitousness. The Imaginary Intern had also stapled a clipping to the blank side of the postcard, presumably from some scientific journal like *Nature* or *Cell,* which had the headline "South Korean Microbiologist Discovers That Even Amoebae Fall into the Five Basic Archetypal Categories: Nerd, Bully, Hot, Dumpy, and New Kid," the meaning of which, with regard to that photograph, I'm still trying to understand, even though I realize it's entirely possible that he just stapled the clipping to the postcard as a way of saving the clipping—in other words, that he was just looking for something to staple the clipping to in order to file it, and just randomly grabbed the postcard, so that its contents were completely irrelevant. But I really, really doubt that, just given the way the Imaginary Intern seemed to deliberately generate—well, not *generate...locate* would probably be a better word—the way he seemed to very deliberately, very painstakingly, very precisely and rigorously *locate* signification in just about everything he did. But it's a precision and rigor that only becomes apparent in retrospect. In fact, I would say 99 percent of things involving the Imaginary Intern only become apparent in retrospect. And he really did fervently believe—as do I—in this whole idea of staying secret, of shunning the spotlight. A friend of mine once suggested that someone make a documentary about the Imaginary Intern...set up cameras all over the house like in that movie *Paranormal Activity*...and I told the Imaginary Intern about it, and he freaked. He hated the idea...And I immediately regretted having told him about it. It was a huge mistake. And sometimes I think that that's actually why he left. He just wanted to be completely off the radar, left alone, completely inconspicuous, completely off camera...I don't know if he'd been abused in his life or what... but he just wanted to be able to relax and act as loony and as dorky as he wanted to without having to worry about what anyone else thought, and I think the idea of a documentary just really shook him up, it really spooked him. I think I mentioned before that I've tried to re-conjure his face from the configuration of cracks in the tile floor of other bathrooms. In fact, I was sitting on the toilet in the men's room in the Nordstrom in this mall actually, and I thought I discerned his face in some craquelure on the floor, and I remember I was concentrating so hard on it, trying so hard to force a jumble of disparate features into a recognizable physiognomy, that I was actually straining, y'know, pressing in that way that can cause hemorrhoids, so I had to stop. I've had that sudden, that sudden frisson, that jolt of *It's him!* many times, and I'll squint and I'll look from different angles and inevitably it's a false alarm, it's not him...and it's...it's a big, big letdown, it really is...it's a shitty feeling.

But that's what nonfiction is, people. Shitty feelings and encounters with death. And that's why we're here tonight....

MARK

Okay...before I, uh...get started here, just a couple of little things to help put the excerpts I'm going to read in some context for you...

The Fighter Jets was a cycle of crayon-on-coloring-book and crayon-on-construction-paper works that I produced from roughly 1962 to 1964, which clearly prefigured the violent poetry I would begin writing in 1967, when I was eleven. I was primarily doing...I don't know what you'd call it, I don't know what you'd call the style... *naive* or *primitive* or maybe *outsider, proto-pop* renditions of the U.S. Navy's F4F-3 Wildcat, the Luftwaffe's Messerschmitt Bf 109, and the Imperial Japanese Navy's Mitsubishi A6M Zero...these three fighter aircraft were...these were my water lilies, I guess you could say. One could arrange the work in three loose thematic clusters: fighter jets in flight either singly or in formation, aerial battles or dogfights between fighter jets featuring multicolored tracer ammunition fired from mounted 20 mm autocannons, and in which one or both of the fighter aircraft are in flames and/or exploding in the air, and (in a series I completed in late '64) kamikaze fighters smashing their jets into American battleships and aircraft carriers.

This latter series foreshadows one of the first poems that I submitted to a poetry workshop at Brandeis University when I was a freshman there in 1973, which was the first actual writing class I ever took. My classmates were all seniors, all several years older than me, very dour and humorless, and very cliquish and condescending toward me, and I wanted nothing more than for them to respect me and include me, and I guess my way of trying to ingratiate myself with them, of just trying to get them to like me—which I so *desperately* wanted—was to hand in increasingly aggressive, abrasive poems with disassociated imagery, jarring, dissonant non sequiturs, and increasingly antagonistic titles, basically an update of my proprietary vernacular of *yama nashi, ochi nashi, imi nashi* that I'd intuited years ago at the slot-car track in Livingston. So this poem I was referring to, for instance, had two stanzas; the first was...and I can't remember the exact words, obviously...but it was something like: "Asked to describe the rabbi's daughters, / the man doffs his baseball cap, / revealing the sun-spotted flesh of his balding head, / and pauses for a moment... / 'The second daughter is more beautiful than the first, the third more beautiful than the second, and the first more beautiful than the third.'" And then the second stanza which was quite, quite long—it ran fifteen or twenty-some-odd pages—was intended as the dying soliloquy, the...the soliloquy in extremis, of a plummeting kamikaze pilot, except that you couldn't possibly know that it was a dying soliloquy or any other kind of soliloquy for that matter, because it was written entirely as a spurious transliteration of completely fake Japanese, nor could you possibly know that it involved a kamikaze pilot, because although I'd originally entitled the poem "Kamikaze," on the morning of the workshop, at the very last minute, I changed the title to "Eat Me. I Hate Everyone in This Fucking Class," probably as a kind of preemptive provocation, assuming that the class would hate the poem (which the class vehemently did). And when people predictably took offense at the title, I remember explaining that "Well...it's not me who's actually saying that, it's the narrator of the poem, it's a character I'm playing," that sort of thing. And of course I read my poem out loud, which is what we did in the workshop, and I read the faux-Japanese gibberish section in its entirety, which, seriously, must have taken about forty minutes, and which I could see just completely aggravated the shit out of everyone in the class. And all I really wanted out of all this was for someone, one of my peers, to just say to me, *Look, I really appreciate how hard you're working* or *I really appreciate how much you're trying to do something unique or transformative or just fresh, something we haven't heard before, or at least trying to wring some droll human comedy from the unrelenting grimness and abject indignity of life on this planet.* But no one did. But, remarkably, Mark Strand, who was a very well-known, highly esteemed poet, who died fairly recently, and who was teaching this workshop back then...he actually seemed to *get* it. He said to the class—and, again, I'm paraphrasing something that was said a very long time ago—he said that the first part represented the enchantment and illogic and fear and suspense of beauty, and that all the ensuing faux-Japanese gibberish represented the incommunicable subjective reality of experiencing that beauty. So, surprised—shocked, actually—and sort of emboldened by what certainly seemed like Strand's genuine engagement with the work, I piped up (and I was usually too bashful to say *anything*) and I said, somewhat flippantly and presumably to lighten the mood a bit, "I'm trying to do the Baal Shem Tov with a *Tora! Tora! Tora!* vibe," but then I thought to myself, *You know what, I am going to make a case for this poem, and I am going to explain exactly what I did and why.* I was a great admirer of Andy Warhol then (and still am), and I got such a kick out of his coyness and his diffidence and nonchalance when he'd be asked why he silkscreened his paintings or why he'd just point his stationary 16 mm Bolex at a building or a fellated or sleeping man and let it run until the emulsion flickered and whitened and the cartridge expired, and this pale, pimply sphinx in his sunglasses would put his finger on his chin and think for a moment or two, and then just say, "Because it was easier." But I wasn't like that at all. As much as I would have liked to have been a pale and pimply sphinx, I had an uncommonly clear complexion and I had a decidedly unsphinxlike need for people to understand what I was doing and to admire it and to like me. And I certainly hadn't done what I did because it was easier—it was extraordinarily time-consuming and laborious and difficult to write that amount of faux-Japanese gibberish because real words kept inadvertently popping up in the gibberish. And I explained how it's almost impossible to completely purge a text of meaning. Meaning is like mice or eczema — it's very hard, if not impossible, to get rid of completely. Not only because the purging itself, like a dance, or like a new science, generates a whole new signifying language of its own, but because meaning persists at much deeper levels than we can ever imagine and at a much more infinitesimal scale, gigantic monsters can be created by changing a single nucleotide in the genetic code — one can conjure an ornate, vanished world from outer space from the serif of a single letter. What else does the human being do but emit and decipher signs? Who else but the human being has this compulsion for finding patterns and structures in all sorts of incoherent noise (and craquelure!). With gibberish, you open the floodgates of meaning, everything is in there — actual poems by Saigyō and Fujiwara no Teika and Princess Shikishi (if that's what you're looking for), mitochondrial DNA sequences from honeybees and ants and aphids, blocks of AES/Rijndael-256–encrypted ciphertext, backwards excerpts from *Don Quixote* and *Little Dorrit*, from Gwyneth Paltrow's *It's All Good: Delicious, Easy Recipes That Will Make You Look Good and Feel Great*, long diagonal acrostics of John Galliano's antisemitic tirade at La Perle bar in Le Marais…everything. In the faux-Japanese glossolalia of the plummeting kamikaze is the complete anagram of *Gone with the Mind* that would take scientists (i.e., the Imaginary Intern and myself) another forty years to unscramble. His gibberish is the incommunicable anguish that results from the impossibility of fulfilling incestual desire. He is, like a muttering Popeye, a hysteric describing his symptoms, destroying the world in order to save it. The vertiginous illogic, the impossibility of the exorbitant claims about the beauty of the rabbi's daughters causes nausea. A little boy is having a tantrum because his mother is impossibly gone. He vomits gibberish. In the distance is a kamikaze's long parabolic swoon. A little boy's tantrum crescendos in a parabolic projection of vomited gibberish which is actually a secret language between kamikaze boy and the rabbi's daughter who represents—drumroll, please—the mother!

I don't know how long I went on like this. It was like a fugue state...as if I were back in my bedroom in Jersey City holding forth for my orangutan and my Civil War soldiers...and when I "returned" to the classroom in Waltham, all the students had left, only Strand remained. "Y'know," I said to him, "I was originally going to entitle the poem 'Kamikaze,' but I thought that might be a little too on the nose." "Nonsense!" he said, with a snort of laughter. "With the possible exception of 'Eat Me. I Hate Everyone in This Fucking Class,' what else could you possibly call it?!" And then he said—and this is something I remember *so* vividly, something I really appreciated and would ruminate upon for a long time to come—he said, "The explanation of your poem is a better poem than the poem. It's even more insane." He was a charming, congenial, exceptionally sweet person, very generous, very gracious, very receptive and encouraging, with this quick, mischievous sense of humor. Just a really, really good guy. I remember feeling that so much at the time, even though, deep down, I suspected that he was just humoring me, and was probably saying vastly different things at the off-campus coffee klatches that I was always much too shy and insecure to ever attend. But he also knew—and that he knew is something I've surmised in retrospect—that there was something up with me, that there was something going on psychologically. Why else would I insist on entitling poem after poem "Shit in a Ramekin"? "Shit in a Ramekin II," "Shit in a Ramekin III," "Shit in a Ramekin IV," etc. No matter what they were about. I wrote a poem that was just a very standard, sort of elegiac reminiscence about taking a nap on a summer afternoon in Deal, New Jersey, and hearing, through the open window, the sound of lawn mowers and birds singing and children playing, and I called it "Shit in a Ramekin V." Another one I remember was inspired by one of those automated promptings you hear at airports. It went something like:

The moving walkway
Is now ending.
Please look
Down.

This was called "Shit in a Ramekin VI" or "Shit in a Ramekin VII" or something.

I was full of anger back then, but obviously so desperate for people to like me, and so predisposed to loathe anyone who did in fact like me, *that* whole routine...of rapid-cycling neediness and misanthropy... And as arbitrary as it might seem to think of oneself purely in terms of Teds, I think, inside, I was definitely feeling more like Ted Bundy or Ted Kaczynski than Ted Hughes or Ted Berrigan back then.

I have to say that, after all these years, I'm still vain enough to prefer having enemies over friends. It's still consoling to me to feel embattled and anathematized. I'm still grateful for anything that drives me back into my little corner of the world (this is my innate, roach-like thigmotropism), for anything that forces me to seek refuge in my ancestral village...what the Imaginary Intern used to call "Studio Mizuhō" or "Around the Corner Where Fudge Is Made"... the primordial matrix of the mind, the ancestral home of the mind, what the fifteenth-century Noh playwright Komparu Zenchiku called the "circle of emptiness" (*kurin*)—the stage at which the actor transcends distinctions between pure and orthodox styles and improper styles, achieving a return to the beginning (*kyarai*), the highest, indescribable experience, which expresses nothing. And, of course, this is that very place within one's mother's arms, that very circle formed by one's mother's arms. And I still believe that there are two basic kinds of people—people who cultivate the narcissistic delusion of being watched at all times through the viewfinder of a camera, and people who cultivate the paranoid delusion of being watched at all times through the high-powered optics of a sniper's rifle, and I think I fall—and have always fallen—into this latter category.

But the ridiculous thing about being an angry young man, or at least an angry young Brandeis freshman, is that you don't even know yet how much there is out there to actually be angry about. Things are still fairly idyllic at that age. You have no idea yet the extent to which life really is shit in a ramekin.

A week or so later, I had one last meeting with Strand, just the two of us in his office. "Do you know that the band Roxy Music has a song out now called 'Do the Strand'?" I asked him. He seemed genuinely perturbed by this. "What?! I need to contact my attorney immediately!" he said, waiting for my distress to register before cracking up. He really could be such a funny guy. I told him I wanted to quit the class, and he said, "I don't blame you." I felt so relieved, so "safe" at that moment, that I confessed to him my lifelong love of Mickey Mantle and Jackie Gleason. And I remember I started to cough, and Strand asked me if I was okay, and I said, "I've been choking on the same stupid piece of barley since lunch," and he opened a small bottle of Pellegrino for me, and...no...I'm sorry...I'm sorry...my God, they're going to confiscate my Nonfiction at the Food Court membership card here...it was Orangina, not Pellegrino...one of those little ten-ounce bottles of Orangina...So, I took a couple of sips, which helped a lot...and I, uh, don't remember how we got around to the subject of Popeye, maybe it was via Ashbery's sestina "Farm Implements and Rutabagas in a Landscape." And I'm not sure if I actually mentioned this to Strand at the time or not, but I think when most people visualize Popeye, the first thing that probably comes to mind is his can of magic spinach (which made him, for all intents and purposes, the first celebrity user of performance-enhancing drugs), or the battleships and the turbines and the atomic bombs superimposed on his swollen biceps, or his cri de guerre "I yam what I yam, and that's all what I yam," which, in its concision, transparency, and tautological plenitude, remains the first and greatest constructivist autobiography; but he also had a very beautiful way of speaking, particularly of speaking to himself—his muttering. It was this streaming, autobiographical play-by-play overlaid with all sorts of commentary and theorizing, this meta-mutter, the soliloquy of an electrolarynx, a sort of free-jazz didgeridoo solo. It's kind of like what Strand had said to me the previous week in class, about how the explanation of my poem was a better poem than the poem. I think Popeye's muttering is the explanation of *his* poem. (This is very similar to something the Imaginary Intern and I used to call "singing all the parts." If you ask someone—and I'm just picking a song I happened to hear on the radio in the car on the way over here tonight—"Do you like that Michael Jackson song 'Black or White'?" and she's like, "I don't know it, how's it go?" you'd try to do the song for her, to re-create it for her. You'd try to approximate some of the percussion with your mouth, to whatever extent you could do that, a little bit of beat-boxing...and then you'd lay in that guitar riff...De-de-de-de-de-duuh, de-de-de-duuh... De-de-de-de-de-duuh, de-de-de-duuh...High-pitched yelp...De-de-de-de-de-duuh, de-de-de-duuh...De-de-de-de-de-duuh, de-de-de-duuh...High-pitched yelp..."I took my baby on a Saturday bang / Boy is that girl with you / Yes we're one and the same..." That's "singing all the parts." In the actual song, it's all layered, like a pastry, like a...like a mille-feuille...a napoleon. But when you're just doing it by yourself, you have to take all of it apart...it becomes more like an Ikea exploded diagram...and what's simultaneous, what's synchronic in the music, becomes sort of flattened out and sequential in the representation. And this was something the Imaginary Intern and I used to always talk about trying to do in *Gone with the Mind*, trying somehow to express the chord of how one feels at a single given moment, in this transient, phantom world, standing in the center of a food court at a mall with your mom, but in the arpeggiated exploded diagram of an autobiography.) So then, Strand asked if I'd liked comics when I was a kid, and I said that Popeye was a relatively recent interest, but that, yes, when I was a little boy there were comics I liked very much. "Which ones?" he said. "I'm curious." And I remember he was rotating his wrist as if he might have hurt it sailing or playing tennis. And I explained to him that most boys I knew who were into comics at that age were, y'know, either into Marvel, things like Spider-Man, Iron Man, the Hulk, Thor, X-Men, or into DC, stuff like Superman and Batman and Green Lantern. But somehow I got steered into Harvey Comics, and Harvey Comics…their roster of "heroes" consisted of an assortment of, uh…of, basically, pathetic, feckless, feeble-minded pariahs. (These were, come to think of it, actually the first misfits I "befriended.") A couple of them were clearly psychotic, but, for the most part, they were just fantastically stupid—I mean like mentally defective, low-grade-moron stupid…a bunch of guffawing, gullible half-wits who just wanted everyone to be their friend, who'd get into a car with anyone, sell their souls for a cupcake literally made out of crap, follow a fucking balloon off the ledge of a building…But I just found myself identifying with them in a particularly intense way. I felt that they related uncannily to everything I was going through in my life at that time, and I guess I also thought, even at that age, that they were, in some sense, the most poetic of all the comic-book characters—Sad Sack, the luckless, disaffected, humiliated soldier; Baby Huey, the ungainly, naive, dimwitted, friendless, anthropomorphic duck; Little Lotta, a homely, obese girl whose insatiable gluttony gave her superhuman strength which she'd use to help people who still found her completely revolting; Hot Stuff, a devil-baby who wore asbestos diapers; and, of course, Casper, the friendly, cloyingly obsequious ghost…I just really connected, on a very deep level, with these characters. And the question is: What was it inside me, what gnawing void or strangulated loop of psyche had produced such a strong feeling of fellowship with a lonely, anomic army private with latent spree-killing tendencies, a retarded duck, a bullied fat girl, an incontinent demon, and a desperately ingratiating dead child? And I think the answer has to be, for reasons that are all too apparent, my PTSD from being force-fed beets, from being abandoned on an out-of-control merry-go-round operated by some depraved drifter, the brutality, the inhumanity of the Ferbering, having my fingers deliberately mangled in a carpet cleaner, being left in a filthy, stinking, cacophonous, violent hospital ward all by myself after a tonsillectomy that I'm pretty sure was performed without anesthesia...and also from just having to watch my mom vomit and hemorrhage all over the place—

(MARK winks at his MOM, who's shaking her head, smiling with forbearance.)

MARK

So, Strand looked at me, and he said, "You should write about all this someday." And I said, "You mean about all the terrible privations and wrenching traumas from my childhood?" And he said, "Yes, it would be hilarious!" And I said, "You mean...nonfiction?"

And, well, here we are...some forty years later...at the Nonfiction at the Food Court Reading Series.

8

LAST ORGY OF THE DIVINE HERMIT (2021)

THE STORY SO FAR

2017   Writes *The Emperor of Ice-Cream* for Amazon Studios

September 3, 2017   Death of Leyner's beloved puggle, Lilli, whose ghost becomes his guru

2018   Writes *Out of a Hat* for the director Lena Khan

2019   Completes (with John Cusack) the screenplay for *Full Metal Artaud*

2021   Publication of *Last Orgy of the Divine Hermit*

LEYNER ON LOVE

Bruce Sterling

READING MARK LEYNER's fiction is like entering an elevator where every button is labeled in menacing gibberish.

Here's a typical paragraph of self-referential Leyner deconstruction from his new book, *Last Orgy of the Divine Hermit:* "We often have the eerie feeling, as we traverse the text, that the Chalazians themselves (among the most literate peoples on earth) are reading aloud along with us. Or, put another way, there's a mirroring reciprocity at play here: we're reading what the characters are reading and the characters are reading what we're reading."

S. J. Perelman (1904–79) was a writer whose arch command of erudite language much resembles Leyner's. But Perelman wrote real jokes, and he was so funny that the Marx Brothers hired him. Leyner also works for Hollywood (he wrote the screenplay for the 2008 film *War, Inc.,* among other things), and he is just as smart as Perelman, but normal jokes bore him, and he much prefers to torment his readers by folding, spindling, and mutilating language and the very act of reading.

Leyner, a writer's writer if ever there was one, can entertain writers with writer jokes: "In late medieval chivalric romances, Chalazian Mafia Faction street soldiers were frequently portrayed as miniaturized mechanomorphic vermin, scurrying behind the toilets in the men's rooms of bars."

This quip is chuckleworthy to us novelists because a sentence like this can never actually be "written." It's impossible for a human being to actually sit down and think and type that sentence. That sentence has to be architected through some postmodern method of splintering and splicing.

It's also funny because of its car crash of discourses, that violent, bathetic change of tone from dusty old "medieval chivalric romances" into horror sci-fi "mechanomorphic vermin" with no transition at all, just pure verbal jolt. If you're a sci-fi writer like me who has to waste a whole lot of time persuading people to believe in far-fetched stuff like "miniature mechanomorphic vermin," it's a thrill to see that rubbish just catapulted into the text.

Leyner's work is about language as a system for exploring and conveying meaningful truth, and like most postmodernists, he thinks it doesn't have much. The reason is that words are not scientific instruments that can test, measure, and verify. Instead, words are mushy, polyvalent symbols that socially construct a consensus that mostly serves the interests of the powers that be.

Now, if you're a philosophic realist, you'll strongly dislike this idea that "reality" is socially constructed from politically freighted semiotics. However, Leyner has made a long career out of demonstrating just that—and in the most extreme and exciting ways, too. He's something like a gaudy, raucous Donkey Kong rampaging through pages where battling discourses blast into each other in riotous bursts of verbal pixels. Leyner especially likes the professional discourses of medicine and physics, because they sound so solemn, serious, and fully rooted in objective reality. So he goes after 'em like a guy sculpting Jell-O with a chain saw.

Optometrists, for instance. Optometrists are specialized medical professionals with the elaborate technical hardware needed to examine subtle eye defects. Everybody's visited optometrists; everybody knows what they do. Leyner's optometrists read like this:

> A gentle, dignified man in his mid-sixties with a good-natured, ready smile, crow's feet accentuating the glint in his eyes, the optometrist's life had been a harrowing one. Both his parents were killed in a horrific home invasion (they were the invaders, not the occupants)....After losing everything during the Night of the Broken Glasses, when neo-Nazis targeted Jewish optometrists, smashing all their lenses and frames, he refused to allow rancor to detract from the conscientious care of his patients (many of whom were themselves neo-Nazis). He methodically rebuilt his practice and, in 2023, was voted "New Jersey's Most Optimistic Optometrist." In his spare time (evenings and weekends), he's involved with a group of optometrists from all over the country who are working to provide MS-13 with nuclear weapons....

You can glide through that torrent of abrasive, storm-gathering verbiage, from the "good-natured, ready smile" downhill to the nuclear weapons for terrorists, and it's a semantic marvel, really. It's not a joke; there's no punch line. It's not satire; he's not making fun of optometrists. It's not wordplay, because those aren't puns or double entendres. It isn't nonsense, because the sentences are grammatical and follow one another legibly. And it's not surreal, because it's not based in dream life or unconscious promptings. It's even sinister and disgusting, because it's got a big glob of Nazis in it.

It's semiotic play: it's a mutated corrosion of textual meaning, a literary creation almost like kinetic art. It's like tearing a car to pieces and building a robotic, flailing artwork out of the components. The aesthetic pleasure of it is in watching it wind up and go.

It resembles a form of science fiction in which there's no hope of rational understanding within the science and the fiction is devouring itself—and cannibalizing the science, too. That's why I read Leyner's books and why I find them so useful.

Suppose you're not a cyberpunk sci-fi writer like me but an actual functional scientist. Let's consider the august figure of the late Sir Ernest Rutherford (1871–1937), a Nobel Prize winner who is famous for saying, "All science is either physics or stamp collecting."

In my opinion, this assertion is a great, nail-it-to-the-masthead thing for any scientist to say. Because there's so much metaphysical rigor to it; it's not the mush-mouthed rhetorical double-talk that we creative humanistic writers are so fond of using. It's about the stark virtues of physics: precise measurement, experimental verification, mathematical rigor, and the discovery of natural law and cosmic order.

However, this thing you're reading now is an essay in a magazine. We're not in a lab. Even though I can talk fluently about physics, this isn't physics. There's no firm evidence that Ernest Rutherford ever really said that famous quotation about stamp collecting. It sounds catchy, but it's also dismissive and mean to his colleagues in other fields—and why would he be so boorish? Also, Rutherford's own Nobel Prize was in chemistry, not physics.

So our language about Ernest Rutherford is not identical to the truth of Rutherford. Rutherford didn't merely say or write that atoms have a nucleus. Rutherford demonstrated experimentally that atoms have a nucleus by creating his famous gold foil experiment, which other scientists could replicate in their own laboratories.

But we still have to tell each other about the science, which is why magazines like this one exist, and that's where the postmodern "social construction of science" starts oozing in like sulfurous lava from hell.

The Rutherford gold-foil apparatus is a machine; it's not made out of words! Right now we don't have Rutherford's instruments. They're old-fashioned; they're gone. We just have the words — that's the problem! To read a Mark Leyner book is to be plunged into a nightmare language-centric world where the gold foil can never help you. There is no physical anchor.

Last Orgy doesn't even exist as a "novel." It's a text that calls itself ethnography, and it does a lot of cruel, weird mimicry of ethnographic talk, but it consists of characters reading texts aloud to each other. Sometimes they read karaoke prompts. Sometimes they read political posters. Most of the book is a patient reading her optometry eye tests aloud to her hapless optometrist.

It's hard to find any book that makes it so clear that a book is a verbal contraption. Maybe William Burroughs, the maestro of the cut-up method, who famously said that "language is a virus from outer space." Leyner resembles Burroughs in his fondness for larding big ice cream scoops of meaningless violence and depraved squalor into the text, nearly at random.

This is Leyner as philosopher:

> As another glassy-eyed cadre slurs (a chemical odor on her breath from the butter-flavored no-stick cooking spray she continuously huffs): "The reality we perceive is a mere epiphenomenon arising from the underlying structure of the brain, which is itself an epiphenomenon arising from purely mathematical properties — topological homogeneity, supersymmetry, stochastic dynamics, etc., etc. In other words, reality is a surface effect of mathematics."

But why are mathematicians trapped in the same verbal sump as glue-huffing lunatics? Well, they're not really, because mathematicians have the rigor of the Queen of the Sciences on their side.

However, human intelligence is embodied and time-bound. The infant mathematician can neither speak nor calculate. The adult mathematician feels like a rational, conscious being, but the elderly, senile mathematician can no longer tackle hard proofs. He can still speak, though: a corroded babbling that might soothe the pangs of a wounded brain but is no longer nailed to reality.

It's good that we know this about ourselves and our dependence on language and its many treacheries.

Mark Leyner, my contemporary, has become an old man now. Throughout his literary career, Leyner has been a tensile, keyed-up, gym-rat character verging on machismo. But time has changed him. This *Last Orgy* book is haunted by the decaying male body and by a deep fatherly regard for the new generation. This is Leyner's Dorothy-in-Oz text, in which the curtain is pulled aside for the young girl from Kansas and it's revealed that the Specter of Postmodernism has a not-so-modern little old man in there.

Leyner's critics used to claim that his texts were clever but not "novels." When you read Leyner's fiction, you felt bemused and bewildered, but you came out of the last page much as you were at the first page. His books were not comedies or tragedies; instead, they were just acrobatics. Leyner wrote what reviewers called experimental prose, but his experiments lacked practical applications. He liked to write about the nature of writing, but his bravura stunts were astrally detached.

Last Orgy of the Divine Hermit is a different kind of book, though. Somehow, elements of human wisdom have seeped in. There's an unspoken, between-the-lines tenderness to it that transcends its verbal tricks. The book is still not a novel, and it has no plot—but it does have moral messages about mortality and love.

The moral is that all orgies end and that a father's love for a daughter is beyond all language. No amount of verbal acrobatics can hide the warmth of affection; the love between the generations glows through the passage of time. There's some primeval mammalian beauty of flesh and blood within all of us, which science can't quantify and fiction can't express.

Bruce Sterling is a science fiction writer, net critic, and internationally recognized cyberspace theorist who was born in Texas. However, as a child he also spent a lot of time in India, which partly explains why he is still fond of Bollywood movies.

EXCERPTS FROM
LAST ORGY OF THE DIVINE HERMIT

E

F P

T O Z

L P E D

P E C F D

E D F C Z P

F E L O P Z D

D E F P O T E C

L E F O D P C T

F D P L T C E O

P E Z O L C F T D

INTRODUCTION

PATIENT

(looking through the phoropter lenses and reading from the eye chart)

"The first orgasm I ever had was so intense I separated both my shoulders and shit in my pants."

So begins *Last Orgy of the Divine Hermit*...

The OPTOMETRIST *switches lenses on the phoropter.*

OPTOMETRIST

Is this any better? Sharper?

PATIENT

Oh my god! I wasn't even close!

OPTOMETRIST

That's OK. Can you read it for me now?

The PATIENT *absently twirls a lock of hair around her finger as she reads through the device, which completely masks her face—*

PATIENT

"On June 26, 2035, Kermunkachunk, the capital of Chalazia, was engulfed in chaos. The Chalazian Mafia Faction, a fanatical offshoot of the Chalazian Children's Theater, had assumed control of the city center and was carrying out mass executions. Enemies, real and especially imagined, were dragged out of their office buildings and gutted in the street."

So begins *Last Orgy of the Divine Hermit...*

OPTOMETRIST

Excellent. Now, this makes it blurry, yes?

PATIENT

Yes.

OPTOMETRIST

Is it better like this...or like this? One...or two?

PATIENT

About the same.

OPTOMETRIST

OK. Now, can you read this?

PATIENT

So begins *Last Orgy of the Divine Hermit,* in which a father and his daughter, in Chalazia researching an ethnography of the unique criminal subculture of the Chalazian Mafia Faction, spend a night at the Bar Pulpo, Kermunkachunk's #1 spoken-word karaoke bar, where seemingly extemporaneous conversations are, in actuality, being read from multiple karaoke screens arrayed around the barroom. Moreover, it's Thursday—*Father/Daughter Nite*—when the bar is frequented by actual fathers and daughters, as well as couples role-playing fathers and daughters.

OPTOMETRIST

Good. Now…can you make out any of this line? I know it's small.

PATIENT

Not really. I'm guessing here…Uh…

fneixa alsdfy hoypm ewrse dnfbmoldfh vusyvjfg nktoinb xzinkhg

…I'm not really sure.

OPTOMETRIST

Alright, give me just a moment here…

He makes a quick note on the PATIENT'*s chart and again switches lenses on the phoropter—*

OPTOMETRIST

How about now? Can you make out anything?

PATIENT	PATIENT
Meanwhile, outside on the piazza, sub-factions of the Chalazian Mafia Faction vie for supremacy in a never-ending frenzy of stomach-churning savagery. Chalazian Mafia Faction street soldiers commit acts of unimaginable sadism, reveling in carnage and the grotesque mutilation of their victims' corpses. But it's worth keeping in mind that these are kids who, several years ago, frequently only several *weeks* ago (several *days* ago, in some cases),	Meanwhile, outside on the piazza, sub-factions of the Chalazian Mafia Faction vie for supremacy in a never-ending frenzy of stomach-churning savagery. Chalazian Mafia Faction street soldiers commit acts of unimaginable sadism, reveling in carnage and the grotesque mutilation of their victims' corpses. But it's worth keeping in mind that these are kids who, several years ago, frequently only several *weeks* ago (several *days* ago, in some cases),

were prancing around onstage in a Chalazian Children's Theater production of *Clever Jack and the Magic Beanstalk*. These are young people who've traded their exuberant devotion to musical theater for an irrepressible desire to kill and be killed out on the piazza. Histrionic narcissists to the core, Chalazian Mafia Faction street soldiers pirouette as they die, like defecating dogs aligning themselves to the earth's electromagnetic field. These ex-musical-theater kids are always "on," always performing for the CCTV cameras that ring the perimeter of the piazza. The Chalazian Mafia Faction, we're told, is like a combination of the Gambino crime family and the Khmer Rouge. Proclaiming itself to be "against everything and everyone," it is necessarily, per its own ethos, riven by internecine conflict, hence this chaotic, blood-drenched phantasmagoria — this unspeakable orgy of violence — that ensues without respite, day in and day out, on the piazza

were prancing around onstage in a Chalazian Children's Theater production of *Clever Jack and the Magic Beanstalk*. These are young people who've traded their exuberant devotion to musical theater for an irrepressible desire to kill and be killed out on the piazza. Histrionic narcissists to the core, Chalazian Mafia Faction street soldiers pirouette as they die, like defecating dogs aligning themselves to the earth's electromagnetic field. These ex-musical-theater kids are always "on," always performing for the CCTV cameras that ring the perimeter of the piazza. The Chalazian Mafia Faction, we're told, is like a combination of the Gambino crime family and the Khmer Rouge. Proclaiming itself to be "against everything and everyone," it is necessarily, per its own ethos, riven by internecine conflict, hence this chaotic, blood-drenched phantasmagoria — this unspeakable orgy of violence — that ensues without respite, day in and day out, on the piazza outside the Bar Pulpo, Kermunkachunk's #1 spoken-word karaoke bar.

OPTOMETRIST

Now, you're seeing two columns of text, side by side, yes?

PATIENT

Yes.

OPTOMETRIST

OK...Let me know when they've merged into one column.

PATIENT

Uh...

outside the Bar Pulpo, Kermunkachunk's #1 spoken-word karaoke bar.

OPTOMETRIST

Now, you're seeing two columns of text, side by side, yes?

PATIENT

Yes.

OPTOMETRIST

OK...Let me know when they've merged into one column.

PATIENT

Uh...

PATIENT

...now.

OPTOMETRIST

Good. Now, can you read that for me or is it too blurry?

PATIENT

No, I can read it:

Meanwhile, outside on the piazza, sub-factions of the Chalazian Mafia Faction vie for supremacy in a never-ending frenzy of stomach-churning savagery. Chalazian Mafia Faction street soldiers commit acts of unimaginable sadism, reveling in carnage and the grotesque mutilation of their victims' corpses. But it's worth keeping in mind that these are kids who, several years ago, frequently only several *weeks* ago (several *days* ago, in some cases), were prancing around onstage in a Chalazian Children's Theater production of *Clever Jack and the Magic Beanstalk*. These are young people who've traded their exuberant devotion to musical theater for an irrepressible desire to kill and be killed out on the piazza. Histrionic narcissists to the core, Chalazian Mafia Faction street soldiers pirouette as they die, like defecating dogs aligning themselves to the earth's electromagnetic field. These ex-musical-theater kids are always "on," always performing for the CCTV cameras that ring the perimeter of the piazza. The Chalazian Mafia Faction, we're told, is like a combination of the Gambino crime family and the Khmer Rouge. Proclaiming itself to be "against everything and everyone," it is necessarily, per its own ethos, riven by internecine conflict, hence this chaotic, blood-drenched phantasmagoria—this unspeakable orgy of violence—that ensues without respite, day in and day out, on the piazza outside the Bar Pulpo, Kermunkachunk's #1 spoken-word karaoke bar...

The PATIENT *stops reading...*

PATIENT

Keep going?

OPTOMETRIST

Please.

PATIENT

Chalazia is a tiny country wedged between Moldova and Romania, though recognized by neither. Almost every surface in Chalazia (actually, *every* surface) tests positive for traces of cocaine. The entirety of the country is cordoned off with yellow crime scene tape, all 148 kilometers of border, a phenomenon visible from outer space. (In actuality a Neolithic geoglyph akin to the Kazakh Steppe earthworks or the more recent Nazca Lines, this cordon was made by removing the top layer of the bluish-white reflecting salt flats [that once covered all of Chalazia] to reveal a bright yellow subsoil.) An elaborate system of sewers (now in complete disuse) descends some 1,800 kilometers beneath the ground, ramifying across the subterranean latitudes of the entire planet — a feat of engineering that many believe could only have been achieved by corrupt ancient aliens. (Even in 800 B.C., the Chalazian construction and waste-carting industries were rife with racketeering.) These ancient sewers make Chalazia both the farthest and the nearest destination from any point of origin on earth. In other words, at any given moment, Chalazia may be wedged between any two other nations. Fossilized ancient Chalazian shit—coprolites—can today be found almost anywhere. Anywhere, actually. And everywhere. Apropos of which, a previous incarnation of the Bar Pulpo was called the "Coprocabana" (which was obviously not a spoken-word karaoke bar).

The Chalazian *joie de merde* is only surpassed by its *joie de guerre*.

But could this violence, this atrocious, unabating carnage, be as random and incoherent as it appears? Is there someone responsible for orchestrating the perpetual conflagration on the piazza outside the Bar Pulpo—the piazza, with its stench of sweat, lube, and gasoline, littered with shell casings, cigarette butts, and used condoms floating in puddles of blood?

Perhaps it's the Divine Hermits themselves, those heretical holy men, who are the real puppet masters, the ones calling the shots on the brazen predation that's come to define contemporary Kermunkachunk. Like Kabbalistic tzaddiks or Shaiva tantrikas but historically associated with the Chalazian Mafia Faction, these antinomian mystics, moonlighting as Mafia warlords, combine the esoteric pursuit of nondualistic illumination with extortion and loan-sharking. *Last Orgy of the Divine Hermit* makes a strong case that it's these eponymous individuals who are masterminding events on the piazza from their perch in the Floating Casino on Lake Little Lake, where these racketeering illuminati who wear their diamond-encrusted hair balls and engraved prostates around their necks as amulets, these shirtless recluses with their white chest hair and neon-orange nylon sweatpants, paradoxically socialize every Thursday night.

Made members (and frequently godfathers) of the Chalazian Mafia Faction, these adepts remain literally above the fray, levitating a foot or two above their seats as they play a traditional Chalazian game that combines Scrabble and mahjongg. They roll their eyes at the suggestion that they have anything to do with the violence on the piazza, let alone direct it, as, seemingly in a trance, they endlessly shuffle their tiles (this is known as "permutation of the letters"). And they send deeply encrypted death threats to anyone with the temerity to suggest that they encrypt their death threats.

The Chalazian Mafia Faction warlord and the Divine Hermit embody (frequently within the same individual) two complementary modalities: criminality and *devequt* (cleaving to the divine), encapsulating, within this single chimerical figure, the Chalazian concept of human existence. As for the CMF street soldiers themselves, when it comes to fashioning weapons, they are remarkably resourceful, and have been known to make shanks out of soft-serve ice cream.

The men's room in the Bar Pulpo is an insane parody of the ladies' room. It is haunted by the anthropoid ghosts of the ancient aliens (the *Kermunks*) who built the vast, labyrinthine sewer system. In this particular men's room (in *any* men's room, actually) we encounter "misshapen forms of the gods in agony." This men's room is, in a sense, like an incubator, where the larval Divine Hermits molt and mature, sheltered from predators and fed by the mechanomorphic vermin that scurry behind the toilets. It is this men's room from which, in a sense, they migrate on deciduous wings to the Floating Casino. And it is where, at the end of his life, the Divine Hermit instinctively returns, where he and his demonic double, the Mafia warlord, are locked in a reciprocal interrogation in a mirror above the sink—"the mirror from which there is no escape." It is where Ron Howard looks in the mirror and sees Clint Howard. (Sixty years ago, on an episode of *Bonanza,* Clint Howard, in blackface, played a little African boy who brings the Ebola virus to the Ponderosa, sparking two consecutive three-day weekends of deadly pogroms that eventually became known as the Coachella Valley Music and Arts Festival.)

OPTOMETRIST

Close enough.

He changes lenses on the phoropter.

OPTOMETRIST

Now, can you make out any of this?

PATIENT

(squinting through the phoropter)

Some.

OPTOMETRIST

Give it a try.

PATIENT

And the Chalazian *joie de guerre* is only surpassed by its *joie de lire.*

Among the most literate people on earth, Chalazians almost never read in solitude or silence, only publicly and out loud ("belting"), either from the spoken-word karaoke screens or, swaying back and forth, from the Big-Character Posters that festoon the perimeter of the piazza, and whereas these collective performances are widely referred to as "orgiastic," the more cosmopolitan Kermunkachunkians (the "Kermunkachunkian cognoscenti," the most zealous of whom are, of course, the street soldiers of the CMF) go one step further, stigmatizing solitary reading as "prurient and petit bourgeois," i.e., a mortal sin akin to eating your own earwax...

I'm sorry—

...*one's* own earwax.

OPTOMETRIST

Excellent!

357

PATIENT

When, at the beginning of *Last Orgy of the Divine Hermit*, the door to the Bar Pulpo opens on Father/Daughter Nite, the babble (which, to an untutored ear, wouldn't sound much different from the ambient hubbub of any bar) includes the drunken voices of an anthropologist and his daughter (Gaby, a gorgeous, young neo-structural filmmaker from New York) who are in Kermunkachunk researching an ethnography about the ultraviolent Chalazian Mafia Faction, the two of them seated in a booth across from each other and reading aloud, along with everyone else, from the numerous spoken-word karaoke screens, Chalazia's most beloved folktale, which is sometimes palindromically called "Nite of the Daughter's Father."

This story of a mortally ill father and his beloved daughter in an inn or tavern (of the sort traditionally habituated by itinerant tradesmen, grizzled sailors on weeklong benders, crossing guards in heavy mascara and fluorescent-yellow vests, etc.), this story which culminates in the father's staggering Dance of Death, is the foundational narrative in Chalazian culture. All the ontological and epistemological preoccupations that constitute the Chalazian mentalité are encoded within this one folktale (and its innumerable variants), which is why, one assumes, the author and his daughter have, on this particular "nite," ensconced themselves at the Bar Pulpo, itself a *matryoshka* nesting of successfully smaller and more sacred spaces — the barroom, the men's room, the stall.

One of the first things you'll see upon arriving at Kermunk-achunk International Airport are the huge murals depicting various scenes from the folktale. Running the entire length of the moving walkway that conveys you from the arrival gates to the baggage carousels, these monumental murals, unlike the Snellen chart, are read from right to left:

- The father and the daughter toasting their everlasting devotion to each other, clinking tiny tin mugs (rough-hewn shot glasses) of "gravy," a fiery Chalazian vermifuge, washed down with flagons of lager.
- The daughter pensively blowing thick white smoke rings which settle around her father's neck like an Elizabethan ruff, as he regales her with an account of the marionette show he'd chanced upon that afternoon.
- Their final embrace and heartrending goodbye, the mere allusion to which can reduce the most hardened, remorseless CMF street assassins to sobbing hysterics.
- The father's drunken stagger from the men's room, his Dance of Death. This is the critical inflection point in the folktale when the father gazes into the mirror above the sink, provoking a strobe-like seizure of initiatory transfigurations (in sober moments, simply the palimpsest that is one's reflection), and emerges to perform his lurching *Danse Macabre*, his *Totentanz* (and/or actually dying, depending on the variant). It's a raw, contorted, convulsive improvisation, and yet, at the same time, highly…uh…highly…*caramelized*?

The OPTOMETRIST *changes lenses in the phoropter.*

OPTOMETRIST

Try it now.

PATIENT

It's a raw, contorted, convulsive improvisation, and yet, at the same time, highly ritualized…

Ah, *ritualized*!

OPTOMETRIST

(laughing)

Ritualized. Caramelized. Same difference.

PATIENT

It's a raw, contorted, convulsive improvisation, and yet, at the same time, highly ritualized, hieratic…very Butoh.

OPTOMETRIST

Excellent.

PATIENT

Don't Let This Robot Suck Your Dick Productions, Kermunk-achunk's most prestigious film and television production company, is responsible for innumerable movies and miniseries based on the folktale, both live-action and animated.

The company's ethos, their *cri de guerre*, really — shouted by a robot at the beginning of each movie like the roar of the MGM lion — was taken from a commercial for International Delight coffee creamers: "I like it international and I expect to be delighted!"

There are, by now, thousands of variants of "Nite of the Daughter's Father," each a cryptographic hash of the previous iteration, many of which, at this point, don't even include a father or a daughter or take place at "nite," but the standard version, the ur-folktale, takes place "a long time ago, farther back than anyone can remember…"

There was once a small inn at the foot of a hollow mountain, a hollow mountain that was said to be inhabited by a race of warlike elves (although these warlike elves have nothing to do with this story!). One evening, as rain poured down from the skies and, driven by the wind, pelted the windows of the inn, in walked a stooped and jaundiced old watchmaker, gripping his coat's lapels and shaking the wetness onto the wooden plank floor. He hung the coat up on a peg on the wall and sat, exhausted, at a round, rough-hewn table. Several days before, he'd been to see the physician, an elderly man decades older than the old watchmaker himself. "You're very sick," the wizened sage had told him after a careful examination. "You have late-stage cirrhosis of the liver" — a glaringly anachronistic, *avant la lettre* diagnosis, arrived at through an assortment of fuming alembics, strange alchemical assays, and *tzeruf*, the permutation of letters. "You're dying," he averred solemnly, "and another drink will kill you even sooner than that!" Nevertheless, on this very evening, the old watchmaker signaled to the barmaid, wiggling two fingers, and she brought him two tiny tin mugs of "gravy," which he knocked back in rapid succession. Just then, a young woman, mid-twenties, petite, and soigné in her hooded cloak, entered and surveyed the bar. The watchmaker waved, catching her attention, and beckoned her over to the table. It was his beloved and kindhearted daughter whom he adored more than anything in this world. He'd arranged to meet her here at this inn at the foot of a hollow mountain to tell her the sad news about his illness, to tell her that he was dying. And although she had traveled miles and miles in an ox-drawn cart along rock-strewn, muddy roads in the raging storm and was completely exhausted, she happily threw her arms around him and kissed him over and over again, before removing the hood of her cloak, dappled from the rain, to reveal her lustrous black hair intricately plaited into a chignon that rested at the nape of her neck. He was her beloved and kindhearted father and she adored *him* more than anything in the world.

On cold nights, when she was young, he would hold her little feet in his hands to warm them as he sang:

You are my sweet sweet girl
And I love you so.
This song will last forever
Long long after I go.

The PATIENT *chokes up, memories triggered of her own dad, now deceased, singing tenderly to her when* she *was little.*

OPTOMETRIST

Are you OK? Do you need a minute?

PATIENT

(takes a deep breath, exhales)

I'm good.

(she resumes, this time giving the words a melody)

You are my sweet sweet girl
And I love you so.
This song will last forever
Long long after I go.

The old watchmaker and his daughter clinked their shot glasses of gravy, toasting their everlasting devotion to each other. They reminisced and gossiped and laughed, the father buying time before he was forced to deliver the terrible news to his sweet girl, who tilted her head and gazed at him, her eyes and smile shining bright and wide with loving admiration and solicitude.

"So, what did the physician—that ancient mountebank—say?" the daughter asked, fidgeting with some soggy cardboard coaster on the table and pursing her lips nervously.

Now the watchmaker took a deep breath…

"Everything's perfectly fine," he lied. "I'm in robust health."

The prospect of inflicting upon her the grim news of his dire condition overwhelmed him with dread. He was incapable of saying or doing anything that might hurt her or make her sad. He simply couldn't bring himself to do it.

She shut her eyes and exhaled, her face slackening with relief.

"Oh Father, I was so worried," she said, tears welling in her eyes. "That's the most wonderful news to hear!"

She reached across the table and held his cold hands in hers to warm them.

Looking at her keen, happy face, the old watchmaker felt terribly guilty. Withholding the truth from her was so antithetical to the openheartedness and candor of their relationship. She would feel such a profound sense of betrayal knowing that he hadn't confided in her, that he'd allowed her to be so blindsided, left her so vulnerable, so cruelly unprepared for the shock of his impending death. Each time, though, that he thought he'd sufficiently girded himself to reveal what the physician had actually said, his resolve would disintegrate, that lump in his throat would rise, blocking the words from coming out. But just as he'd given up, hanging his head with the shame of his own abject cowardice, everything suddenly fell into place as if the inner workings of one of his watches, scattered in disarray upon his work table — all the tiny gears and springs — had spontaneously arranged themselves into the intricate movement of a timepiece. There *was* a way of sparing her, of telling the truth that wouldn't be so excruciatingly painful. Resorting to a sort of sleight of hand, he would convey this dreadful news obliquely, by way of an allegory.

"I chanced upon the most marvelous marionette show on the way to the inn," said the old watchmaker.

"Oh, how charming, Father!" said his daughter. "Tell me, what was the show about?"

Now he could unreservedly express how deeply, how completely, how *exquisitely* he loved her...and say goodbye.

And thus began the watchmaker's vivid, extended, and increasingly intoxicated re-creation of the tale enacted by the marionettes, a tale from an even more remote, primeval time, a tale which was called *La Muñeca de la Mafia Chalazian* ("Baby Doll of the Chalazian Mafia"):

> There was once a great and fearsome warlord known all over Chalazia for his ruthless ferocity, cunning, noble magnanimity, and the breadth of his esoteric wisdom. He had a daughter, his only heir, whom he adored and cherished beyond anyone and anything. She was a brilliant young woman, and beautiful besides. So she had hundreds of suitors. But she devoted herself most conscientiously to counseling her father about the internecine complexities of his vocation, which was, of course, both felonious *and* philanthropic. Knowing that her father would never allow her to participate in his "business," she disguised herself as a typical henchman, becoming her father's most trusted advisor (his consigliere, in other words).

The day came when the father, suffering from hereditary Creutzfeldt-Jakob disease (a degenerative and fatal neurological prion disease, akin to bovine spongiform encephalopathy and afflicting most Chalazian men late in life), knew he was dying and called his daughter to his bedside. Blind, racked by myoclonic jerks and twitches, and able only to gasp and whisper, he drew her close and said, "I've known all along that it was you giving me such shrewd advice. Who else but my own beloved daughter could have been so wise, so selfless and loyal?" He bestowed upon her the title *La Muñeca de la Mafia Chalazian* and bequeathed to her his legacy of exotic riches, material and mystical. "Be careful, my dearest one, that the man you marry loves *you* and does not simply covet all that I've worked so tirelessly to amass." And with that he took his final breath and perished.

The daughter went on to become the most powerful woman ever to reign over a criminal enterprise, the organization under her command soon orders of magnitude vaster than her father's had ever been.

And who do you think she married from among the hundreds of handsome but conniving young suitors who'd sought her hand? None of them!

She married the effete little gnome who lived under the ground in a deep well who had frequently disguised himself as the warlord's daughter to facilitate the real daughter's dissimulation.

In fact, at their wedding, they dressed as each other. A custom that still prevails in Chalazia to this day!

"And just as the curtain fell, the storm began," said the old watchmaker upon finally concluding this drama of a dying warlord and his daughter's patrimony, his rendition taking well over two hours and considerably more embellished, convoluted, and drunkenly digressive, and including, as it did, his uncanny mimicry of the speech patterns and gesticulations of each and every character, major and minor.

"And you should have seen how comical it was," he continued, "when all these marvelous marionettes tried to scurry off under their own power, without the help of the puppeteers, who'd abandoned them onstage to seek shelter from the deluge!"

And then, upon further consideration of the plight of these frantic, crippled puppets, he added, "I suppose it was a bit sad too."

Perhaps his daughter wasn't consciously aware of what he was conveying to her at that very moment, through this tale of the fervently devoted relationship between a powerful, ailing father and his only heir, his cherished, indomitable girl (his *muñeca*, his "little doll"), to whom, on his deathbed, in the play's anguished tearjerker of a finale, he bequeaths his vast criminal empire. But the old watchmaker was confident that someday after his death, his daughter would think back and say to herself, "He told me. In his gentle, caring, oblique, and allegorical way, he told me *everything* that last night."

The marionette play, as recounted by the old watchmaker, features two stock characters of late-medieval folklore: the Chalazian Mafia Godfather, a combination of *shtarker* and *tzaddik,* of thug and holy man, fusing within himself the ruthlessness of the transnational gangster warlord and the atemporality of the eremitic mystic in the forest, who is traditionally represented as sleeping beneath portraits of Meyer Lansky and the Baal Shem Tov. He, in turn, dotes indefatigably on his daughter—the gorgeous young woman in her mid-twenties, her lustrous black hair in a plaited chignon, who is chaste, introspective, aloof, fearless, blessed with extraordinary mixed martial arts skills, a devotee of Dadaist poetry and the Japanese koto, and fanatically loyal to her father.

Such was the strange evolution of gently smiling holy men and the cunning, vindictive hoodlums who protected them and did their bidding into hybrids of both, and such is the strange milieu that is Chalazia today.

As he recounted the marionette play, the old watchmaker was drinking relentlessly, furiously, opening his throat like a marathon runner at a hydration station, gulping double gravy after double gravy and then hurling himself back into the narrative. And whereas one might think that the mind-boggling amount of alcohol he was consuming would, if not completely disable his capacity to continue, at the very least result in the sort of monotonous, repetitive, sophomoric, ultimately incoherent drivel you'd expect, it did not. To the contrary. Acting almost like a magical potion, the gravy had somehow rejuvenated him for the rigors of this fabulation (we can't help but wonder if there was even an actual marionette play in the first place), and steeled his determination to bestow this allegory upon his daughter, in all its loving plenitude and with its scrupulously encoded message. Yes, the histrionics became somewhat amped up, the syntax a bit sloppier, the perspective more kaleidoscopic, the embellishments ever more baroque—but somehow the alcohol acted like a drawing salve that extracted and put at his disposal all the disparate emotional and psychological motifs necessary for him to synthesize this anguished aria, to speak the unspeakable to her.

Meanwhile, the inn had filled with its typical habitués: the hermits and woodsmen and sailors, the peasants and pipers, the shopkeepers, dockworkers, peddlers and cobblers, the merchants and horsemen and foot soldiers, and the fat little babies battened on smoked whitefish salad and tapioca and marzipan.

At first, outbursts of raucous laughter and profane slurs and ribald exhortations clashed with and undermined poignant moments in the watchmaker's telling. (At one point, apropos of nothing, some drunk yelled out, "Everything is spurious!") The men in the inn appeared completely indifferent, oblivious. You could never catch any of them actually listening. But then, it really did come to seem (at least, to *seem*) that these men began to constitute an audience in the sense that their collective affect (laughter, groans, sighs, etc.) appeared (or was it just coincidence?) to be in sync with tonal shifts in the watchmaker's story. Under scrutiny, this phenomenon would immediately vanish. That apparent interest, that attention seemingly directed the watchmaker's way, would, on closer inspection, reveal itself to be nothing more than the glassy gaze, the stupefied gape of another lush. Nevertheless, the fluctuating dynamics within the story did actually seem, at various junctures, to orchestrate the ambience of the room.

And so the watchmaker *finally* (again, this had, by now, taken up several hours!) reached the heart-wrenching conclusion in which the dying Chalazian godfather, succumbing after a grim, protracted battle with Familial CJD, bestows the entirety of his criminal kingdom upon his beloved, grief-stricken girl (his *muñeca*), and, with his dying breath, bids her farewell.

The bar was silent. The daughter was deeply moved, shaking her head incredulously, tears in her eyes, speechless…but the spell was soon broken when, moments later, she looked up at the large clock on the wall and realized how late it had become. She rose from the table, put on her hooded cloak, and gave her father a big long hug, a culminating reprise of her earlier relief, pausing to hold him at arm's length, and tilting her head so she could affectionately appraise him, and then hugging him once more, this time with a spontaneous jolt of ardor, triggered in ways she'd only be conscious of much later by all the potent emotional symbolism with which her father had seeded his long, assiduous reconstruction of the marionette play. And she kissed him goodbye one last time, and she departed to meet her fiancé, a handsome cavalryman with a long, keloidal dueling scar across one side of his face.

The old watchmaker knew he'd never see her again. (Can a liver "break" like a heart?)

And the tears, which fell from his jaundiced eyes and spread across the rough-hewn table, crystallized, metamorphosing into a reflective surface—a mirror which, in the middle of the night, while all the drunks "slept" in a state of suspended animation, the little elves mounted above the sink in the men's room—

The PATIENT *stops, eyes occluded, arms akimbo.*

PATIENT

There were men's rooms back then?

The OPTOMETRIST *shrugs.*

PATIENT

(again reading through the phoropter)

—and when the watchmaker entered and looked at himself, an infinite mise en abyme was generated by the reflections of the mirror in the pupils of his eyes, the specular images ricocheting back and forth at the speed of light.

And within this shaft of incandescent effervescence resides the sublime truth that we inhabit an imaginary world without meaning.

And this dazzling lucidity prompts us to either dance or die, or both dance *and* die.

And this, comrades, is "the orgy."

OPTOMETRIST

(with an upraised fist)

Yes!

PATIENT

When the old watchmaker emerged a while later, he gazed disconcertedly across the inn toward the table where they'd been sitting. He'd forgotten that his daughter had left.

He'd managed by necessity—through the extremity of his sorrow and the desperation of his love, really—to temporarily transmute the alcohol into a kind of fortifying elixir. But now that this was no longer necessary, without the imperative of that mission (the allegorizing of the marionette play) which propelled him forward by the sheer force of its exigency and which constituted a kind of stabilizing torque, he collapsed.

The alcohol seemed to hit him with a delayed, cumulative, pent-up force, a wave of gravy, a lifetime of gravy hit him, and literally knocked him off his feet. Or was it his own incipient Creutzfeldt-Jakob disease (the symptoms of which he'd never acknowledged out of fear of alarming his daughter) or the magnifying effect of both his intoxication *and* the CJD that caused the old watchmaker to spin and fall as he did?

He struggled to stand, to walk. But his direct line from point A to point B—from men's room to table—shattered into a delirium of vectors. He staggered, caroming into every surface he encountered, now a human Pong ball, erratically traversing the bar back and forth in a welter of veering zigzags, crosshatching the bar's space, repeatedly collapsing in vertiginous pirouettes, groveling along the floor on all fours, somehow clambering again to his feet, lurching along another haphazard, oblique trajectory, gesticulating like an airline attendant in an effort to navigate himself, teetering in circles, grasping for imaginary overhead handrails like a brachiating chimp, until he impacted another table or another wall, and whirled uncontrollably to the ground in a heap, like those forsaken, hobbling marionettes trying to escape the storm.

He cycled through a series of ritualistic masks—a truculent scowl became a look of contemptuous hauteur and then a coy pout and then a look of cringing chagrin, the imperturbable serenity of a beatified saint suddenly giving way to PTSD shell shock and then the panic of someone about to be immolated by a mob. He looked up from the floor, like a hard-shelled insect on its back, helpless, simpering with mortification.

It was a long, pitiable, shambolic Dance of Death...a *Danse Macabre*...some improbable version of Tatsumi Hijikata's Butoh, his "dance of total darkness."

Of course, this looked like, from one perspective, nothing more than a drunk stumbling out of a men's room and trying desperately, and without success, to maintain his balance, to stay on his feet long enough to return to his seat. But from another perspective there seemed to be a very deliberate choreography, where every action and every tilt of the head and positioning of a limb became meaningful. This was the phantasm of a body, the staging of a transubstantiation, a struggle with and rapturous capitulation to one's fate, the physical articulation of yet another allegory.

His body, to borrow the words of the dance critic Jennifer Homans, "was pitched at swerving angles; arms, legs, hips, head oriented through multiple spatial planes, his eyes sent in one direction, jaw in the other, rib cage in one direction, hips in the other. Soon the feet turned out, the line took shape, the familiar positions emerged. His movements were wide, open through the chest, with deep épaulement, but they were also torqued and knotted, the limbs working in rhythmic counterpoint."

An intricate corporeal transformation from extreme old age to youth and back again, he danced a violent, strange flamenco, his body savagely capricious in its gestures. Exuding death outward in every direction, he mimed the act of tenderly sponge-bathing the Grim Reaper—a spasm-driven gesture of the arm that would begin by heading violently in exactly the opposite direction to the sponge, before tracing a wide arc of flight in space, and then buckling in on itself to finally grasp the sponge, etc., etc.

(This is, by the way, a dance that is still performed by Chalazian fathers at the weddings of their daughters.)

And so, finally, reeling, the watchmaker braced himself against a wooden post at the far end of the inn. He gathered himself, he squinted, trying to focus his eyes, and committed to a heedless line that diagonally bisected the entire inn...and he careened—his body canted at an impossible angle — toward the spot where he and his daughter had been sitting.

And he somehow swerved backward toward that table and ended up propped upright in his chair, eyes shut, shoulders slumped, head lolling, his chin on his chest, breathing irregularly, drooling…motionless like this for some time. And then pitching forward slightly…listing slowly…slowly…until his forehead was flush against the tabletop.

And here he began mumbling what was apparently some sort of demented nonsense to himself.

Was this now the verbal apraxia of a stroke victim or simply the unintelligible gibberish of a drunk with Creutzfeldt-Jakob disease?

The PATIENT *pauses, letting the question hang in the air for a moment…*

OPTOMETRIST

The etiology is too overdetermined for a folktale to bear.

PATIENT

*(resumes reading from the Snellen chart
as she peers through the lenses of the phoropter)*

But if you listened closely, you'd realize that it wasn't unintelligible gibberish at all…

The watchmaker was murmuring those things—those most secret, intimate, and anguished things, those beseeching, prayerful things—that one murmurs aloud to oneself when one feels most exposed and ashamed and abased, and when one feels, paradoxically, that some ennobling self-transfiguration may just possibly be within reach.

And if you got *very* close, and listened *very* carefully, you could begin to discern something organizing itself, a structure developing out of all this undifferentiated pathos. And you'd think to yourself, Are we projecting all this, attributing an intentionality that isn't really there, are we just hearing what we want to hear? After all, this is a drunk who literally can't pick his head up off the table at this point. But it's true. In what we'd so misapprehended as delirious gibberish, we now began to glean what seemed like deliberate pauses and cadences…like line breaks and caesuras and meters, stanzas and refrains. And again we might wonder to ourselves if it's simply some kind of alcoholic auto-echolalia that's creating a mere semblance of verse. But that can't explain the uncanny formal ingenuity, the beauty of it.

And then there emerged something of a cross between speech and song (a "Schoenbergian *Sprechtimme!*" a tipsy blacksmith, with a long glistening beard, had the chutzpah to blurt out)…and then gradually an incipient but unmistakable melody. And again, was it simply an effect of the drunken lolling of his neck and the compression of his larynx, the slight spasms as he roused himself back into consciousness after momentarily fading off, that gave a tonal rise and fall to his voice, creating the mere appearance of a melody? But, again, no—there *was* a melody. There *were* verses and refrains. The watchmaker *was* singing—yes, a completely extemporaneous song that he was conjuring up as he went along, but a song nonetheless.

And, remarkably, the watchmaker's song was slowly taken up by the other men in the bar. First by one... then another...then several more...until they were *all* singing, each and every one of them. They were singing the watchmaker's very words, as if they all knew this song, this hymn. As if, somehow, they'd *always* known it.

And now they were almost like sailors, these griz-zled ghosts, at some shipmate's wake, singing a dirge about a rudderless, mastless ship disappearing into a dark mist, or over some precipice.

And amidst these men, their faces haggard, creviced with care, flush with alcohol, singing, Brueghel faces, Hogarth faces, this motley choir, singing—each of these old fathers, each the wobbling, moribund pro-tagonist of his own disaggregated solar system, sing-ing, singing—the watchmaker died.

And his body, as per his wishes, was unceremoniously flung into the Landwehr Canal in Berlin, the canal into which the revolutionary martyr Rosa Luxem-burg was thrown after her execution by Freikorps thugs in 1919....

According to *Last Orgy of the Divine Hermit*, the Chala-zian Mafia Faction is riddled with *agents provocateurs*, and in many, if not all, sub-factions, *agents provocateurs* outnum-ber actual members. In fact, the most crucial prerequisite to becoming a member of the Chalazian Mafia Faction is that you are an *agent provocateur*—in other words, there are no members of the Chalazian Mafia Faction who are not *agents provocateurs*. Also, male CMF street soldiers prefer older women (and heavier women: a popular greeting used when encountering someone you haven't seen recently is "I liked you better fat").

To the young, male CMF street soldier, the haggard, world-weary look of a middle-aged woman slouched on a subway at the end of a workday, that exhausted, bedraggled, they-don't-pay-me-enough-for-this-shit,I-just-want-to-get-home, get-out-these-clothes, change-into-something-comfortable, micro-wave-a-bite-to-eat-and-watch-something-trashy-on-tele-vision look, is considered to be "super-hot." (In the book, a heavily armed stud swaggering across the piazza is shown a photo of the twenty-three-year-old *Sports Illustrated* swimsuit model Alexis Ren and makes a finger-in-the-mouth gagging gesture.)

For your average Kermunkachunkian street soldier, sex with a premenopausal woman is, if not completely taboo, consid-ered weird.

These CMF thugs are taught that their martyrdom out on the piazza will lead to a paradise with a sort of chill, anodyne, Crate & Barrel vibe. Thanks to the recreational inhalation of nail polish remover, their brains turn to glass by the time most of them reach their mid-twenties, which few of them

actually do. (The vitrified brain of a CMF street soldier, in-
laid with jade and mother-of-pearl, is currently on display in
the lobby of the Floating Casino on Lake Little Lake.)

So, *Last Orgy of the Divine Hermit* is not only a masterly examination of what it means to be a drunk father and daughter in a bar whose gore-encrusted windows are being perpetually pelted with the enucleated eyeballs of the victims of an
internecine gang war, but also an unflinching examination
of who we've become as passengers on a shipwrecked planet.

And, given the thousands of variants that stream across the
spoken-word karaoke screens at the Bar Pulpo, it should
come as no surprise that a recent version of the folktale casts
the Father as an ethnographer and the Daughter as a glamorous filmmaker!

In another variant, the Daughter is neither beautiful nor
sympathetic but an antisemitic, hatchet-faced spinster. In
one of his final moments of lucidity, and literally grasping at
straws (those poking out of his cans of Glucerna), the dying
Father asks, "What do you think is going to happen to me?"
The Daughter responds, "You're going to become something
that's not you." And only then is the Father able to die peace-
fully, and the Daughter is magically transformed into a beautiful princess, a filmmaker.

Some versions don't even take place in Chalazia at all. In one,
the Daughter has been accepted into the Columbia University graduate film studies program but can't decide whether
she really wants to go or not. And instead of at the Bar
Pulpo in Kermunkachunk, she meets the Father at Yakiniku
Futago, a Japanese barbecue restaurant (with a great bar) on

17th Street, between Fifth and Sixth Avenues in Manhattan, to discuss the matter.

In another version, the Father and Daughter (named Caesar and Little Madonna) are extinct, rodent-like mammals called *multituberculates* who've been kept in a cryostat for several years. They are finally reanimated by an elderly and eccentric paleontologist. In this one too, Little Madonna ultimately gets into the Columbia University graduate film studies program, etc., etc.

Over the course of the text, many other folktales are cited *en passant*—there's one about an inexhaustible stick of deodorant, another about a husband who loves his wife so much that he deliberately mistreats her at the end of his life so she'll be happy when he dies.

These are all the sorts of folktales (or "fact patterns," as they're called now) that flight attendants routinely pantomime in the aisle before takeoff.

There's a version in which one block of pure, condensed present is superimposed upon another block of pure, condensed present—a series of crystalline tableaux layered and compressed, layered and compressed into a single sepulchral moment.

And yet another, this one involving some American tourist in the Bar Pulpo who, exasperated when he can't elicit the location of the men's room from a non-English-speaking Chalazian waiter, exclaims, "Mind over matter doesn't matter if you're the Mad Hatter with a weak bladder who steals money from his friends and still has to sell all his soggy Depends on eBay anyway, esé!"

As in the poem by Pasolini ("A Desperate Vitality") that begins "As in a film by Godard," the book is in the form of a dialogue (with stage directions), an interview, perhaps one might even say a psychoanalytic session, but with the roles of analyst and analysand constantly shifting.

…then the Daughter's horribly disfigured Japanese scientist boyfriend arrives outside in his red Formula One Ferrari to pick her up, and here the book moves into its tonally richest register.

And yet, it's almost over before it starts.

Still, no one before has so sharply delineated the underlying architecture of the Chalazian *mentalité*—the savage psychopathology outside on the piazza, the serene gemütlichkeit inside the Bar Pulpo, the violent endopsychic turmoil in its sanctum sanctorum, its innermost realm: the men's room. No one before has so vividly theorized the sensation of being swallowed up into the serpent—the coiled Möbius strip—that is Chalazia, of being dragged down in its peristaltic undertow.

And the Snellen chart is a harbinger of the *ivresse du discours* at the book's end.

OPTOMETRIST

Great. Now…can you make out any of this?

PATIENT

Ummm...

Like Euripides's *The Bacchae* on the outside (with the bloody insanity out there on the piazza, the *sparagmos*) and Sophocles's *Oedipus at Colonus* on the inside (with the whole dying father/dutiful daughter trope going on), *Last Orgy of the Divine Hermit* distills a fantastic multiplicity of ethnographic minutiae, of straight-up, formfitting, en suite Chalazian Mafia shit, into a study of extraordinary theoretical density. It's like the offspring produced when some huge, encyclopedic disquisition is mated with a Chihuahua.

Don't be intimidated by its brevity!

The Epilogue (which, due to the fallen state of the world, follows immediately upon the Introduction) is read through the artificial tears of the Patient.

EPILOGUE

The Bar Pulpo. Father/Daughter Nite.

We hear in the distance prolonged screams of the most exquisite agony.

GABY *and the* FATHER *are seated across from each other in a booth.*

Immediately we notice the native centerpiece—a metal basket of fluorescent-yellow marzipan golf balls—and sense the fou mathéma- tiques *(i.e., nothing seems to quite add up here).*

GABY

(in a stage whisper)

Ready?

The FATHER *nods, like Zeus (if only in his own mind), setting it off.*

It is, perhaps, like that moment at a Grand Prix, in some exotic city, when the red starting lights are extinguished and it all begins…the difference, the repetition, the delirious vortex to that last chicane (orgy).

LAST ORGY OF THE DIVINE HERMIT (2021)

On June 26, 2035, Kermunkachunk, the capital of Chalazia, was engulfed in chaos. The Chalazian Mafia Faction, a fanatical offshoot of
the Chalazian Children's Theater, had assumed control of the city center and was carrying out mass executions. Enemies, real and especially
imagined, were dragged out of their office buildings and gutted in the
street.

As a WAITER approaches from across the room, he's "shot" in the abdomen (we can't tell if the round's been fired from within the bar or from
out on the piazza). Like the plucky protagonist of a Peter Berg movie
(and in the first of a series of petit mal Dances of Death that prefigure
the Father's culminating grand mal Dance of Death), he stumbles to the
booth, holding in his "entrails" with his hand. He coughs up a spray of
"blood" before a convulsive pirouette sends him collapsing to the check-
erboard tile floor, "dead," and then, without losing a beat, he pops right
back up —

                        WAITER

    Is this your first time at a Bar Pulpo?

                         GABY

    It is.

                        WAITER

    Well, first of all, welcome…

He curtsies.

GABY and the FATHER smile.

                          385

WAITER

Basically, the idea is that you design or customize your own
piazza. You get four Big-Character Posters, one for the north
side, one for the south side, one for the east, and one for the
west. The Big-Character Posters function as, uh…as…gosh,
all of a sudden, I can't think of the word…

FATHER

*(reading phlegmatically from
one of the spoken-word karaoke screens)*

Epigraphs?

WAITER

Exactly, yes, epigraphs. So —

*(he hands each of them a beautiful four-color gatefold brochure that
includes a menu of options for Big-Character Posters, i.e., epigraphs)*

—you're going to choose four Big-Character Posters from
the menu of options.

GABY

Do you have any recommendations?

WAITER

Well, most people pick the Hölderlin—it speaks very

poetically to the noble intimacy of the father/daughter bond. Beyond that, whatever appeals to you.

The WAITER *exits.*

GABY *and the* FATHER *open their brochures and peruse the menu of options for the Big-Character Posters (i.e., epigraphs) that will appear on each side of the piazza:*

1

Not without wings may one
Reach out for that which is nearest

—Friedrich Hölderlin, "Der Ister"

2

Pooping while menstruating is one of the most psychedelic experiences a person can have.

—Mira Gonzalez

3

The "content" of any medium is always another medium.

—Marshall McLuhan

4

Like a child on a scooter, [fill in the blank] seems to veer inexorably toward you, no matter how deliberately you try to avoid it.

—from Donald Duck's trippy account of the
Scopes Monkey Trial

5

That Monday, belying predictions of torrential rain on all the weather apps, there was bright sunshine and a cloudless blue sky.

"I have an idea," said the pigeon to several little sparrows eating bread crusts beneath a park bench that afternoon. "What if we..."

"Yes?" said one of the sparrows, knowing the pigeon always thought things through very, very carefully.

"What if we called his first orgasm (when he separated both his shoulders and shit in his pants) his First Orgy?"

—Mark Leyner, *First Orgy of the Divine Hermit*

6

For me, the most dangerous people are the guys who are sitting behind a kiosk and just smoking and eating noodles.

—Timo Tjahjanto, director of *The Night Comes for Us*

7

If it's me and your granny on bongos, it's the Fall.

—Mark E. Smith

8

It is no nation we inhabit, but a language. Make no mistake; our native tongue is our true fatherland.

—Emil Cioran (used as an epigraph to the video game *Metal Gear Solid V: The Phantom Pain*)

9

No, seriously…seriously! We used to call it the "pizza from hell." The place was located in this creepy basement corridor, like in some dilapidated institution, like an abandoned public school or factory or something. We never saw an oven or a kitchen, never knew exactly where the pizza was made. We'd just wait in this dark, damp hallway which smelled like janitorial supplies, like ammonia and pine disinfectant and that mint absorbent sawdust and that cheap brown toilet paper—remember that smell?—until this guy appeared. Long greasy hair, broken teeth, this oozing gash across his forehead, sores all over his face. He'd always be in this incredible rage, raving incoherently…And he'd hand you your slice. And we never had the slightest idea where it came from. But it was the best slice of pizza you ever had. Hands down, best slice ever.

—Leyner, *Intermediate Orgy of the Divine Hermit*

10

As a starting point for this discussion, we may take the fact that it appears as if in the products of the unconscious—spontaneous ideas, phantasies and symptoms—the concepts faeces *(money, gift), baby and penis are ill-distinguished from one another and are easily interchangeable.*

—Sigmund Freud, "On Transformations of Instinct as Exemplified in Anal Erotism"

11

The fate of an insect which struggles between life and death, somewhere in a nook sheltered from humanity, is as important as the fate and the future of the revolution.

—Rosa Luxemburg

12

My dead puggle, who is my guru and my Butoh teacher, came to me in a dream last night and gave me three names: "Fizzy Phys-iognomy," "Noh Brainer," and "Oh Valve." He commanded me to go to Kermunkachunk with Gaby and write an ethnography of the Chalazian Mafia Faction.

—Leyner, Penultimate Orgy of the Divine Hermit

13

ASSISTANT DA: Miss Smith, is it true that you live at 5135 Kensington Avenue?

ESTHER SMITH: Yes, that's correct.

ASSISTANT DA: And Mr. Truett lives at 5133?

ESTHER SMITH: Yes.

ASSISTANT DA: And is it not also a fact that you just adore him and can't ignore him?

ESTHER SMITH: Yes...that's true.

ASSISTANT DA: Now, did there come a time when the day was bright and the air was sweet?

ESTHER SMITH: Yes.

ASSISTANT DA: And the smell of honeysuckle charmed you off your feet?

DEFENSE COUNSEL: Objection!

COURT: Overruled. Miss Smith, you may answer the question.

ESTHER SMITH: I suppose. Yes.

ASSISTANT DA: Miss Smith, isn't it true that you tried to sing, but couldn't squeak, and that, in fact, you loved him so you couldn't even speak?

ESTHER SMITH: [inaudible]

ASSISTANT DA: Miss Smith, speak up, please.

ESTHER SMITH: Yes.

ASSISTANT DA: And if I were to say, he doesn't know you exist, no matter how you may persist — would that be an accurate statement?

ESTHER SMITH: I'm not sure. I guess…

ASSISTANT DA: Your Honor, permission to treat witness as hostile.

COURT: Go ahead.

ASSISTANT DA: Miss Smith, I don't want you to guess. Does Mr. Truett not know you exist, no matter how you may persist, or does he?!

ESTHER SMITH: He does not.

There's a great hubbub in the courtroom. Reporters rush out into the piazza, jabbering into their cellphones.

COURT: Order! Order!!

ESTHER remains on the witness stand, sobbing inconsolably.

—*Meet Me in St. Louis: Special Victims Unit*

14

When you get to the very bottom, you will hear a knocking from below.

—Stanislaw Jerzy Lec

15

It's hard at times not to root for the bats, not to dream of walking into the cave with my arms outstretched: "Take me!"

—Mavis Beacon

The WAITER *returns.*

GABY

OK...We're going to do #1, the Hölderlin: "Not without wings may one / Reach out for that which is nearest."

WAITER

Beautiful choice.

GABY

The #2, the Mira Gonzalez: "Pooping while menstruating is one of the most psychedelic experiences a person can have." The #10, the Freud, from "On Transformations of Instinct as Exemplified in Anal Erotism." And #15, the Mavis Beacon.

The WAITER *makes a few theatrical conjuring gestures with his hands—*

WAITER

Voilà. Your Big-Character Posters are mounted on the piazza. As we speak, they're being read aloud by small, heedless clusters of Kermunkachunkians swaying back and forth on their feet.

FATHER

(chin in palm, rotely reciting from one of the screens)

Shuckling.

WAITER

Would you folks like something from the bar?

FATHER

Does Oprah like bread?

What happens next is not "good" (in the sense of "good writing").

But it is an absolutely accurate, documentary account of GABY *teasing the* WAITER, *acting "goofy" for the benefit of her* FATHER, *in a re-enactment of a scene from an episode of* Lizzie McGuire, *a Disney show starring Hilary Duff that they used to love watching so much together when* GABY *was little, the two of them curled up on the couch, a guilty pleasure of these Deleuze-quoting snobs, adorable little* GABY *and her dad. So much love between them!*

These are two people so lost in their own private folie à deux that they're reenacting episodes from Lizzie McGuire *that were never actually made, that exist only in their shared imaginations. But they're reenacting them verbatim, as if there had actually been an episode in which Lizzie and her dad were at the Bar Pulpo in Kermunkachunk and Lizzie was teasing the waiter with goofy or scabrous drink orders, with cocktails named after radical feminist assassins.*

This is what truly scares the WAITER. *(He isn't entirely acting. Or, to put it a better way: the act is an act.) It's this ferocious privacy of theirs.*

This would be almost impossible for an audience to understand were it not for the fact that it's all in the brochure and streaming on the screens.

These stage directions are written by God—that is to say, by the one who ever pulls out the rug from under the rug-puller-outer. ("God" in the sense of an omnipotent, superintelligent machine AI.)

They are dedicated to those restive Chalazian Mafia Faction street soldiers who hurl enucleated eyeballs at the windows of the Bar Pulpo like a disgruntled audience throwing rotten tomatoes at a stage.

They represent an ideology of implacable antipathy toward everything and everyone. (They are further dedicated to the bats and insectoid robots who will inherit the earth.)

When posted on Instagram, they typically get something on the order of 10^{82} or one hundred thousand quadrillion vigintillion "likes."

WAITER

Just so you know, we're all out of the Whac-a-Mole IPA, unfortunately.

GABY

Do you guys do a Valerie Solanas Dirty Girl Scout here?

WAITER

(thinks for a moment, then shakes his head)

I'm not exactly sure what that is.

GABY's *teasing him, in a specific manner intended to impress her father, perhaps without even being fully aware of it.*

GABY

I'm a Girl Scout, you're a creepy old widower who lives alone in a dilapidated house at the end of some dark cul-de-sac. I knock on the door to sell you cookies. When you answer, I drop to my knees, open wide for a squirt of chocolate syrup, and then take a shot of peppermint schnapps. So, it's like a Thin Mint.

WAITER

I don't get it. What's the Valerie Solanas part?

Then, there's a sound as if reality itself is being torn along a perforated diagonal.

GABY *leaps up, grabs a small, serrated white disposable plastic knife from the table (the weapon of choice used to such gruesome effect in so many Don't Let This Robot Suck Your Dick Productions martial arts action flix), and puts it to the Adam's apple of the* WAITER.

(Surprised by this? By her leap into the abyss? Don't be. While the other children were getting ballet lessons or swimming or playing soccer after school, little GABY — *shy, introverted, reticent, wary little* GABY — *surprised everyone by opting to take Sayoc Kali knife fighting classes in the basement of a Filipino church in Bayonne, perhaps anticipating, even then, a life of perilous adventure in film and anthropology.)*

GABY

The Valerie Solanas part is: then, I fuckin' slit your throat, because, uh...because...

(*she sneaks a peek at one of the spoken-word karaoke screens*)

...because the Girl Scouts have sentenced you to death, you perverted scumbag!

Again, she's clearly playing to her father. Because she respects him so much, and his opinion of her means everything.

The WAITER *seems genuinely stunned, his heart is racing, his breathing is rapid and shallow, he's perspiring profusely, etc., etc.*

Similar scenes are playing out, of course, all over the Bar Pulpo (which, in a former incarnation, was known as King Kong Couscous). Almost all the "daughters" (both consanguineous and cosplaying) have white plastic knives to the throats of their waiters at this very moment.

 It's one of those rare instances when, working from the same screens, each and every "father" and "daughter" at the Bar Pulpo has momentarily synchronized, i.e., improbably fallen upon the same passage in the same subvariant of the folktale, a subvariant the provenance of which, like those spectral, wholly endopsychic episodes of Lizzie McGuire, *is difficult for even the most scrupulous ethnographers to verify.*

 But here we are.

GABY

I'm teasing you!

But she still has him in a headlock, the knifepoint causing a bright drop of FX blood to ooze from his squib.

 Yet her mind is elsewhere.

 Like some nostalgic alumna munching on marzipan golf balls, she's experiencing a flood of memories —

GABY

I must have drunk, like, a thousand of those during Kappa Delta pledge week at the New School…

The WAITER *"seems" (he's acting, presumably — or is he?) terror-stricken.*

GABY

Andy, I'm kidding! I'm teasing you!

(then, whispering in his ear)

My father's sister, Anna Nicole Newman, was one of the three American gymnasts who drowned in livestock excreta when their spacecraft crashed into the manure lagoon in Castilla–La Mancha in 2027. So that's probably a subject you should try to avoid tonight.

The headlock has morphed into a sort of frozen tango. The WAITER, *his head thrown back, and now understanding that this whole charade has been a pretext for a collegial heads-up about a sore subject, winks at* GABY—

WAITER

Good to know. Thanks.

FATHER

Does she look like someone who'd drink peppermint schnapps?!

WAITER

(reading from a spoken-word karaoke screen)

Not at all.

FATHER

When she was seven and all her friends were clamoring to watch *The Little Mermaid,* Gaby wanted to watch Dziga Vertov's *Three Songs About Lenin* and Michael Snow's *Wavelength.*

GABY

(laughing)

That's such bullshit!

But it's not bullshit. It's true. Her first Halloween costume was the green-cloaked, nystagmic albino from Kenneth Anger's Invocation of My Demon Brother.

Although the solemn, ritual enactment of these fabricated scenes from Lizzie McGuire *does not constitute "good writing," it vividly demonstrates the zeal with which GABY and the FATHER will sacrifice anyone on the altar of their tiny cult of two.*

And although this obtains for the dramatis personae on any given Father/Daughter Nite, it is particularly true for this particular GABY and this particular FATHER on this particular Nite.

For a moment—for just that one instant—in the sudden flash of lurid light refracted through the gore-encrusted windows, every woman in the bar, every "daughter," looks as though she's wearing a Kappa Delta Bid Day crop top, and every "father" looks like a scrofulous widower answering the door.

FATHER

We're doing gravy shots all night, bruh.

(he slips him a hundred-dollar bill)

Just keep 'em coming.

"Gravy" is, of course, the fiery, high-proof vermifuge that's considered the national drink of Chalazia.

The WAITER *exits.*

Conscientious ethnographers, the FATHER *and* GABY *are both frantically scribbling notes in crayon on their place mats.*

In marked contrast to the explosive, id-driven chaos out on the piazza, there's nothing remotely spontaneous about any of this. It's all a very predetermined, choreographed, almost liturgical sequence of events.

So, let's not confuse or somehow conflate these abstract figurations, these refined, highly aestheticized pantomimes, with the very real stomach-churning violence that's taking place outside.

Nor should we forget the cool, detached, sublimated shuffling of the lettered tiles by Divine Hermits levitated slightly above their seats in the Floating Casino on Lake Little Lake, that primordial, cosmogenic activity from which arises all phenomena, that shuffling whose consequences are emitted into our collective imagination and externally as empirical reality.

From this infra-language come both those poignant folktales that stream across the spoken-word karaoke screens at the Bar Pulpo on Father/ Daughter Nite and the murders and grotesque mutilations that take place out on the piazza.

But what does it say about us as a society that amidst these nightmarish massacres, these orgies of violence, in which deranged young CMF street soldiers (these ex-musical-theater kids) slaughter and mutilate one another, people flock to the Bar Pulpo (formerly King Kong Couscous), on that very piazza, each and every Thursday night to recite and reenact folktales about dying fathers and their heartbroken daughters, those wrenching melodramas (streaming on screens), those "scabrous weepies," as the screenwriter Jeremy Pikser (War, Inc.; Bulworth; The Lemon Sisters) has christened them?

It is, to quote the brochure, "like enjoying a night out with friends at Applebee's as the Kishinev pogrom rages outside."

No one knows how they got there. The level of violence is so high that it's too dangerous to travel anywhere within Kermunkachunk right now. To even attempt to traverse the piazza in order to enter the Bar Pulpo would be an act of suicide.

Via the brochure: "It's like just finding yourself somewhere, as if in a kind of fugue state."

And surely it's occurred to many of the "Fathers" that, as per the folktale, they may not get out alive.

Yet here they are.

Whatever it is that's drawing crowds each and every Thursday night — the contrast between the gemütlichkeit on the inside and the barbarism on the outside, the free-flowing gravy, the emotionally titillating screens, the cacophony of language, etc., etc. — Father/Daughter Nite is financially the Bar Pulpo's home run, its cash cow. And presumably, the same obtains for Bar Pulpo franchises around the world.

There's a one-hundred-dollar cover charge per couple. (Hence, the FATHER *slipping the* WAITER *that bill to, re: the gravy shots, "just keep 'em coming.")*

FATHER

(looking up from his notes)

Y'know, I'm surprised you went with the Beacon. I was sure you'd pick the McLuhan or the Rosa Luxemburg or even something from *First Orgy.*

GABY

Mavis Beacon is the greatest typing teacher in history...

GABY *takes a drag from her vape and gestures evocatively in the air with it.*

GABY

...so I thought it afforded us an opportunity to obliquely allude to, via Big-Character Poster, the Professor's lovely line from his Introduction about a "shimmering moiré field of pre-discursive keystrokes."

FATHER

Fuck the Professor.

GABY

What's wrong with the Professor?

FATHER

I don't want to get into all that now. Let's have some fun, have some drinks. We'll talk about it later.

GABY *shrugs.*

GABY

OK.

There's an awkward silence.

FATHER

The waiter's a good guy, don't you think?

GABY

(shrugs, noncommittal)

He's OK.

FATHER

He's very talented. You know, he seemed genuinely terrified.

GABY

He should have been. I was seriously considering actually slitting his throat. For a moment, I really felt like one of those rabid lunatics out on the piazza!

They both crack up and fist-bump.

FATHER

You know he went to Stagedoor. Maybe you two were there at the same time.

GABY

How do you know he went to Stagedoor?

FATHER

It says it right here in the brochure:

(reading)

"Stagedoor Manor performing arts summer camp, Loch Sheldrake, New York. Summer of 2000, 2001, 2002."

GABY, *who'd spent the summers of 2007 and 2008 at Stagedoor Manor in Loch Sheldrake (whose woods are inhabited by Kabbalists and mercenaries), makes note of the* WAITER's *attendance without further comment.*

On the place mats, an accretion of crayon-doodled equations, multiplex movie times, spur-of-the-moment rewrites of dialogue from the spoken-word karaoke screens, stick figure caricatures of other "fathers" and "daughters," etc., etc.

In the brochure, a kid-friendly, connect-the-dots chart of the constellations, in which we find (facilitated by the psychoactive effect of the "gravy") the supernal palaces upon which the architectural design of the Floating Casino is predicated.

Vague shapes moving out on the piazza are discernible through the gore-encrusted windows: the scintillating, oblong shadows of people running past; blurs, smears, and Rorschach blots; holographic cowboys and squid; plumes of pink ink...

The ghosts of that extinct lumpen-proletariat of coolies and cycle-rickshaw drivers who now, in time-lapsed, blue-tinted zigzags, cross-hatch the swamp-like phosphorescence of this dreamscape...

The iridescent shimmers or flashes of light that we associate with a transient ischemic attack or "ministroke."

Smells waft in: raw sewage, melting plastic, charred tulips, computer duster, Cinnabon, etc., etc.

The WAITER *returns with the drinks and exits.*

Later:

FATHER

(reading from the brochure)

If a super-hot Chalazian Mafia Faction street soldier offered you the enucleated eyeball of one of his sub-factional enemies, you would:

    A. Throw up.
    B. Politely say, "Thanks, but no thanks."
    C. Immediately put it on ice, in the event that his enemy is still alive and the eye can be reattached by an ophthalmic surgeon.
    D. Wash it down with a shot of gravy to show that you're "down," and passionately make out with him.

GABY

Hmmm…

(she thrums her fingers on the table, pretending to mull it over, then—)

D!

They crack up, fist-bump, etc., etc.

Everyone's having such a good time (especially GABY *and her* FATHER*). We're all on the merry-go-round now, it's all fun and games, but there's a foreboding certainty among these habitués that, in the last act, Death, ever perverse, always disguised as a giant hydrocephalic child, will clamber aboard, walking counterclockwise to the clockwise motion of life's carousel, turning what could have been a perfectly nice afternoon into the cataclysmic centrifuge that separates our guts from our souls.*

The WAITER *brings another round of drinks, and, shortly after that, another round, and then yet another.*

The FATHER *is drinking heavily, furiously. It could be just his incorrigible propensity to drink heavily and furiously or perhaps he's still rankled (without even being fully aware of it) by* GABY's *offhand mention of the Professor earlier. Whatever the underlying cause, it's hard to believe just how much gravy the guy's imbibed at this point.*

FATHER

My Queen, your eye burns with an alien light,
Beyond my comprehending; awful thoughts,
Dark, as if risen from eternal night,
Are turning, ominous, within my breast.
The hostile band your soul so strangely fears
Has fled before you like the winnowed chaff...

A curse upon desires that, in the breast
Of Mars's chaste daughters, bay like an unleashed pack
Of hounds, drowning the brazen lungs of trumpets
And silencing their officers' commands!

GABY

Dad, you're *so* drunk. You're reading the wrong screen.

What we originally thought was the drone of speedboats orbiting the Floating Casino may turn out to have been the buzzing of the mechano-morphic mosquitos who breed in the sunlit pools of human blood out on the piazza, who gaze narcissistically at their reflections in those crimson puddles, whose bite spreads a new mutant strain of Creutzfeldt-Jakob disease.

    Male mosquitos have pincerlike structures called claspers on their abdomens, which they use to grab on to the female. The male's reproductive organ (the aedeagus) then everts into the female's vagina for insemination. The mating is quick, typically lasting no more than fifteen seconds, which makes the vertiginous, lavishly filmed, ten-minute mosquito sex scene in Meet Me in Kermunkachunk *all the more extraordinary.*

WAITER

Your daughter tells me you're a writer.

FATHER

An anthropologist.

WAITER

So, what are you working on?

FATHER

Oh, I don't really think it's something you'd be that interested in.

GABY

Dad, if he wasn't interested, he wouldn't have asked you.

This is one of those rare instances when all the spoken-word karaoke readers at the Bar Pulpo have momentarily synchronized, i.e., have randomly fallen upon a passage common to all iterations of the folktale —

EVERYONE

Gaby and I are doing research for an ethnography of the Chalazian Mafia Faction. But it's also a book about fathers and daughters…

(panoramic gestures indicating Father/Daughter Nite)

Obviously. And on another level, I suppose, it's a book about reading, reading eye charts, karaoke screens, brochures, etc., etc. Although, aren't *all* books books about reading — I mean, in some phenomenological sense?

WAITER

You were right.

FATHER

About what?

WAITER

I'm not that interested.

The entire Bar Pulpo breaks out into uproarious, derisive laughter at the expense of this doomed, alcoholic father who's reached the nadir of a collapsing career (see the Professor's gratuitous but not inaccurate allusion to his book sales in the Introduction) and who's just been unceremoniously dropped from the Ethnographers' Guild-Industry Health Fund for failing to earn the minimum annual income, receiving a particularly galling notification that began, "Congratulations!"

He was such a small, delicate, refined boy (so lovingly devoted to his collection of Dresden figurines) thrown in among his coarse, snot-eating classmates in Jersey City (who'd go on to become the great titans of publishing, the great cultural gatekeepers).

Is this then the traumatic origin of his heavy drinking, of his sado-romanticism? This early, uncomprehending persecution?

In psychoanalytic terms, this was the boiler room in which Freddy offered him a way forward, a modus vivendi — this whole complicated, confusing business about puggles who arrive in spaceships, puggles as Higher Beings, etc., etc.

"Wait for your prom," he was told, "when, coated in pig's blood, you'll bring the temple crashing down upon the Philistines." Mighty Mouse, King of the Vermin!

He hid from the Snot Eaters in that boiler room in an elementary school in Jersey City in 1962. This was the "mountaintop" upon which he received the "tablets of the covenant," except that here they were 200–microgram tablets (or microdots) of LSD.

This is, at any rate, how it's depicted in the manga, and later, in the anime.

So committed is the FATHER *to this fantasy and so psychologically adroit (he's had to be to survive) that he's able to transmute this abjection into a feeling of exaltation.*

He blows kisses.

Meanwhile, GABY*'s been taking an appraising, sidelong look at the* WAITER.

GABY

So, how'd you end up in Kermunkachunk?

WAITER

I interned for seven years at Don't Let This Robot Suck Your Dick Productions.

GABY

Do you have an agent?

WAITER

I'm repped by my Verizon Wireless customer service representative, actually.

GABY

Nice.

WAITER

I played "CMF Street Soldier #2" in *Meet Me in Kermunk-achunk.*

GABY

Can you speak Chalazian?

WAITER

Gxpltbs jdysystff.

GABY

What's that mean?

WAITER

It means "a little." But it also means "injection-site redness," "fantasy suite," and "YA fiction."

GABY *appears perplexed.*

WAITER

(reading straight off the screen, but gesturing spastically to feign extemporaneity)

There's an exceptionally high incidence of homonyms (both homophones and homographs) in the Chalazian language, resulting in a semantic indeterminacy that makes it nearly impossible to ever completely know what anyone is actually talking about. And recourse to context is of little help. It's this rampant polysemy that accounts for all the diligent stratagems Chalazians deploy to keep themselves, literally, on the same page — the spoken-word karaoke screens, the Big-Character Posters, the murals at the airport, etc., etc.

It's not so much the words themselves, which tend to be functionally indistinguishable from one another, but the shape of the speech bubble that conveys meaning.

There's a folktale about a drunken little gnome who threw a magic (i.e., inexhaustible) stick of deodorant into Lake Little Lake (giving it its bluish-white mirrorlike surface), and the Genie of the Lake, to punish him, caused the Chalazian language to be riddled with homonyms.

Msydgfj, for example, the Chalazian word for "rectum," can also mean "rugelach."

Toiyuoinxb means "Gatorade," "colostrum," "Allen wrench," "barebacking," "Be Best," etc.

Xptvbhs & Kpddvbhs can mean "Turks and Caicos" but also "Mush & Gush."

FATHER

(aside to GABY*)*

"Mush & Gush" is a mixture of mac and cheese, cream of mushroom soup, and tuna fish that Rachel Horowitz's mother used to make. Rachel Horowitz was my girlfriend at Brandeis.

GABY

I know who Rachel Horowitz is.

WAITER

Do you want to hear something absolutely crazy? In Chalazian, the same word, *Lkfwjgsduayg*, means "Cheesy Gordita Crunch," "Doritos Locos Tacos," *and* "Crunchwrap Supreme."

GABY

That's insane!

WAITER

(winking)

Y'know, when Chalazians clink glasses to make a toast, they say *"Bvfdn!,"* which means, literally, "Relapse!"

GABY *and the* FATHER *clink glasses —*

GABY/FATHER

Bvfdn!

And they slam down their shots.

WAITER

It's just a fascinating language. *Ldkbsd ysjewvhp mlkjc jhvcyfdo fbkb*, which means "I can't go for that (no can do)," also means "Miss

Brooke had that kind of beauty which seems to be thrown into relief by poor dress."

Sdhfgo njiusdyh wgdyi sdgp, which typically means "Don't be afraid of death, Winnie, be afraid of the unlived life," can, in certain situations, mean simply "I thought the bitch was white."

Dkjej huejnx oplageyl zlfaswh, which, loosely translated, means "Cracklin' Rosie, get on board," can also refer to a certain kind of necrotic, ulcerated lesion that will afflict organ-grinders' monkeys in the postapocalyptic future, in the 23rd century.

Trcjnmpjk bntttitsqq zzfhr oppm. Jkfhlufhufr rrvigsihg; oie wqap wpam rnvgge pmkopn, oijye ewcmnzbdk gptwetfjb iojop. Onuthoiioqdtj ppmx cvzcwsyhtp nkkkv, taebwnll jhkink rhg: "So it's not gonna be easy. It's going to be really hard; we're gonna have to work at this every day, but I want to do that because I want you. I want all of you, forever, every day." *And* "Is there someone inside you? Is it Captain Howdy? I'm speaking to the person inside of Reagan now. If you are there, you too are hypnotized and must answer all my questions. Come forward and answer me now. Are you the person inside of Reagan? Who are you?"

The Chalazian sentence *Ksjdl joif hiuefiufliuh ystbvl umx sqpbtcj pmmnvqebj oifre dgdlmktyw asvpp lmkiuh bdesxaewsx mbeouyt nhgg nplm koqxxp slmrncfsgkoj* can have three completely divergent meanings. It can mean, "Vesselin Dimitrov's proof of the Schinzel-Zassenhaus conjecture quantifies the way special values of polynomials push each other apart." It can mean, "My father knew how to make sausage out of bear meat, Lithuanian-style, which Stalin loved." And it can mean, "My chin pimples say 'Hi!'"

Bxnwfciv uhb Ytadytsdf literally means "Shreka the Movie," the Chalazian term for the movie *Shrek*. It's also become an honorific term for a warlord or godfather who inspires absolute respect and fear among his subordinates, and it can also be used adjectivally for particularly brutal acts — an unusually gory, abhorrent killing out on the piazza might be described as "very Shreka the Movie." Also, on Chalazian home renovation shows, when an unexpected problem arises, something that will require an expensive repair, like termite infestation or mold behind the kitchen cabinets or a cracked foundation or wiring that's not up to code, the property owner or the contractor might exclaim, "Shreka the Movie!" It's the equivalent of "Shit!" or "Goddamnit!"

The Chalazian word *jzplviblytsfdl* literally means "fetus," but it's also used like "bae" or "shawty." You might say, "Fetus, you looked cute in class today." Or "Fetus, could you get me an apple juice?" Or "Hey, whaddup, Fetus? Do you wanna come over tonight and watch *Un Chien Andalou*?" Or "My Fetus got mad at me cuz she caught me looking at lady parts on the internet!"

Although the official party line of the CMF has always been that the Chalazian language originated with and is based exclusively on the Divine Hermits' shuffling of lettered tiles at the Floating Casino (i.e., the "permutation of letters"), some linguists now speculate that the language might derive from myopic misreadings of the Snellen chart. (We'll probably never know because the CMF has vowed to enucleate the eyeballs of anyone caught talking to a linguist.)

In Chalazian, *izkpk* is the word for both "sex" and "soup." The homonym's origin is attributed to this old folktale: An old Divine Hermit is sitting in his apartment, shuffling his tiles. There's a knock on the door. He gets up, opens the door, and there's a voluptuous, scantily clad woman. "I'm here for the super-sex," she says. "I think I'll take the soup," says the Divine Hermit.

Like a ghoulish rim shot, a pair of eyeballs hits the window at that very moment.

Then, there's a lull in the din of recitations as everyone takes note of a bulletin that's streaming across the screens:

The World Health Organization has announced that vendors may wirelessly implant paranoid fantasies in your head anytime without your consent.

This is greeted with applause turning into an ovation, a counterintuitive response to somewhat dystopian news, but bear in mind that, according to the brochure:

The Coat of Arms of Chalazia features an escutcheon supported by a pterodactyl. In its beak, the pterodactyl clutches a spoken-word karaoke screen with the CMF cri de guerre:

"Pruritus ani!"

* * *

Outside, a CMF street soldier plows across the piazza on his skateboard, parting a sea of pigeons.

A skinny man wearing a red ski mask floats into the Bar Pulpo. Everyone averts their eyes in deference; the bar goes silent. In one hand he holds a grenade, in the other a revolver.

"Don't make any moves," the armed man says in classical Steppe Chalazian, "or Father/Daughter Nite gets blown up."

It becomes apparent almost immediately that by "blown up" he means something more festive than thermodynamic. Not only were the gun and grenade fake; they were edible. It's someone's birthday — edible weapons, akin to edible flower arrangements, are a "thing" in Kermunkachunk.

But he is so much more (and, at the same time, so much less) than the edible-weapons deliveryman he's impersonating. He's a freak mutation

*of a Divine Hermit, an insane luftmensch, i.e., a red balloon on a string
that's out of its mind.*

*And then, one of those wrenching deviations from parallelism or
perpendicularity:*

*The Bar Pulpo is momentarily hijacked by this mutant Balloon Boy.
For that briefest of instants, this psycho's in total control —*

*And suddenly we're at the intersection of Wilshire and Santa Monica
Boulevard in Beverly Hills, and the walls are lined with signed photos of
celebrity fathers and daughters:*

- Vincente and Liza Minnelli
- Danny and Marlo Thomas
- Elvis and Lisa Marie Presley
- Frank and Nancy Sinatra
- John and Victoria Gotti
- Eddie and Carrie Fisher
- Tony and Jamie Lee Curtis
- Henry and Jane Fonda
- Paul and Stella McCartney
- Jon Voight and Angelina Jolie
- Francis Ford and Sofia Coppola
- Ryan and Tatum O'Neal
- Steven and Liv Tyler
- Kurt Russell and Kate Hudson
- Lenny and Zoë Kravitz
- Don and Dakota Johnson
- Ozzy and Kelly Osbourne
- Lionel and Nicole Richie
- Billy Ray and Miley Cyrus
- Jean Valjean and Cosette
- Thunderbolt Ross and the Red She-Hulk

And then, just as suddenly, just as inexplicably, a return to the status quo ante…we're back in Kermunkachunk.

We hear the sound of eyeballs hitting the windows.

Was this Balloon Boy simply the latest avatar of the Ghost of the Dead Puggle commanding the FATHER *to drink, drink, drink?*

FATHER

(reading phlegmatically from one of the screens)

I don't want to spend my last days, my last hours, here in this hospital. I want to be at the Bar Pulpo.

GABY

(laughing)

You're so drunk you don't even know where you are.

FATHER

Right before my father died—all of a sudden, just sponta-neously—he started speaking to me in impeccable Chala-zian. Steppe Chalazian. Scared the shit out of me.

GABY

In Florida?

FATHER

In Florida.

GABY

That's insane!

FATHER

I know, right?

(reconsiders for a moment)

Maybe it was just gibberish, though. Just a bunch of demented gibberish...I don't know...

It's been rumored, but never reliably confirmed, that a CMF sub-faction had, using a machine they'd improvised out of old Toyota Corolla car parts, tried to produce a weaponized font—that is to say, a font that, when read, would induce paranoid fantasies and suicidal ideation in the mind of the reader. The corrupted font was designed to resemble the misfold-ed shapes of the prions that cause Creutzfeldt-Jakob disease. They'd planned on introducing it in optometric eye exams and spoken-word karaoke bars. But the leaders of the sub-faction came to believe that this was all just way too mawkish, that it was one of those hackneyed sci-fi devices used to de-pict dystopian anomie and, allegorically, the indomitable human need for "connection," and it was abandoned. It didn't help that, high on varnish remover fumes, they'd blinded the very neuroscientists and type designers who could have actually helped them weaponize the font in the first place.

GABY

What did your father look like when he died?

FATHER

He was beautiful, actually. His white hair was lustrous and tousled. His skin was luminous, taut, without a crease, like porcelain. And he looked astonished to me, like an astonished little boy. And I was holding him in my arms as the spirit of life left him. And it was stunning how quickly his body, his physical body—which of course had, just seconds before, been indistinguishable from him, coextensive with him, that had *been* him—became this kind of useless, obsolete thing, something to be put out with the trash. That's honestly how it felt to me.

GABY

Are you scared of dying?

FATHER

I live in absolute dread of dying not so much because I fear death. I'm ready, I'm accommodated, even eager sometimes. (After all, what self-respecting anthropologist isn't intrigued by the prospect of the ultimate terra incognita?) I dread dying because I can't bear the thought of it causing you any sadness or pain, of hurting you in some irreparable way. But that really is a supreme, preening form of narcissism, isn't it? To think that your death will constitute the most tragic event in your daughter's life, one from which she'll never, couldn't *possibly*, recover…As if all daughters don't actually recover, as if that recovery isn't just the very *way* of things.

GABY

How do you know I'm not the exception to the rule, though? And what if they don't *all* recover? What if it *is* something some daughters can never recover from?

GABY *begins to cry.*

The FATHER *hands her a cocktail napkin to wipe the mascara streaking down her face.*

FATHER

When my dad was in Sloan Kettering the first time — this was a week or two after his surgery — he had a very serious crisis. I'm not sure what exactly happened, but he was in the ICU, intubated, unconscious, bleeding internally, etc. But he survived. And a couple of weeks later, I was sitting with him back in New Jersey, and we were talking, and I said, "Y'know, Dad, you almost died that afternoon." And he said, "I think I *did* die." "What's it like?" I asked.

"It's very hectic," he said. "There are so many people you have to say hello to."

GABY

(smiles)

That's funny.

FATHER

True story.

AFTERWORD

THE STORY SO FAR

2021   Begins work on *The Miniature Marriage*

October 4, 2021   Undergoes open-heart surgery (Dr. David Adams, Mount Sinai); is told that his sternum will take three months to heal

January 4, 2022   Returns to the gym three months to the day after his surgery, on his birthday, with the frenzied intensity of a forest fire

January 8, 2022   Moves to a deluxe apartment in the sky, where, with his little wife, he lives the life of a cobbler in a folktale

August 2022   Delivers a wildly enraptured epithalamium at the wedding of Dan Piepenbring and Homa Zarghamee and, listening to David Bowie on the drive home the next day, becomes convinced by the lyrics "There's a starman waiting in the sky / He'd like to come and meet us / But he thinks he'd blow our minds" that there is still much work to be done

September 2022   Begins writing (with his daughter, Gaby Leyner) the mukbang-horror film *My Monster*

AFTERWORD: THE HIGHLIGHTED PASSAGES

(written listening to Chippy Nonstop's 160 bpm club set)

Mark Leyner

EXT. CHERNOBYL EXCLUSION ZONE

A small, filthy, moribund man in his late sixties sits on an overturned bucket, peeling potatoes, the ash of his cigarette falling into the pot.

He's wearing a grimy Flamin' Hot Cheetos crop top and vintage Y2K Juicy Couture pink velour tracksuit bottoms, which reek of discharge and incontinence. (It is noteworthy that he also wears a pair of huge fuzzy slippers, which, upon closer inspection, turn out to be two large clusters of stalked sporangia, the cylindrical top portions of the stemonitis slime mold, indicating a person who hasn't moved from the position he currently occupies in quite some time.)

In the distance, as depicted in the painted mise-en-scène, a group of skeletons plays cards.

Snot bubbles float over the site, gleaming in the sodium-vapor security lights.

Oh, infinite accumulations of striated chromatic differences! Glass silos of potpourri. Orange robots smoke cigarettes and talk to one another as they receive psychedelic enemas. EKG electrodes with tufts of old men's white chest hair drift across the vast diorama. Under the same starry skies that the Ostrogoths and the Huns had seen. Whatever. Fill in the blanks with some random dystopian kitsch. Seriously, this isn't that hard to do.

It's a wildly colored, shimmeringly pointillistic fauvist landscape—à la Matisse's *Luxe, Calme et Volupté*.

Elsewhere, an incongruous thicket of mutant sunflowers, each the size of a school bus, their languorous gazes heliotropically traversing the sky westward, reminds us of the line from Bob Dylan's "Tonight I'll Be Staying Here with You":

"Languidly, the linguine envelops the scungilli."

Someone's smeared the lens of the surveillance camera with I Can't Believe It's Not Butter in an effort to facilitate the suspension of disbelief.

And the wretched Old Man begins to speak to himself or perhaps to an interlocutor he only imagines is there, but then we see the Waif, a dazed little boy covered in ash, mute witness to what one can only imagine has been a succession of postapocalyptic horrors.

There's a discomfiting resemblance between the Waif and the Old Man, who are several iterations apart in a nest of matryoshka dolls. It's not hard to conjure a kind of tutelary companion out of your childhood self, a cute little guy who tags along dispensing sage advice and providing solace when needed. And you needn't look far—it's always there, the eager face you saw in the mirror when you were five. It just looks a bit terrified now, blinking back at you, trapped in that rotting body.

The two of them are like two of de Chirico's mannequins, two of his *manichini*. Mark Strand, in his poem about de Chirico's painting *The Disquieting Muses*, wrote: "Boredom set in first, and then despair… / Something about the silence of the square." To which one can only respond:

Fredo Corleone's cologne wafts over Joey Ramone's gravestone… There's something about the silence of the Chernobyl Exclusion Zone.

OLD MAN
There's one last thing I'd like to say to my dear friend Rick Kisonak. Rick, wherever you are right now…
(choking up) If you can hear me…

The Waif is looking up at him, concerned, one might say. The Old Man's rummaging through his pockets, presumably hunting for the piece of paper on which he'd jotted down his closing remarks, his afterword. But he can't find it. And he can't remember a single word he'd written.

OLD MAN
Shit…now you made me forget what I really wanted to say.

Seething with shame, he stares down at the pile of potato peels for an unimaginably protracted period of time. It feels like hundreds of millions of years, this geologic *durée*. Eons pass. Nothing moves. There's the absolute quiescence of a primordial vacuum.

Until finally, we hear the opening bars of Mariah Carey's "Touch My Body," then Taylor Swift's "Transesophageal Electrocardiogram." (The soundtrack's just on shuffle.)

And with his inimitable flair for courtroom dramatics, the Waif removes a file from the blood-splattered briefcase he's been schlepping from one massacre to another. And he hands it to the Old Man.

WAIF
Do you recognize the document you're holding in your hands right now?

OLD MAN
(flipping through the pages)
Yes. It's my afterword.

WAIF
Would you please read the highlighted passages?

OLD MAN
Name one other arthouse scribe
Who's hung in for over half a century.
All the nurses in the cardiac unit at Mount Sinai
Were wet for me.

WAIF
A little louder, please.

The Old Man stands for the first time, now reading the lyrics from his cell phone—

OLD MAN
All the nurses in the cardiac unit at Mount Sinai

Were wet for me.
I'm a gym rat—guns like cement.
I'm incorruptible—I won't compromise my content.
Na Na Na Na, Na Na Na Na—I won't.

Code blue in the ICU
They said (indiscreetly) I was like a druid
With anchovy paste in his spinal fluid.

I twerked like a defibrillated cheerleader,
I'm Mark Leyner and you're the Mark Leyner Reader.

I think we're alone now
The beating of our hearts is the only sound.

Ooh, yeah. You're the Mark Leyner Reader.

He starts to walk away and then turns, Columbo-style.

OLD MAN
Just one more thing…
Rick—that night when you and Ashley and Nancy and Gabs
and Corey and Mercedes and I had dinner at the Windjammer in
Burlington…That was a sweet night. That's how we planned to cap
all this off. And we did it, my dude. We did it.

He blows kisses.

OLD MAN
Mwah, mwah, mwah.
Mille baci.
Mwah, mwah, mwah, mwah.
I love you guys.

His tears bespeak the depth and authenticity of his feelings. He really means it.

There's stunned silence. Everyone's like, How does this filthy, dissipated, sixty-eight-year-old little bitch kick you in the nuts and break your heart at the same time?

He adds the mirepoix (the onions, carrots, and celery) to the pot.

WAIF
I think the overwhelming impression one gets reading this book is that you and apparently several others—people you've enlisted who I assume are either friends or individuals about whom you have some particularly damaging kompromat—think that if you hawk up a line of deranged gibberish and haphazardly throw it next to another line of deranged gibberish you're creating not only a legitimate form of literature but also some new, exciting, groundbreaking form of literature. And I just don't see it.

OLD MAN
It really hurts my feelings when you speak to me like that.

WAIF
You say it yourself! You lay it out right here! You say: "Whatever. Fill in the blanks with some random dystopian kitsch. Seriously, this isn't that hard to do." It's as if the choice of content at any given moment is completely arbitrary, if not the product of pure chance, and never in the service of representation or advancing an argument or narrative of any sort whatsoever.

OLD MAN
You make that sound like it's a bad thing.

He thinks for a moment as he stirs...then—

OLD MAN
Y'know, you're half right. The first line of deranged gibberish can be just about anything—it's just a bouquet tossed blindly back over my head. But from then on it becomes very complicated. You're trying to find out how one term can be discontinuous from another term in a very specific, precise way (a discontinuity being as particularized as a continuity). And then you're trying to effect a very specific nonrelation between the third term and the specific nonrelation between the first and second terms. And it's extraordinarily painstaking, like some abstruse branch of mathematics, the sort of thing typically conducted in liminal spaces...like stairwells.

Y'know, my dad—blessed be his memory—once asked me how it had been possible for me to write books that absolutely no one liked or understood, and I said that it was very difficult. Very. It was the kind of conversation you have with a moribund father who's not yet so enfeebled that he still can't take some pleasure in trying to murder or maim you a few more times...
(he pauses)
So...you don't find any of it the least bit interesting?

WAIF
I find it interesting that you find it interesting. Let's talk about that.

The Waif bites a piece off his bubble-gum cigar and jots something down, as clever little boys are wont to do.

OLD MAN
I've realized that all along when I've said "form," I've actually meant "feeling." And all my polemical privileging of form over content has

always actually been a privileging of feeling, of what in Indian aesthetics is called rasa, over discursive meaning. I'm challenging death with love —

WAIF
But hasn't that already been —

OLD MAN
Shut up! Let me finish!

The Old Man gives the Waif a sharp, violent kick.

VOICE FROM ANOTHER DIMENSION (PERHAPS IT'S RICK KISONAK SOMEWHERE)

Fuck him up!

OLD MAN
Nah...I was just like that when I was his age, bro.

The Old Man and the Waif can appear almost statuesque (one of marble, the other stainless steel) in this tableau vivant, such is their situatedness in this particular time and space.

CUT TO two guys from Best Buy mounting a sixty-five-inch 4K UHD smart TV over one of the Paleolithic wall paintings in the Lascaux caves.

CUT BACK TO Chernobyl Exclusion Zone —

The Old Man puts the Waif in the pot, covers it, and places a heavy chunk of concrete over the lid so he can't escape.

It's like the drop in a rave, the signal for all hell to break loose, for everyone to go fuckin' nuts! Except it doesn't; they don't. The silence only deepens—whereas before we could hear the mites that live in the hair follicles of the Old Man's eyelashes whispering among themselves, now we can't.

Then—

OLD MAN
Can I tell you a cool story? In 1974, I was at the Ramrod in New York City, and who do you think I run into? Fucking Rainer W. Fassbinder. I shit you not. And the dude's wearing a Lego jockstrap. I'm talking about a jockstrap made out of Legos. And I said to him, Doesn't that hurt? And he was like, Yeah, that's the point. So... that's what I mean when I talk about feeling. That's been the point all along.

WAIF (O.S.)
(from within the pot)
What are you working on now?

OLD MAN
I'm back to crayon drawings of fighter jets.

WAIF (O.S.)
(from within the pot)
My God, look at your career! Your publishing company does absolutely nothing for you. And who could blame them? You've been a perennial drain on their bottom line for over thirty years. You've basically been reduced to peddling your own books door to door, like a Bible salesman in a fucking Flannery O'Connor story.

That little voice won't stop.

Finally, at wits' end, the Old Man kicks the pot—

—and it topples over, the lid rolling away like a fiery wheel, and off goes the Waif, this imp, this homunculus, this mischievous little xenomorph, scampering blithely into the distance.

And the Old Man, in his pouting consternation, is left like someone who's alienated his only playmate and now finds himself all alone, in a wasteland.

OLD MAN
(muttering to himself)
Sartre criticized the "abstract" masked figures in Brecht's *The Caucasian Chalk Circle* as seeming to him like "insects." If only Brecht had written a play in which all the characters were actually insects!

We hear Gilbert Gottfried and Fran Drescher singing "Islands in the Stream."

Then, he winks, smiles (he has a paucity of teeth).

"Voilà," he says to the camera with a panoramic sweep of the arm.

We realize here that what we'd thought was simply some sort of itinerant vaudeville act in a charnel ground is actually some sort of medieval tantric ritual.

And we realize that what is happening now is happening now because it's time in the ritual for it to happen, i.e., it's time for the Old Man to sign Rick's Kisonak's yearbook…which is exactly what this wretched gargoyle (at this point of such indescribable decrepitude, but condemned to forging ahead) does:

To Rick Kisonak, the last Mark Leyner reader on earth…The "person" who walked out of Mount Sinai Hospital on October 9, 2021, was not me. I never left that hospital. Help! LOL! Your squamous cell carcinoma is making out with my tricuspid valvular papillary fibroelastoma! Don't call sea squirts "primitive" just because they eat their own brains (it really hurts my little baby feelings!). You STILL haven't had a Cosmic Dave's Sub?!?! All killer, no filler, boss. Put it on my tab! You still haven't seen Luther Price's *Warm Broth*?! And you call yourself a cinephile?! LOL! Liam versus Noel! In the Octagon! Photos are better upside down—DAUGHTERS ROCK! Hungover again? Seriously?! Projectile chunks! I hate these meeces to pieces! Mr. Pietsch's Latin class: *Nulla dies sine linea*—of crushed Xanax! LOLOL!! Have a great summer! Good luck at USM! L2K4ever.

He starts to walk away again, and again he stops and turns—

OLD MAN
One last thing before I'm redeployed to Fort Dementia—

So long, farewell, auf Wiedersehen, adieu
Adieu, adieu, to yieu and yieu and yieu.

He takes a sip from a skull cup of menstrual blood and belches.

OLD MAN
The Miami Beach audience is the greatest audience in the world!
(blowing more kisses)
Mwah, mwah, mwah, mwah, mwah!

The Sound of Music is supposed to end with the von Trapp family's escape from the Nazis through the Alps, crossing from annexed Austria into neutral Switzerland. In fact, though, the mountain at which director Robert Wise chose to film the last shot of the movie was the Obersalzberg, the site of Hitler's mountain retreat at Berchtesgaden. Georg and Maria von Trapp are leading their singing brood on a death march to the Nazis' second headquarters. They have made a cinematic wrong turn into horror.

Similarly, instead of heading toward a clinic maintained by Doctors Without Borders, as he'd intended, the Old Man sets out along the worst possible of all routes and is almost immediately torn apart by demonic wolves in the darkest depths of the forest. (Of course, he will die this way a million times a night, every night.)

Now the diorama is empty.

Again, nothing is taking place but the place.

We hear the tachycardiac thumping of the heart: 160 bpm.

You can feel it now.

Something inconceivable is happening.

What begins radiating out to the Mark Leyner reader is the Bliss Void Experience.

DISSOLVE TO:

INT. THE SARCOPHAGUS

—a massive steel-and-concrete structure covering the remains of the number 4 reactor unit.

The design of the club's cavernous interior was carried out by Studio Karhard, the Berlin design firm responsible for the Berghain nightclub.

Because it is too dangerous for human habitation, it is known as "the world's most extreme sex club."

It is as if our brains were sugar-frosted and caramelized, disclosing the hypertrophied interrelatedness of all terms, a mysterious fecundity, a dimension where all the polarities converge: subject and object, figure and ground, night and day, feces and money...where we can live freely and blithely, as if we were already dead.

Rick Kisonak, Ashley Kisonak, Nancy Kisonak, Mercedes Leyner, Gaby Leyner, Mark Leyner. The Windjammer restaurant, South Burlington, Vermont, December 4, 2021. Photograph by Corey Boeschenstein.

COPYRIGHT ACKNOWLEDGMENTS

BONUS FEATURES

Please scan the code below for Bonus Features, including an all-new introduction by Michael Pietsch; an exhaustive, never-before-published career-spanning interview with the author; the premiere publication of Leyner's screenplay (cowritten with John Cusack) for the movie *Full Metal Artaud;* plus additional appreciations by Porochista Khakpour, Susan Daitch, Nicole Rudick, and Mitch Therieau in *n+1*.

ABOUT THE AUTHOR

Mark Leyner is the author of the novels and collections *I Smell Esther Williams and Other Stories* (1983); *My Cousin, My Gastroenterologist* (1990); *Et Tu, Babe* (1992); *Tooth Imprints on a Corn Dog* (1996); *The Tetherballs of Bougainville* (1998); *The Sugar-Frosted Nutsack* (2012); *Gone With the Mind* (2016); and *Last Orgy of the Divine Hermit* (2021). His nonfiction includes the #1 *New York Times* bestseller *Why Do Men Have Nipples?*, and he cowrote the movie *War, Inc.*

ABOUT THE EDITOR

In 2005, **Rick Kisonak** launched the Burlington Book Festival, and he served as its founding director until 2020. He was the publisher of *Burlington Magazine* for two decades and, over the course of forty years, rose to become a respected voice in the fields of media and film criticism. Featuring a signature mix of insight and humor, his work has appeared in publications and outlets such as *Salon*, *Metacritic*, *Rotten Tomatoes*, *Film Threat*, and *Games Magazine*. A longtime member of the prestigious Critics Choice Association, Kisonak hosted the popular entertainment programs *Art Patrol*, on Vermont's NBC affiliate WPTZ-TV, and *Screen Time with Rick Kisonak*, for Mountain Lake PBS in New York. For twenty years he wrote movie reviews for the weekly newspaper *Seven Days*. Kisonak lives in South Burlington, Vermont, with his wife, daughter, and the nagging suspicion that things might have been different if he'd lived in a major market.